MODERN QUILLING

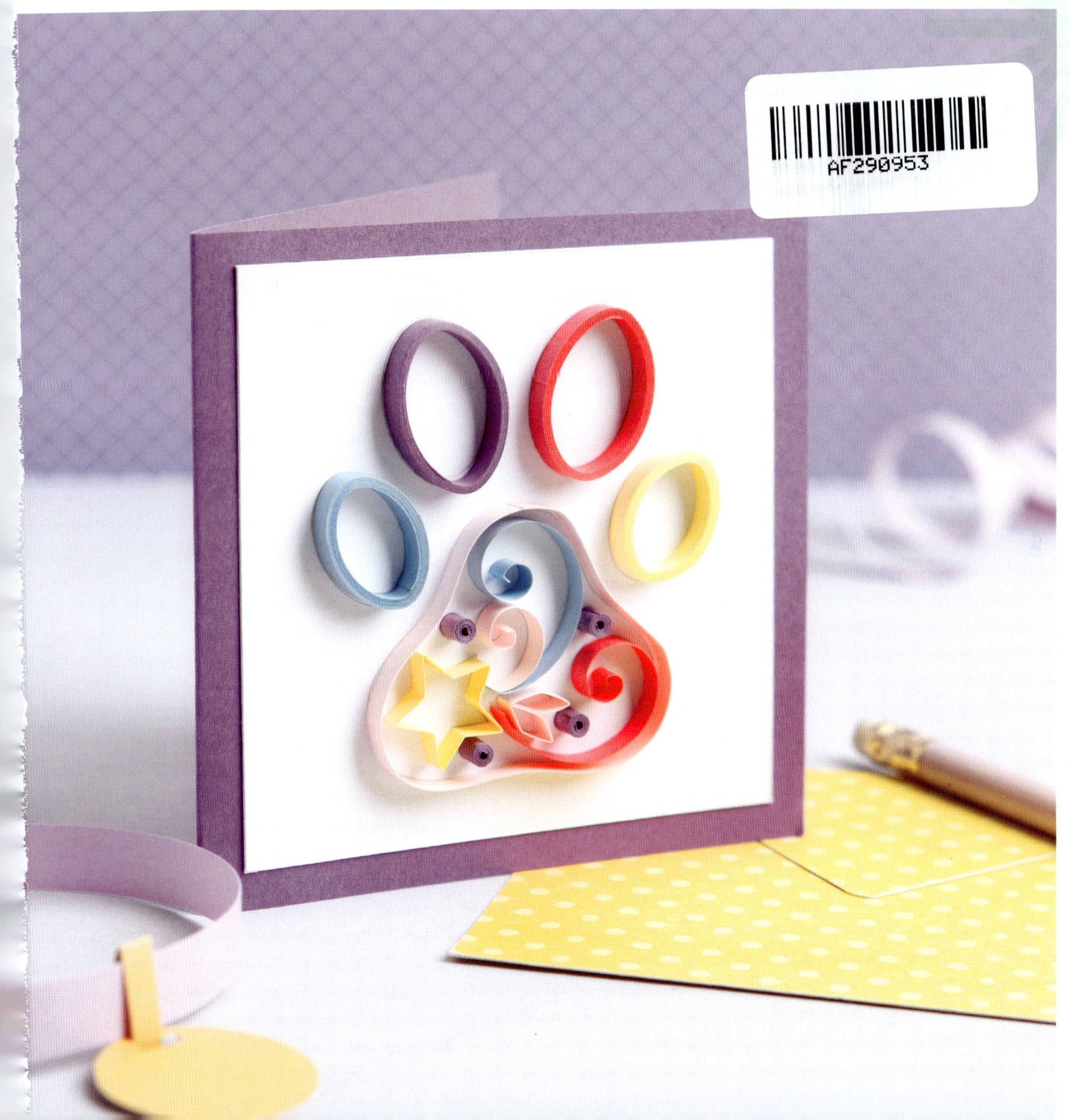

First published in 2025
Search Press Limited
Wellwood, North Farm Road,
Tunbridge Wells, Kent TN2 3DR

ISBN: 978-1-80092-250-1
ebook ISBN: 978-1-80093-249-4

Suppliers
If you have difficulty in obtaining any of the materials and equipment mentioned in this book, then please visit the Search Press website for details of suppliers: www.searchpress.com

Extra copies of the templates are also available to download free from the Bookmarked Hub. Search for this book by title or ISBN: the files can be found under 'Book Extras'. Membership of the Bookmarked online community is free: www.bookmarkedhub.com

You are invited to see more of the author's work at www.tillyviktor.com and @tillyviktor on Instagram.

Publishers' note
All the step-by-step photographs in this book feature the author, Jessica Janiak, demonstrating quilling techniques. No models have been used.

The projects in this book have been made using metric measurements, and the imperial equivalents provided have been calculated following standard conversion practices. The imperial measurements are often rounded to the nearest $\frac{1}{16}$in for ease of use except in rare circumstances; however, if you need more exact measurements, there are a number of excellent online converters that you can use. Always use either metric or imperial measurements, not a combination of both.

This book is dedicated to my sister Ellie – without whom TillyViktor would not exist. Your encouragement and faith pushed me to think big and chase my small business dreams.

MODERN QUILLING

20 beautiful paper art projects to make

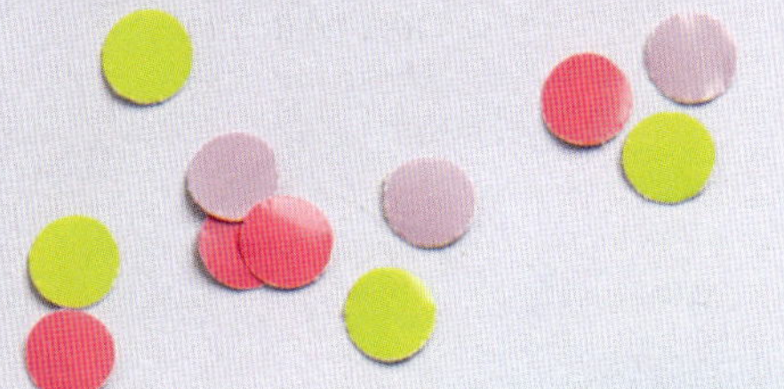

Jessica Janiak

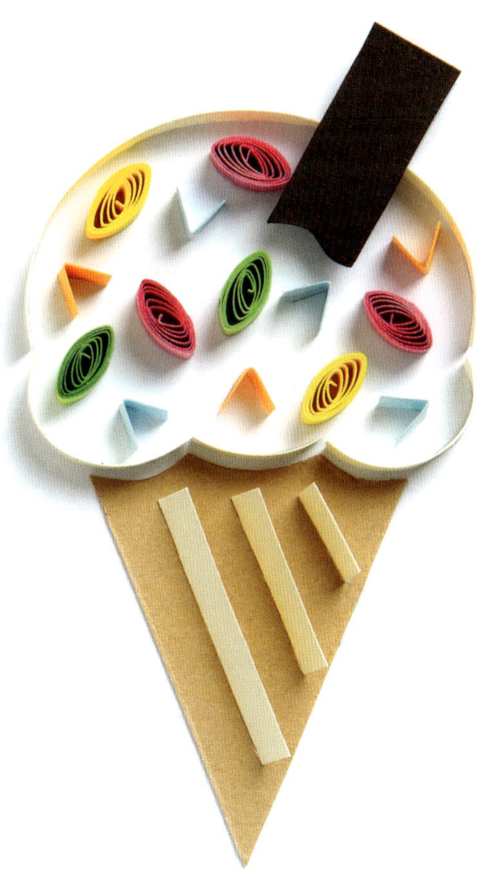

SEARCH PRESS

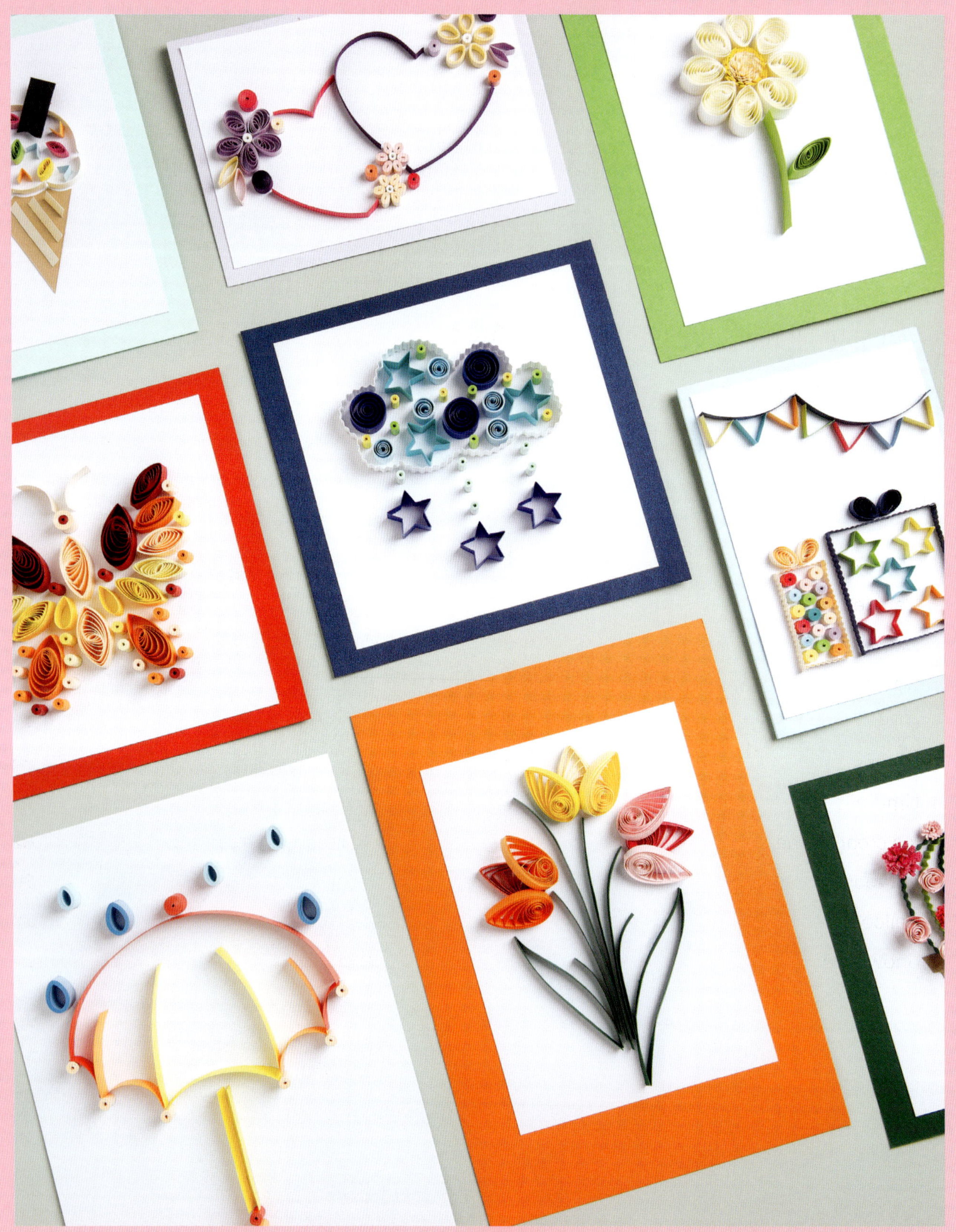

Contents

Introduction

I'm Jess, a professional paper twirler, designer and the all-round paper-obsessed owner of TillyViktor. You will often find me in my home office, buried in a pile of paper strips of every colour imaginable, refusing to throw away even the tiniest scraps of paper, just in case I need it!

I've been crafting for as long as I can remember, and as a child I loved getting messy and creative with anything and everything. My career initially took me into the fashion industry, where I worked as a print designer for nearly a decade. Despite success in fashion, I always felt a strong pull towards paper crafting. During my college and university years, my research sketchbooks were filled with vibrant three-dimensional paper art, reflecting my growing fascination with this versatile craft.

My journey into quilling began while I was searching for ideas to make a gift for my niece, Tilly. She was a toddler at the time and absolutely Disney-mad! I came across a quilled Disney Princess Castle, which was so beautiful I knew she'd love it, so I ordered the tools that day and made my own version. To name my business TillyViktor seemed fitting – Tilly for my niece, and Viktor as a nod to my Dad's middle name and our Polish heritage.

Initially, TillyViktor was a side project that I managed alongside my fashion career. I took commissions and created bespoke quilled art pieces. However, after receiving numerous requests for quilling tutorials, advice and supplies, I was excited to develop my own line of branded quilling papers and tools. I launched my first branded tool kit in early 2022, followed closely by my first quilling kit a few weeks later. The support from the craft community was overwhelming and the brand's rapid growth exceeded all my expectations. That marked the beginning of an exciting new chapter!

TillyViktor is not just about selling quilling supplies; it's about sharing a passion for this ancient art form with a modern twist. My background in design influences my approach, bringing a contemporary edge to traditional quilling techniques.

From a hobby to a thriving business, I would love to continue to captivate and inspire crafters around the world. I get immense joy from teaching others and watching them discover the beauty of quilling, and I'm excited about the journey ahead – one filled with inspiring kits and templates, colourful papers, high-quality tools, workshops and, of course, books and tutorials! Whether you're an experienced crafter or a complete beginner, the designs in this book aim to help you develop and refine your skills as you progress through each project, learning new techniques along the way. Once you've worked through the 20 projects, you'll have mastered all the basic quilling techniques, giving you a strong foundation in this craft.

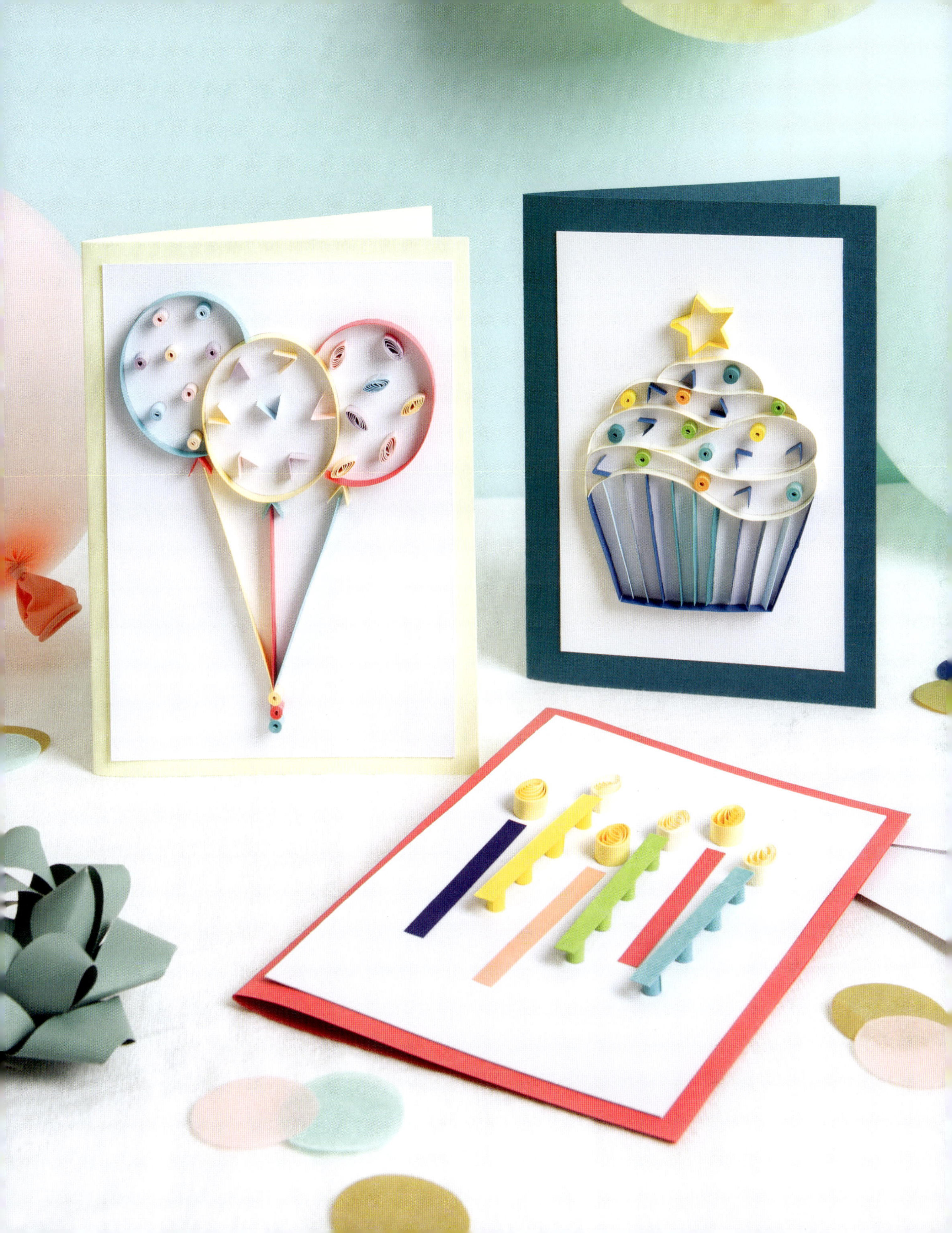

What is quilling?

Quilling, also known as paper filigree, is a fascinating and ancient decorative art form that involves twirling, coiling, pinching and shaping thin paper strips into intricate and playful designs. Imagine transforming simple paper into stunning art pieces! From adorning religious artefacts to being worn as jewellery, quilling has a rich history believed to have originated in Europe during the fifteenth and sixteenth centuries.

In the past, quills or needles were used to roll the paper, but today quilling is much more accessible with the development of many specialized tools, making complex designs so much easier and more precise. Today, quilling typically involves using a slotted quilling tool to coil the paper strips into tight circles, which can then be pinched, twisted and manipulated into various traditional quilled shapes such as teardrops, petals, diamonds, scrolls, hearts and spirals. These individual elements are assembled in simple or complex ways to make beautiful arrangements.

Quilling isn't just about making stunning pieces; it's about mindfulness, education and relaxation. The repetitive actions of rolling and shaping the paper can be incredibly soothing and stress relieving, making it a therapeutic hobby. And although a finished quilling project may look complicated, the basics of this art form are surprisingly easy to master. With a bit of practice and patience, you can create an array of shapes, patterns and designs. From simple floral designs to intricate portraits and even three-dimensional sculptures, quilling allows you to transform simple strips of paper into extraordinary works of art.

From its origins in religious communities to its modern-day revival, quilling continues to captivate and inspire creatives, artists and craft enthusiasts around the world. Its evolution over the centuries is a testament to the adaptability and creative potential of this beautiful and intricate paper craft.

Whether you're seeking a creative outlet, a new hobby or simply a moment to relax, with quilling, you're not just learning a craft; you're embarking on a journey of self-expression and creativity. Quilling opens up a world where you can unwind, explore your artistic side and create something truly unique and beautiful. I always say that with quilling, the possibilities are endless – your imagination is the only limit. No matter what artwork I'm creating, I often use many of the elements featured in this book. By simply adjusting the colours and layouts, you can create countless new designs. Let's get started!

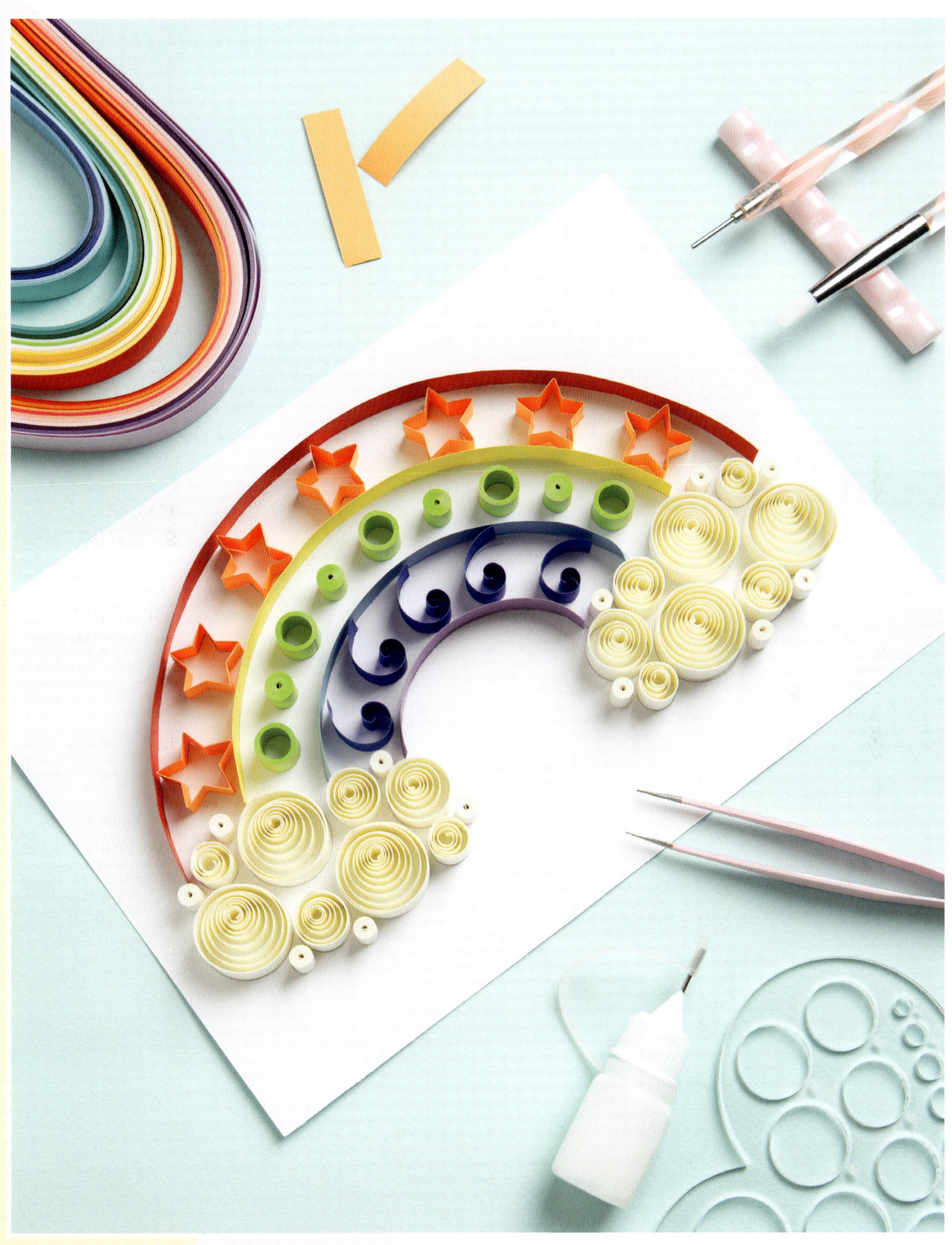

Tools and materials

There are many quilling tools available, but only a few are absolutely essential. Having the right tool is paramount to making your quilling journey simple and enjoyable, and good-quality tools are key to a good-quality piece of work.

I like to work with the TillyViktor tool collection, which I have detailed below. However, if you can't get a hold of the TillyViktor products, there are a few things I would recommend looking out for when sourcing quilling tools and paper:

- Use very sharp scissors to make crisp, even cuts in your paper.
- Source a quilling tool with a 10mm (⅜in) slot; this can be used for all paper widths.
- Tacky PVA is key; you need it to be not too wet, not too tacky.

Tools

1 Manual quilling tool
This is an essential tool for quilling. The paper is slotted into the centre of the tool enabling you to twirl, coil and then shape the elements. I use a 10mm (⅜in) slotted quilling tool.

2 Quilling board
Many basic elements require the use of a quilling board, which allows you to size the elements, and keep the shapes all nice and uniform, for example when making petals on a flower.

3 Tweezers
Craft tweezers are a personal choice when quilling, some people prefer to use their fingers, but I wouldn't quill without tweezers! They make picking up, gluing and strategically placing elements simple and precise.

4 Glue brush
I never craft without a glue brush. When quilling we don't need a lot of glue, but a small amount in exactly the right place. The TillyViktor Deluxe Glue Brush is double ended, it has a spatula tip at one end and a pointed tip on the other, which allows for neat and precise work. I guarantee once you start using one you'll never quill without it!

5 Sharp craft scissors
When I say sharp, I mean sharp to their very tip scissors! As crafters we all have scissors, but I use the Pointy and Precise TillyViktor scissors, they are an absolute game changer when quilling!

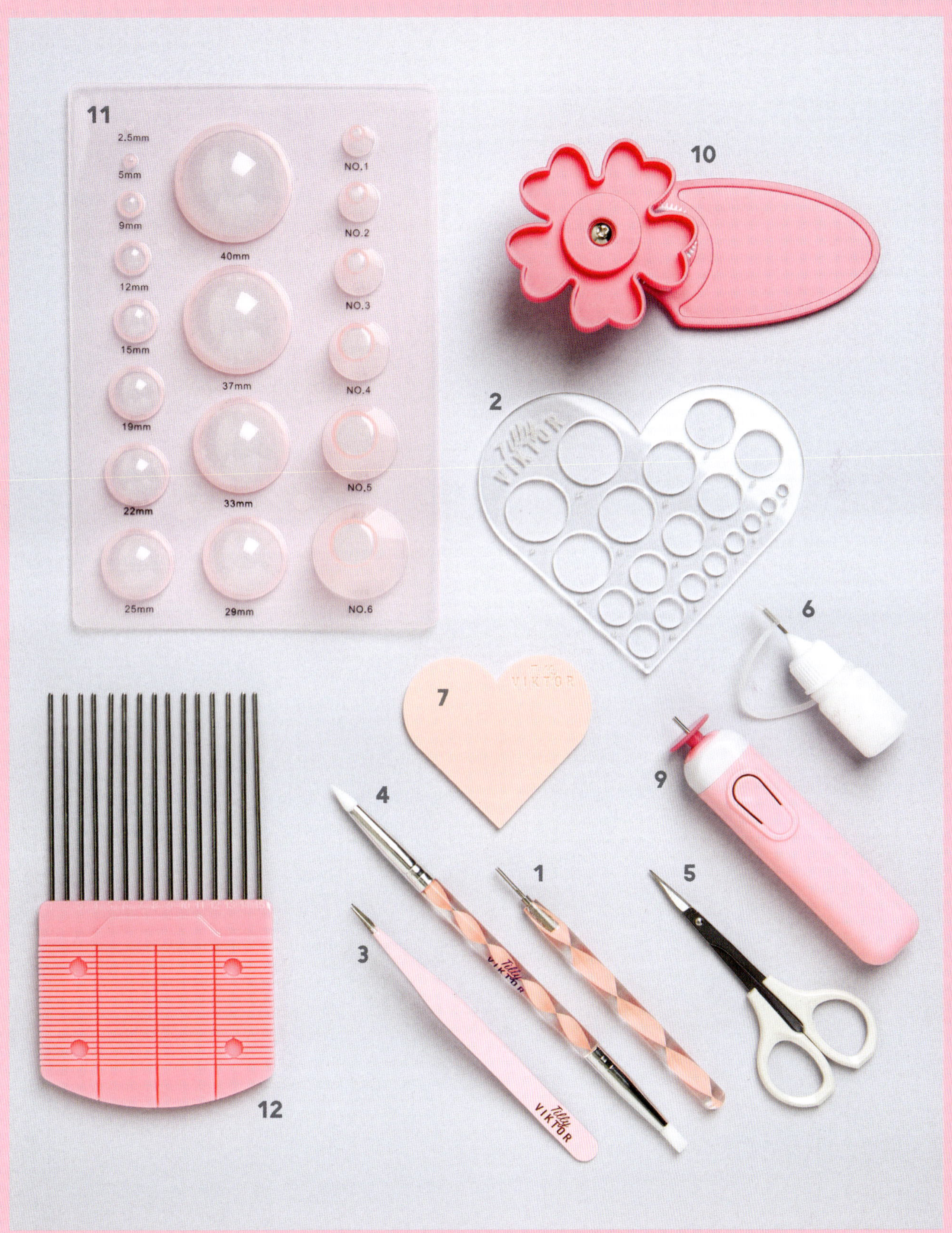

11
2.5mm
5mm
9mm
12mm
15mm
19mm
22mm
25mm
40mm
37mm
33mm
29mm
NO.1
NO.2
NO.3
NO.4
NO.5
NO.6
10
2
7
6
9
4
3
1
5
12

6 Glue

I always use TillyViktor Tacky PVA glue. You need it to be not so wet that it warps the base card, at the same time it's not so tacky that it has dried before you get a chance to use it!

7 Glue plate (optional)

I find having the glue in one specific area to dip your brush into keeps things clean and neat, and once you've finished, any leftover dried glue peels right off.

8 Tool stand (optional)

Another optional tool but one that keeps your crafting area organized, and stops your tools from rolling around your desk.

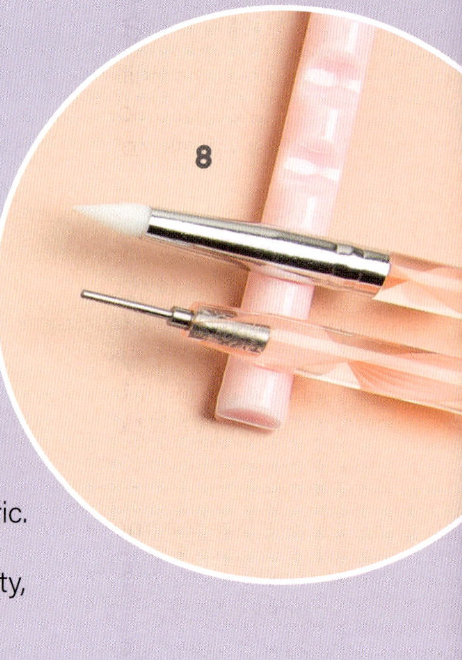

9 Electric quilling tool (optional)

A tool that divides opinion! Some people prefer manual, some prefer electric. I prefer a manual as I like the rhythmic aspect of twirling on a manual tool but for those of you who want a quicker result or those with limited dexterity, maybe the electric tool is for you!

10 Paper crimper (optional)

This is an optional tool that crimps paper, and there are a couple of projects that feature this variation. Simply slot the paper into the crimper and turn the handle to give a corrugated effect to the paper. This can be a great little tool to add interest and texture.

11 Dome mould (optional)

A handy tool which adds extra dimension to quilled elements. You can use the concave side to press flowers into to make them more life-like, and similarly use the convex side to press quilled ellipses onto to give them a more dome-like appearance!

12 Quilling comb (optional)

A brilliant tool to expand upon your basic quilling shapes, this tool can make larger elements like leaves, wings, petals – the possibilities are endless!

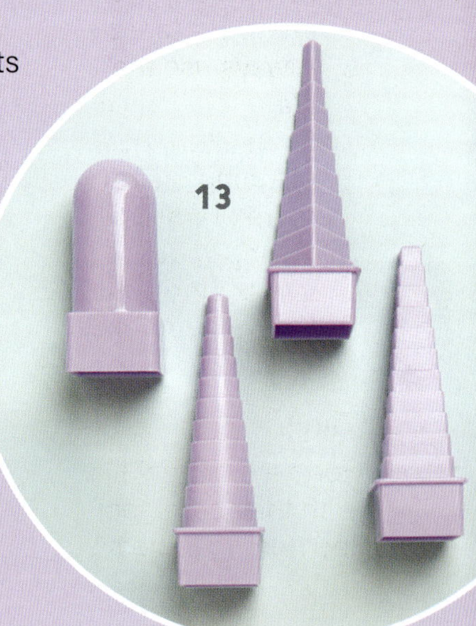

13 Quilling towers (optional)

The perfect addition to your quilling tool range, the towers are an easy way to make hollow bordered elements. You can use these when making circle eyes, square console buttons or maybe even triangle sprinkles on a cake artwork!

Quilling papers

Also known as quilling strips, there are so many variations available on the market. Traditionally many people quilled with 80gsm (50lb) papers, however I prefer to use 120gsm (80lb) papers, as I find papers lighter than 120gsm (80lb) feel thin and fragile, and I find they don't hold the shape, meaning the finished artwork isn't as robust.

I sometimes use heavier papers to edge my work, especially when working with text pieces, however, I wouldn't ordinarily quill with anything heavier than 120gsm (80lb). Thicker papers or card stock can be hard to quill, they can split, become uneven or just look a little untidy.

The projects in this book are quilled using TillyViktor paper (see below for the TillyViktor colours). These papers are available in three different pre-cut widths: 3mm, 5mm and 10mm (⅛in, ³⁄₁₆in and ⅜in) from the TillyViktor website. However, if you can't get your hands on TillyViktor papers, I recommend the guidelines below when choosing papers:

1   Always choose good-quality papers: in my opinion 120gsm (80lb) works best.
2   Always buy pre-cut strips; artwork can look a little untidy if strips aren't cut to a consistent width.
3   Always use the correct width for the desired outcome. If you are planning to send your artwork as a greetings card, use 3mm (⅛in) or 5mm (³⁄₁₆in) paper widths to make it flat enough for posting. If you are planning on framing your artwork, 10mm (⅜in) papers always give more drama, dimension and personality.
4   Mixing widths can give added interest to a piece of work – I like to mix 5mm (³⁄₁₆in) and 10mm (⅜in) strips when working on framed artworks.

TillyViktor quilling papers

For each project I have listed the TillyViktor paper colours used, along with their corresponding number. The colour names and numbers match the quilling papers sold on the TillyViktor website, as shown below.

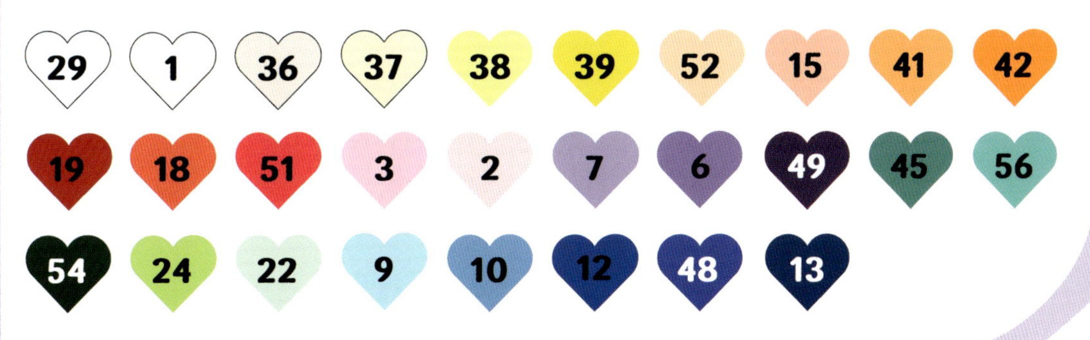

TillyViktor top tips

A finished piece of quilled art can seem overwhelming at first, but when you break it down into simple steps and individual elements, it becomes surprisingly achievable! To help guide you, I've added my top tips below.

Master the basic shapes

Take time to learn the basic shapes we cover in this book before moving on to more complex work.

Good-quality tools

Quilling has come a long way since its ancient roots, there are now many tools to help you create precise work (see pages 10–12). As the bare minimum get your hands on a good set of craft tweezers, a good-quality quilling tool and quilling board, and a small brush to apply glue.

Paper weight

There are many pre-cut paper strips available on the market, however I only use 120gsm (80lb). I find lighter paper flimsy and doesn't hold its shape as well. Heavier paper can be difficult to roll or coil. I only tend to use heavier card for outlines or borders.

Glue

Choosing the right glue is key. I've found the best glue is a tacky PVA glue. Thin PVA glue can soak into the card base, but thicker, tackier glue will bond your papers quickly without warping the backing card in the process. It is important to get the right amount of glue in exactly the right place. Too much glue will leave your work looking messy; not enough will make it less durable. Use a small brush to apply glue, to get it exactly where it needs to go without getting too messy!

Colours

In my opinion, having the right colours can either make or break a piece of artwork. Too many colours can look busy and overcomplicated, and too few can leave your work looking a little flat. I like to get out my coloured papers first, lay them down next to each other and make sure the palette is right before I start crafting.

Keep your paper strips organized

It's so beautiful when your quilling strips are all pristine and flat! To keep them this way once a pack of paper is open, pop a metal stationery clip on the top of each colour and hang them.

Practise, practise, practise!

This one is a given! Like any new skill, quilling takes a little patience and practise. If something doesn't look right, take a deep breath and try again. Go slow and give yourself the time and space to learn.

The quilled shapes

You will learn the techniques to create the 18 different quilled elements listed below (see more on pages 98–115). Once you've mastered those, the creative possibilities for your quilling are limitless. These elements form the foundation of everything I create, no matter the piece!

- Rounded teardrop
- Pointed teardrop
- Tight coil
- Multi-coloured tight coil
- Ring coil
- Ellipse coil
- Loose coil
- Fringed tight coil
- Hollow marquise
- Marquise
- Loose swirl/Open scroll
- Arch
- Triangle
- Pointed heart
- Star
- Hollow teardrop
- Ring teardrop
- Hollow ellipse
- Rose

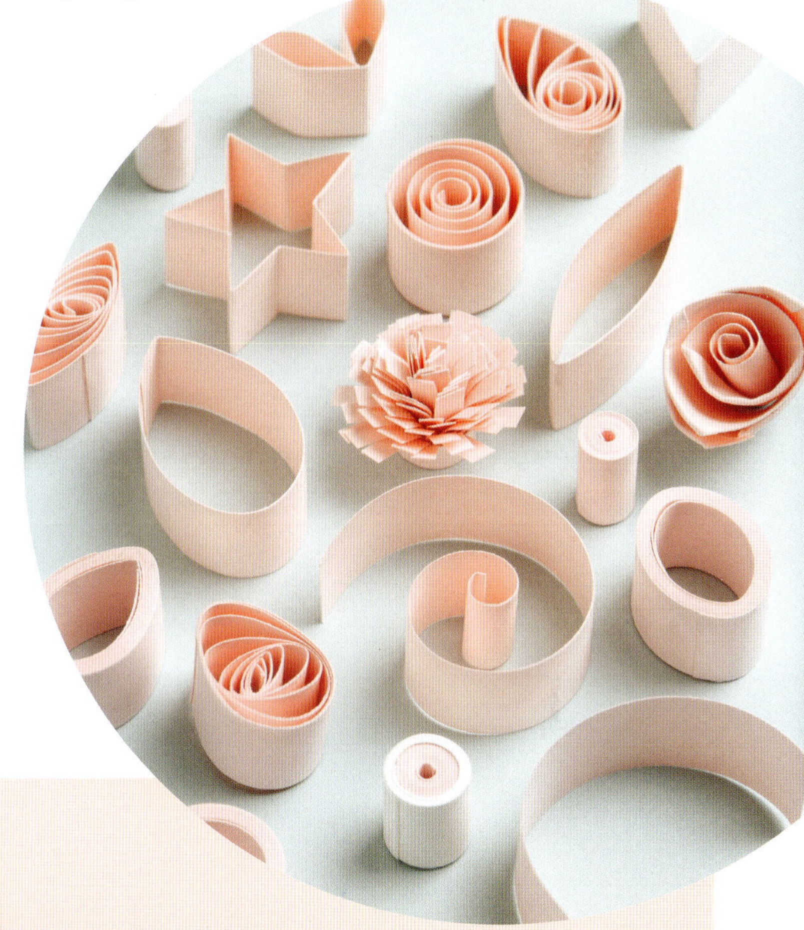

Templates and card bases

Whether you're an experienced quiller or complete beginner, I recommend using quilling templates. There is a ready-made, full-size template for each project in the book on pages 116–128.

Using the templates

You can either photocopy the templates from the back of the book, or download them from the Bookmarked Hub (www.bookmarkedhub.com) to print out. Be sure to print or photocopy onto a sturdy card base, at least 300gsm (200lb), to prevent the base warping from the glue, and to provide a quality surface to work on.

I generally suggest using a plain white base for your artwork, but feel free to choose a coloured base if that suits your style!

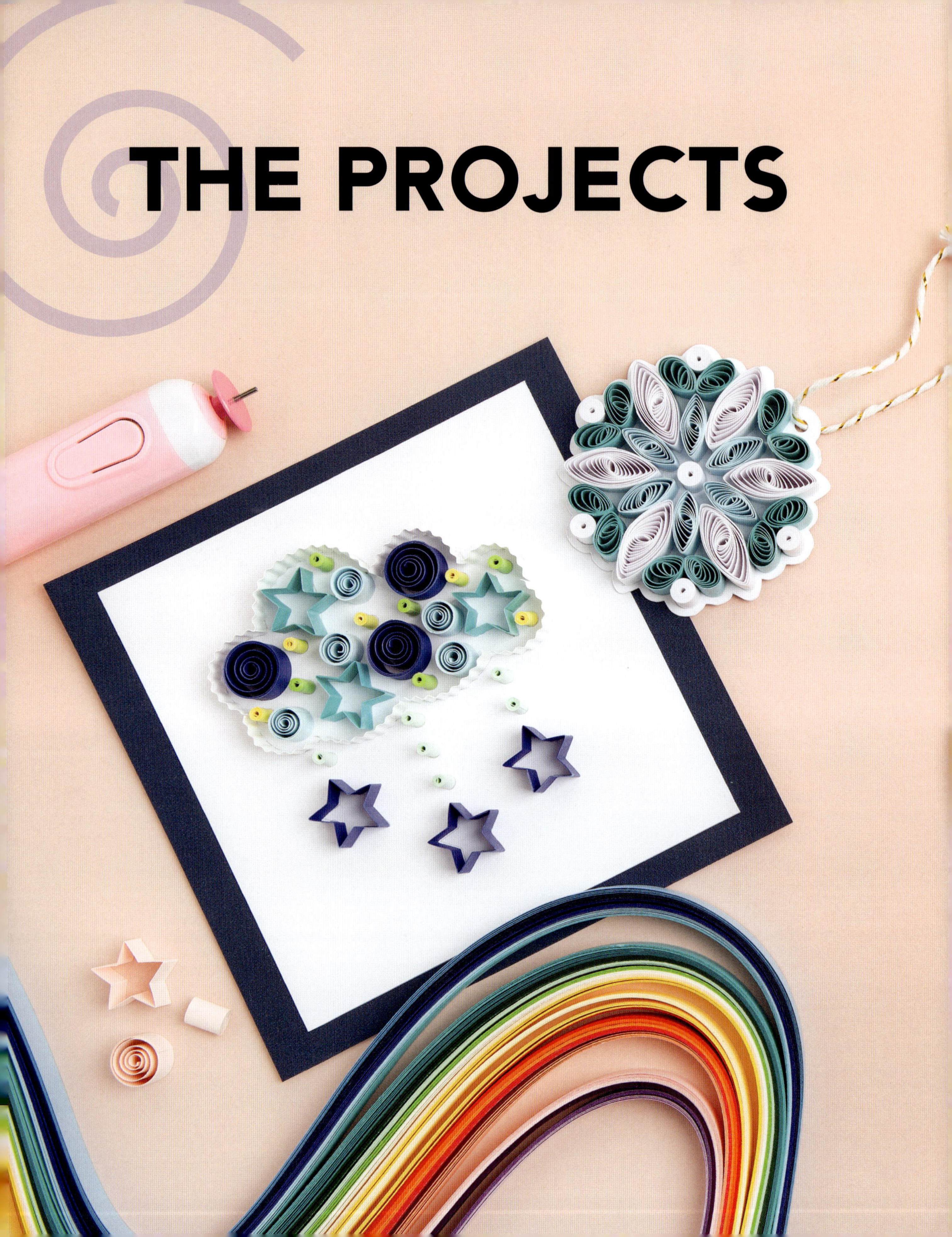

THE PROJECTS

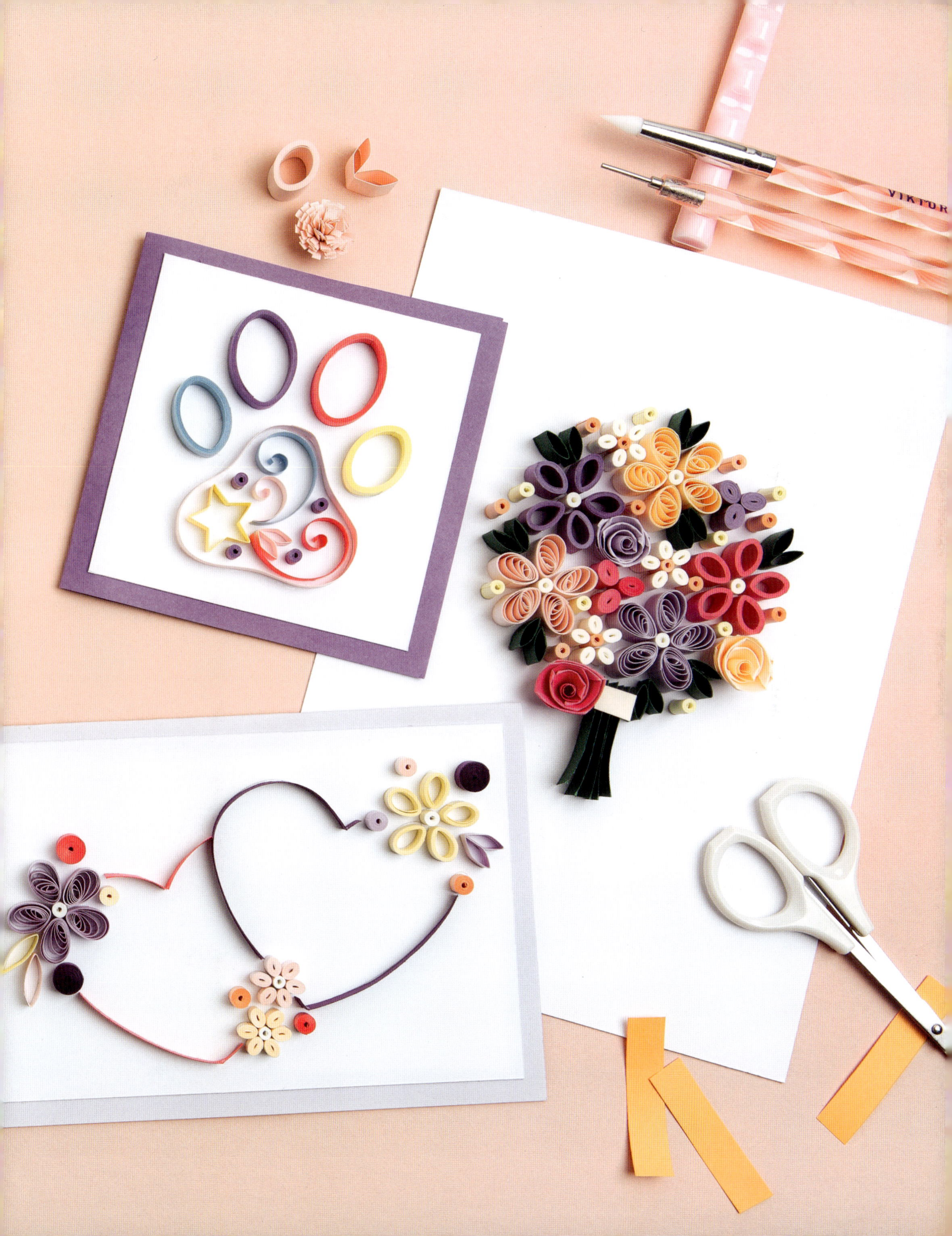

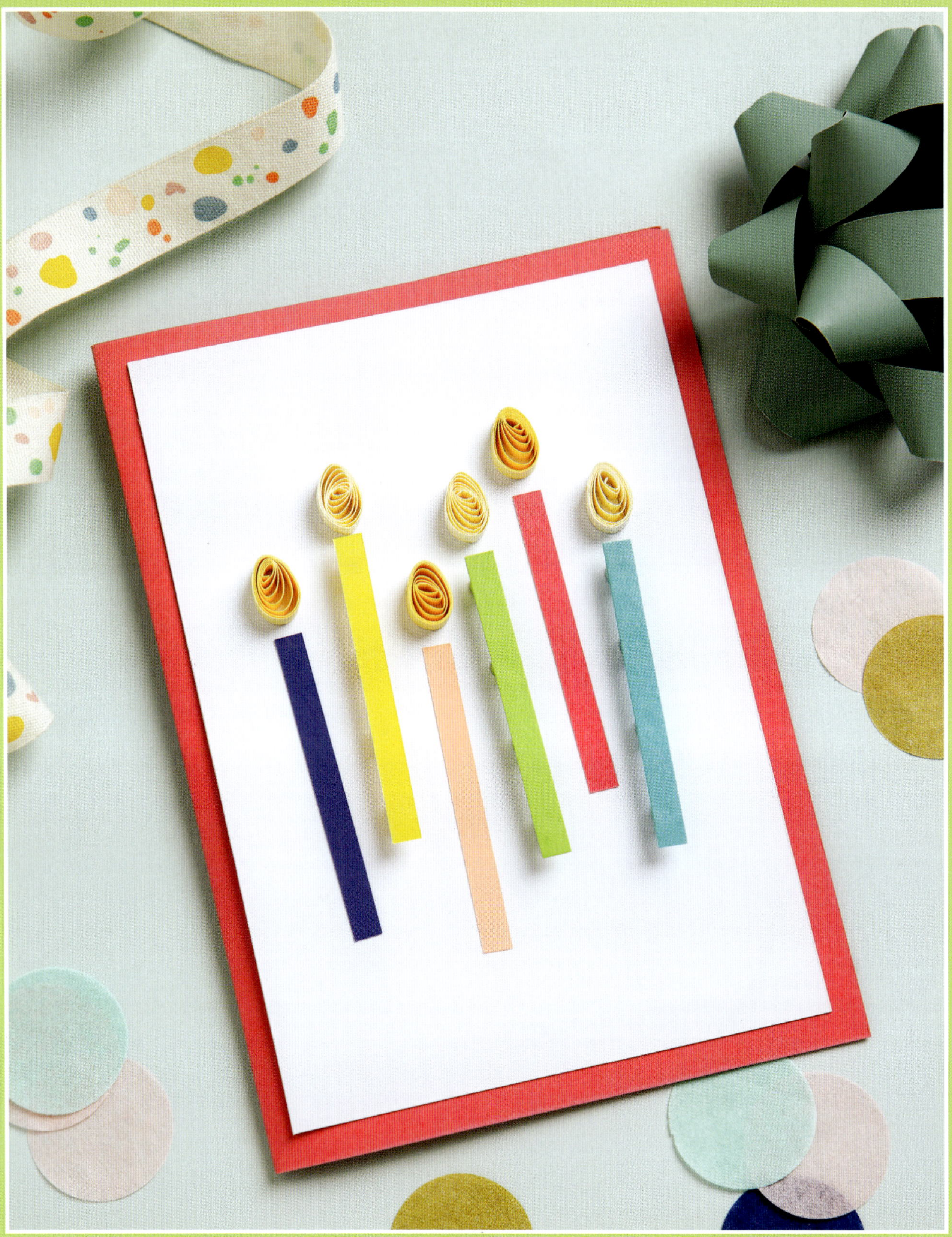

CANDLES

Made using rainbow colours, this candle card is a cute little greetings card. The colours can be changed to suit different occasions and recipients. With the use of just two quilled elements, this is the perfect place to start your quilling journey.

The candles are simple to create. Half the candles are flat, half are raised off the base by sitting them on top of the tight coil shapes.

Candles

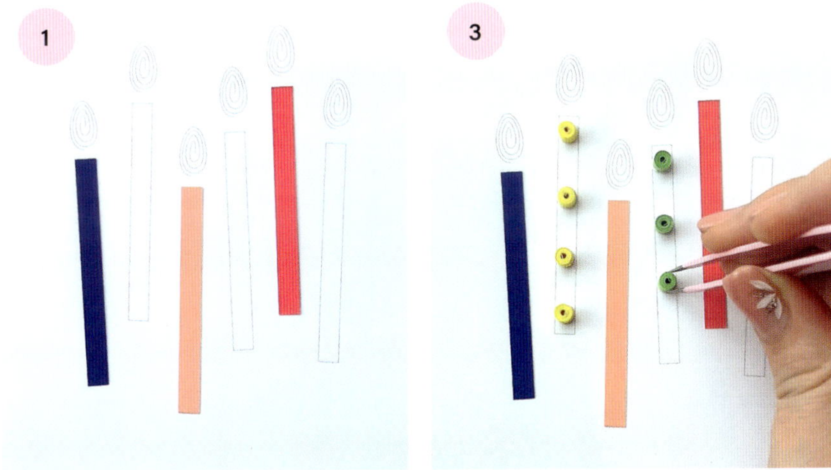

1 Cut six 5.4cm (2⅛in) strips of paper in your chosen colours. I've made the flat candles in royal blue, peach and magenta. Add a little glue to the back of these strips and fix down to the template.

2 Cut four 8cm (3⅛in) strips each in lemon, viridity and turquoise and follow the instructions on page 100 to make four tight coils in each colour.

3 Stick the tight coils down to the template base with an even gap between each coil, ensuring there is a tight coil at the base and the tip of the candle on the template.

4 Add a little glue to a glue brush and dab on top of the tight coils, then overlay the corresponding candle strip on top of the coils. This will give the candle body a raised and more three-dimensional appearance.

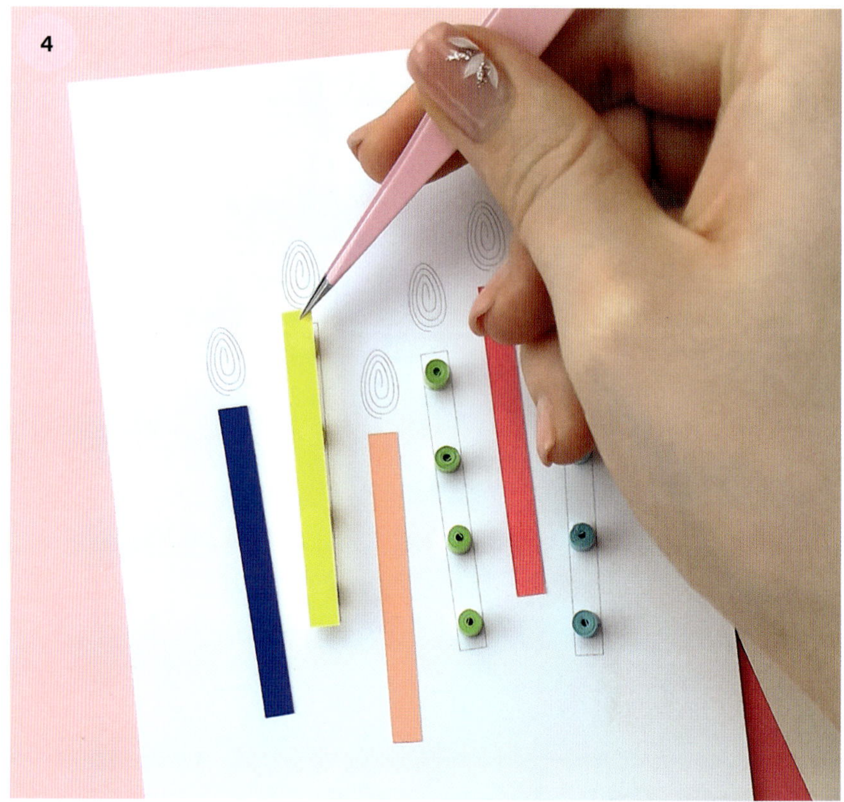

Flames

5 The candle flames are made from simple rounded teardrop shapes. You can use one colour for all six flames or use two complementary colours for added interest: I've used lemon and light yellow. To make your flames, cut six 15cm (6in) strips in your chosen colours. Use the 10mm (⅜in) hole on the quilling board and follow the instructions on page 98 to make the rounded teardrops.

6 Once all six flames have been made, dab a little glue on to the back of the teardrop shape and fix down to the template base.

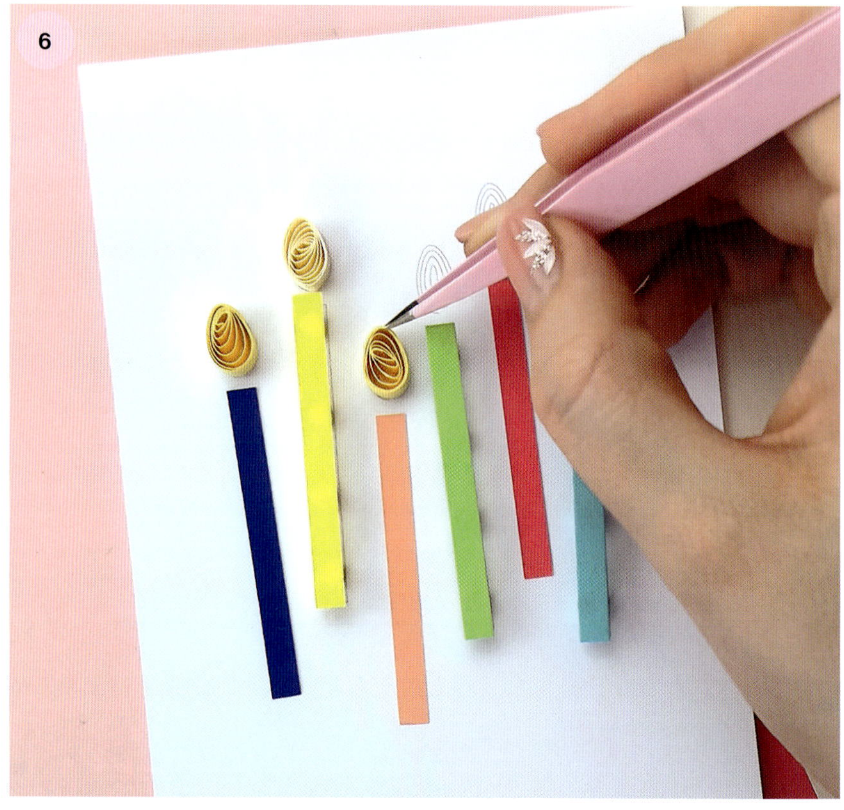

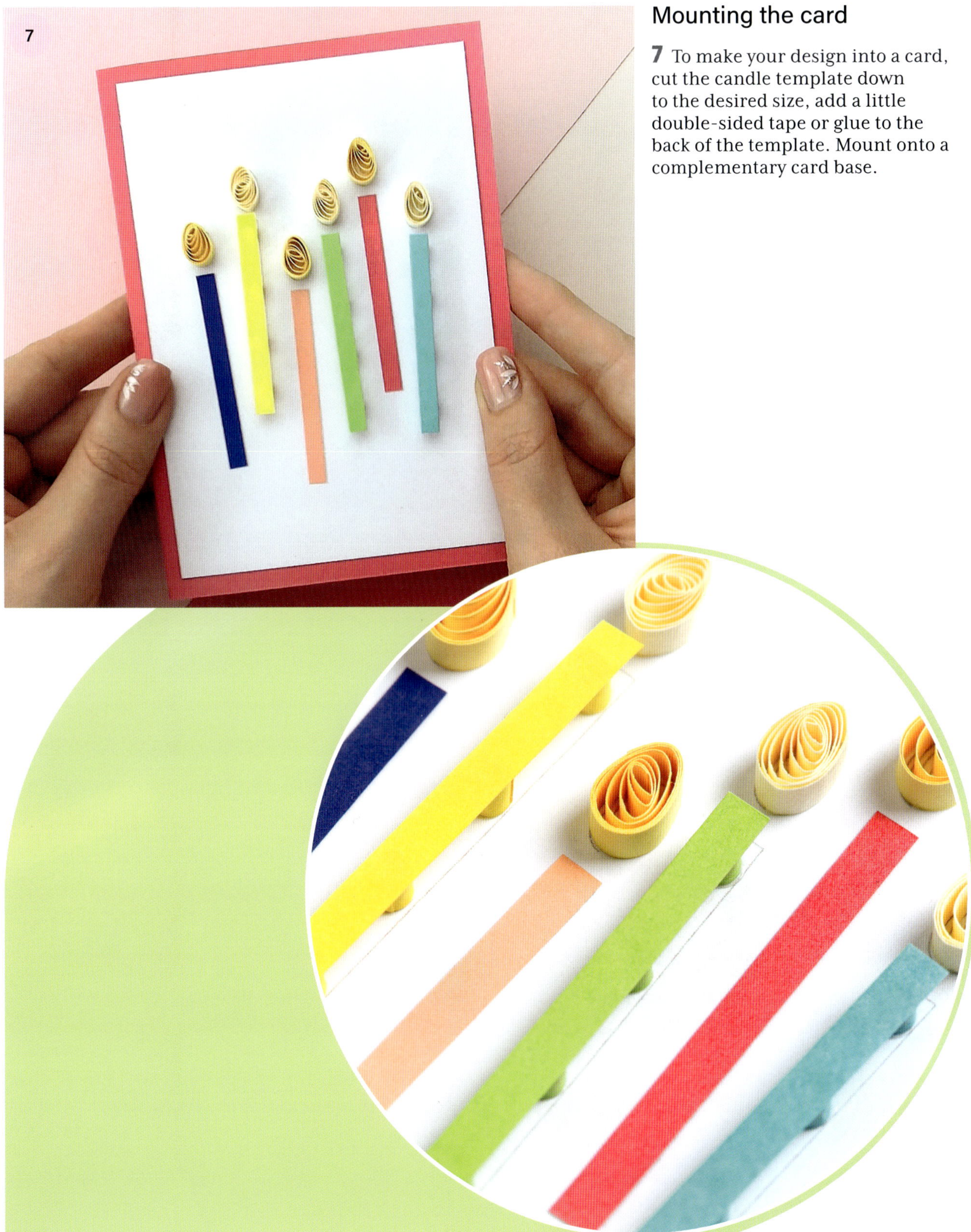

Mounting the card

7 To make your design into a card, cut the candle template down to the desired size, add a little double-sided tape or glue to the back of the template. Mount onto a complementary card base.

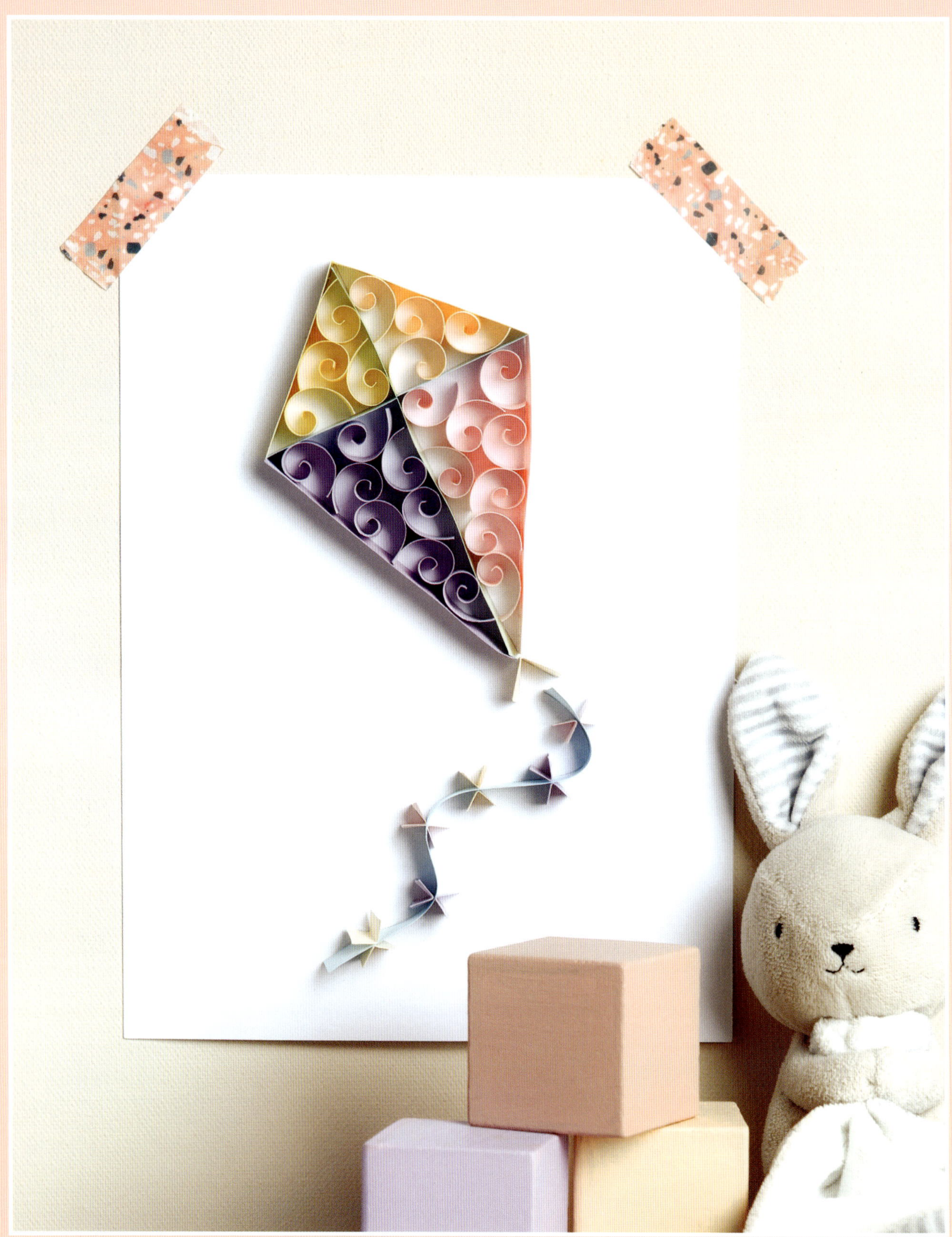

KITE

This pastel kite wall art is super simple and is the perfect piece to continue your quilling journey. A statement piece for a nursery wall or a beautiful framed gift for a friend who loves adventures!

Outline

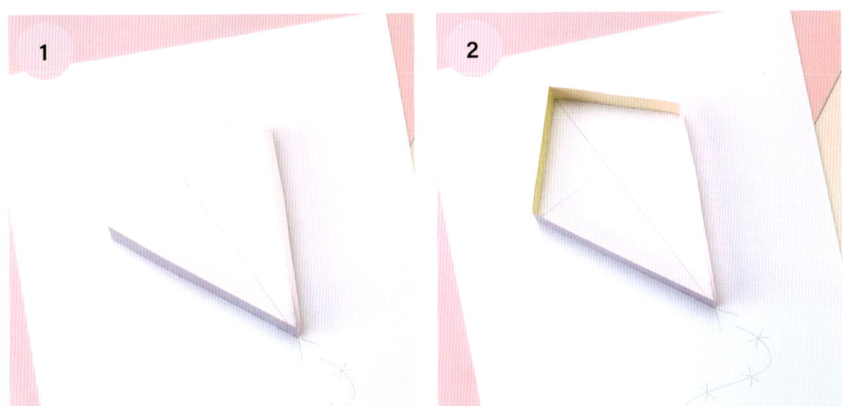

1 Start your kite by assembling the outline. Cut one strip in light purple and one in pink, both measuring 7.6cm (3in) long. These will form the bottom section of the kite outline; sit them in place on the template.

2 Cut one strip in apricot and one in light yellow, both measuring 4.8cm (1⅞in) long. These strips will form the top section of the kite outline.

3 Add a little glue to the thin edge of each of the four strips, using your glue brush. Stick them down on the template using tweezers to hold in place until the glue bonds.

Kite centre

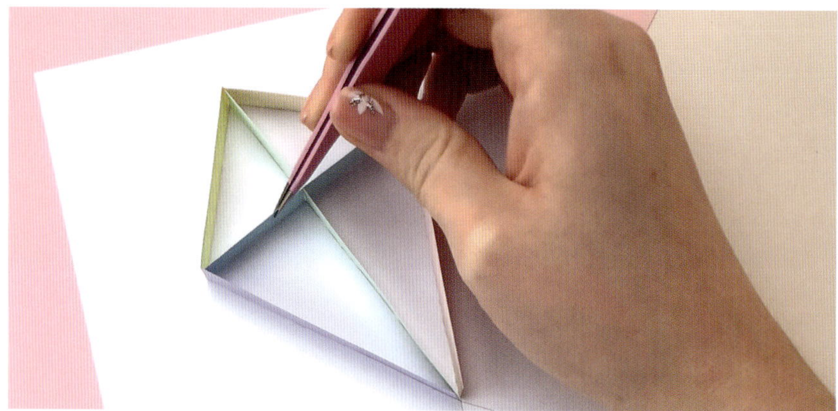 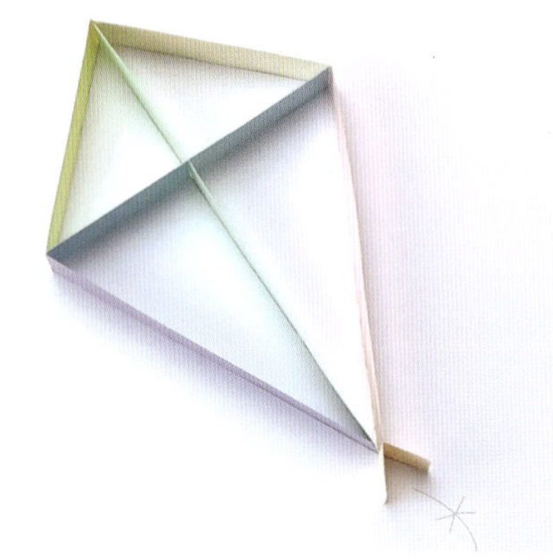

4 There is one long strip running the entire length of the kite and two smaller strips sitting either side of the middle. Cut a 10.1cm (4in) strip in light green and two smaller strips in sky blue, measuring 3.3cm (1⁵⁄₁₆in) each. Apply a little glue to the thin edge of the strips using your glue brush and stick down to the template, using your tweezers to hold in place until the glue bonds.

5 Cut a 2cm (¾in) strip in apricot and fold in half. Add a little glue to one edge and stick down to the template, in an upside-down V shape at the base of the kite.

Kite tail

6 Cut a sky blue strip in half, and add a little glue with your brush to the first few centimetres (an inch) of the thin edge of the strip. Stick the strip down to the template using your tweezers to manoeuvre the strip into place and hold to allow the glue to bond.

7 Once the first section has stuck, apply a little glue to the glue brush and paint it directly onto the template. Use your tweezers to guide the strip in place, as shown, sticking down as you go and trimming off any excess once you reach the end.

8 There are 12 mini V shapes decorating the kite tail. Cut four strips in pale pink, lilac and peach, all measuring 1cm (³⁄₈in) each. Fold the strips in half, add a little glue to the base of each strip, and fix down to the template.

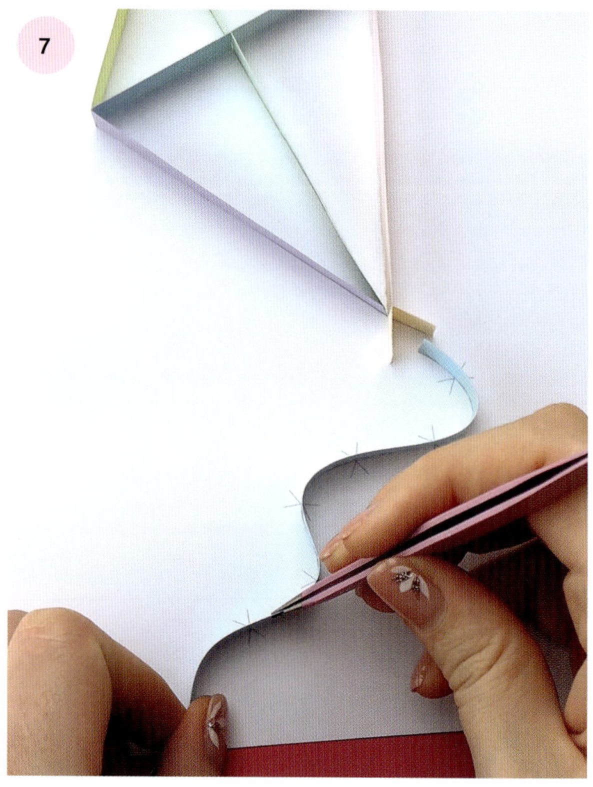

Kite decoration

9 Cut 4cm (1⁹⁄₁₆in) lengths of the following: four strips in light yellow; eight strips in light purple; eight strips in pink; four strips in apricot. Then follow the instructions on page 108 to make loose swirls.

10 Arrange the loose swirls inside each section of the kite. Once you are happy with their placement, add a little glue to the base of each element and stick down to the template using tweezers.

11 If you have some gaps, make a couple of extra loose swirls and add them in.

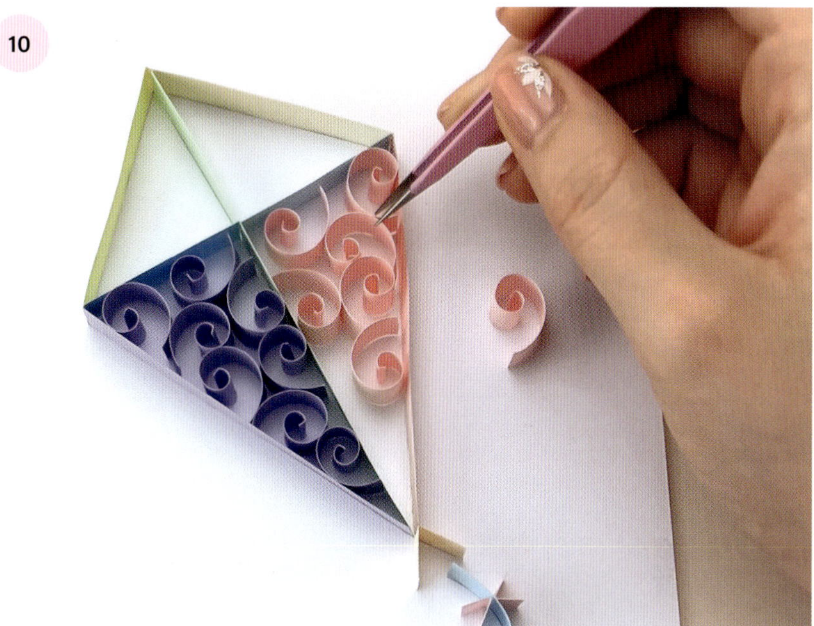

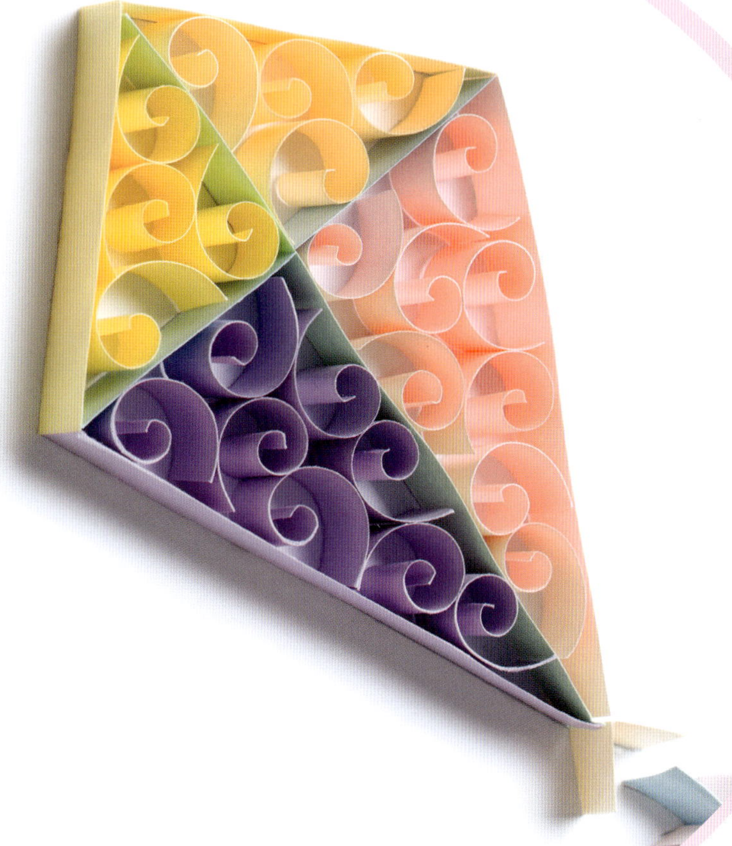

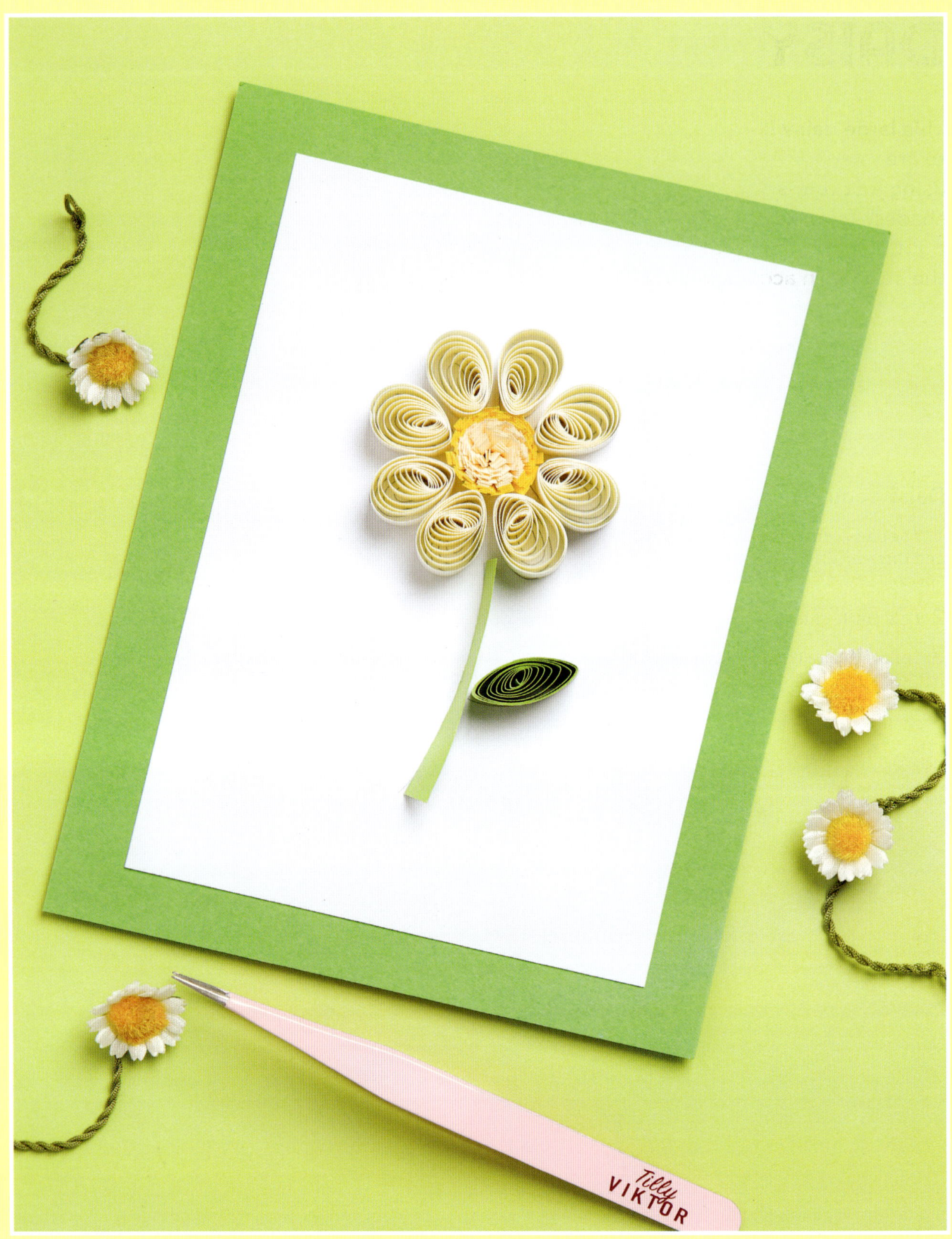

Tilly
VIKTOR

DAISY

This large daisy is definitely a statement piece, simple to create yet so eye catching once completed. It is made using just four simple quilled elements in fresh spring shades. To make the flower, you will attach the fringed tight coil first, followed by the quilled petals and finally the stem with accompanying leaf.

Daisy centre

1 The daisy centre is made by fringing two strips in varying shades of yellow and then making a tight coil. Cut a 25cm (9¹³⁄₁₆in) strip in light yellow and apricot, and fringe with a sharp pair of quilling scissors, as shown below.

2 Dab a little glue to one end of the paler strip and stick both strips together.

3 Follow the instructions on page 100 to make tight coils using the fringed strip, but take care not to wind too tightly as this may tear the fringe.

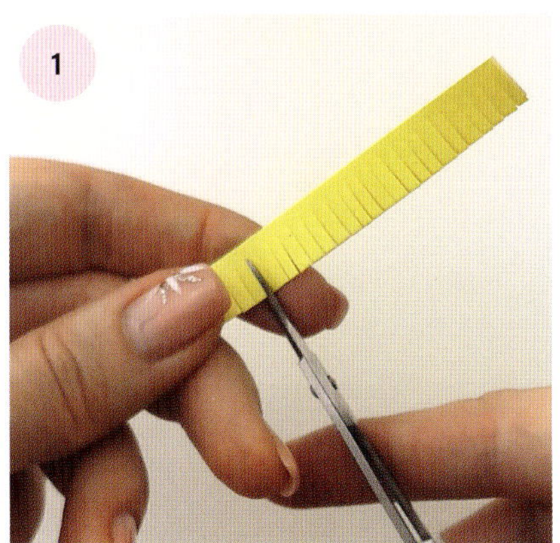

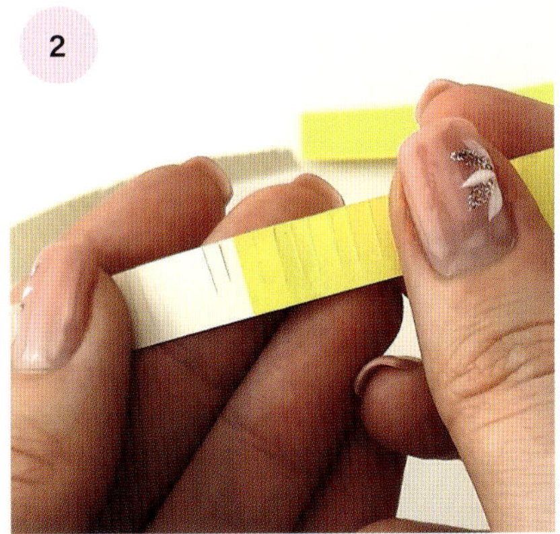

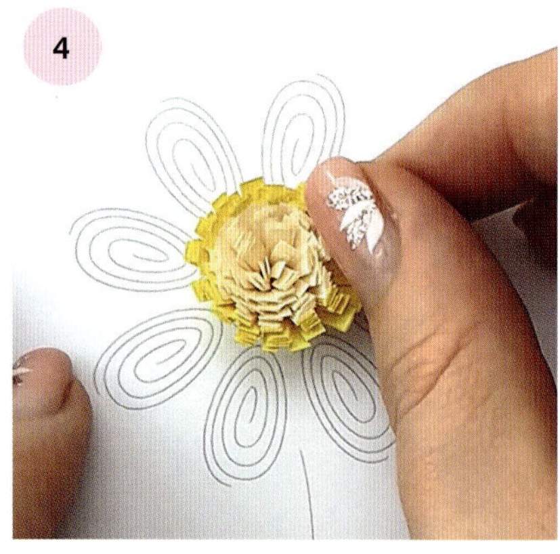
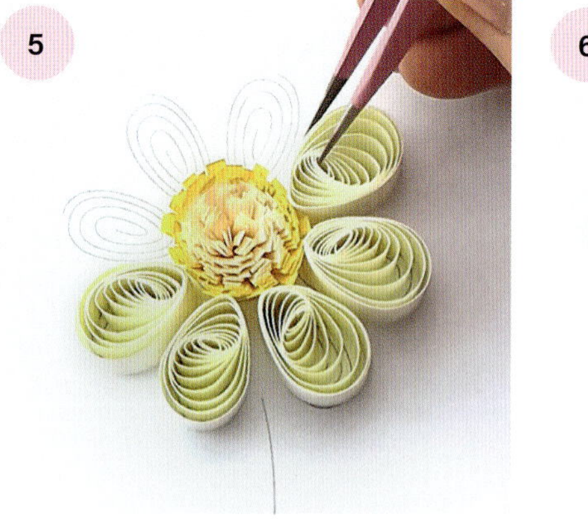
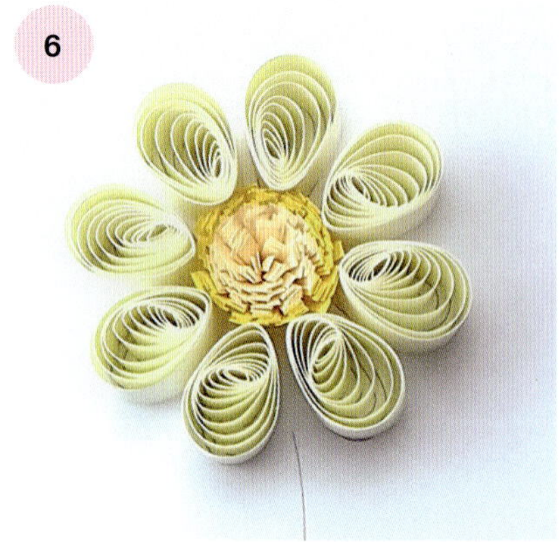

4 Add a generous amount of glue to the base of the fringed element and fix down to the template card, adding a little volume by fanning out the fringe as shown.

Petals

5 The petals are made from rounded teardrop shapes, there are eight in total, these will be placed around the daisy centre to make the flower shape. Cut eight 27cm (10⅝in) strips in beige and follow the instructions on page 98 to make. Use the 15mm (⁹⁄₁₆in) hole on your quilling board.

6 Once all eight petals are made, add a little glue to your glue brush and dab onto the base of each petal, then fix down to the template.

Stem

7 The daisy stem is made by sticking a strip down to the template on its thin edge. Cut a 5cm (2in) strip in viridity, apply a little glue to the strip edge and stick to the template. Hold in place with your tweezers for a moment to allow the glue to bond.

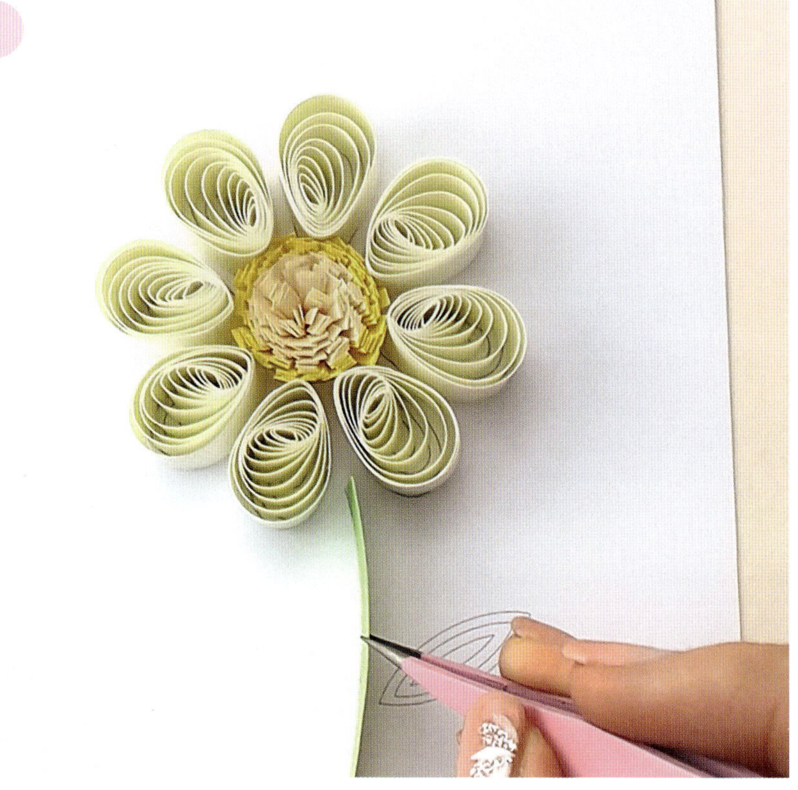

Leaf

8 Finish off your daisy by adding a little leaf to the stem. The leaf is made from a marquise shape. Cut one 27cm (10⅝in) strip in viridity and follow the instructions on page 107 to make. Use the 15mm (⁹⁄₁₆in) hole on your quilling board.

9 Once your leaf is made, add a little glue to your glue brush and dab on to the base, then fix down to the template.

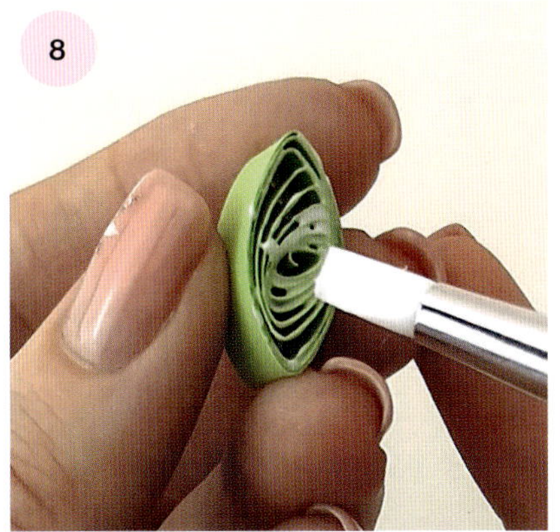

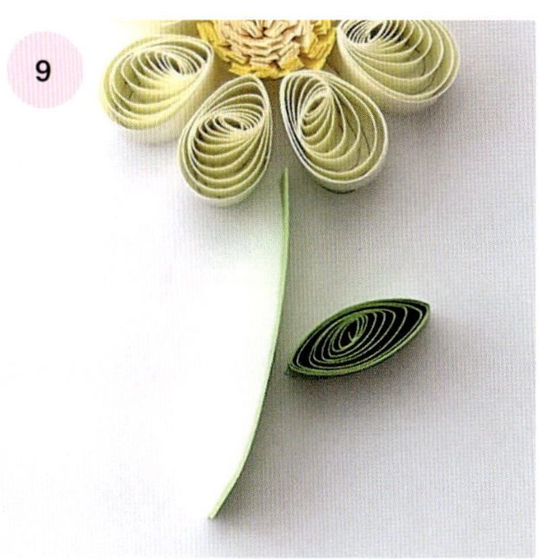

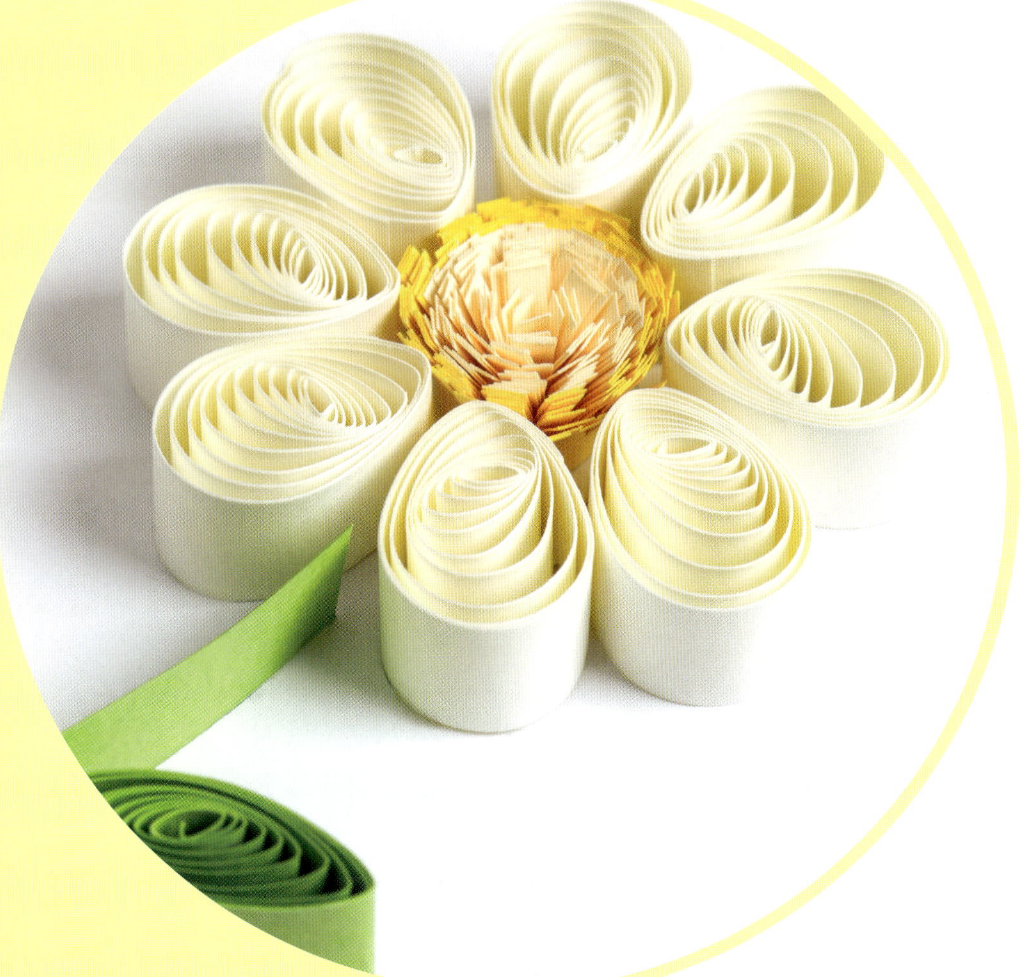

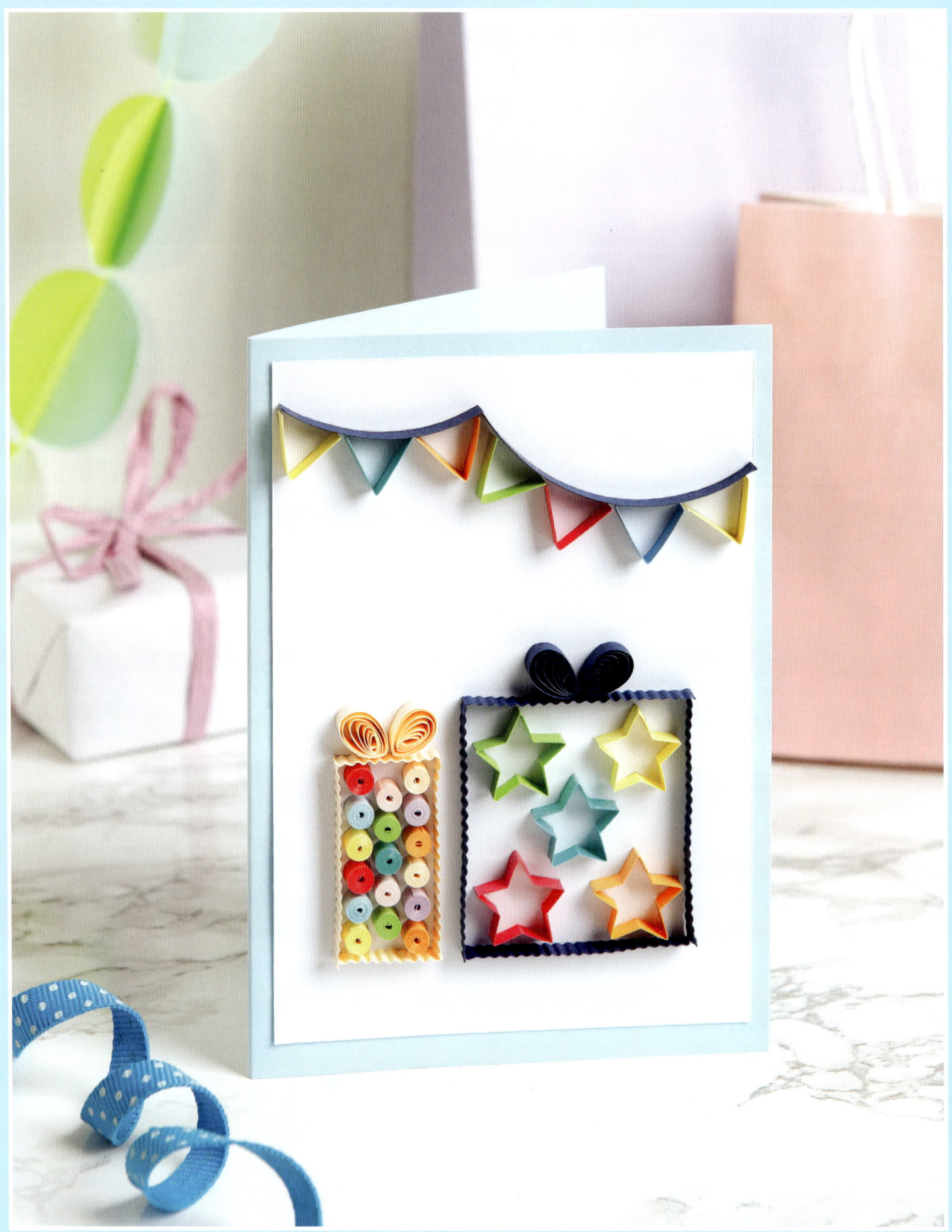

GIFTS

Designed in bright colours, this gift card is perfect for birthday celebrations! The artwork requires just four different quilled shapes in a range of fun colours.

TIP

You can make this piece without a paper crimper, the crimped paper simply adds a little interest to the finished piece.

Outlines

1 Take a strip of apricot and indigo quilling papers and run them through a quilling crimper (this step is optional).

2 The gift outlines are made by sticking strips down to the template on their thin edge. For the smaller gift, cut four strips in apricot, two measuring 3.9cm (1⁹⁄₁₆in) and two measuring 2cm (¾in). For the larger gift, cut four strips in indigo, two measuring 4.4cm (1¾in) and two measuring 4.9cm (1¹⁵⁄₁₆in). Using your glue brush, add a little glue to the thin edge of each strip and stick down to the template, holding each strip in place to allow the glue to bond before moving on to the next strip.

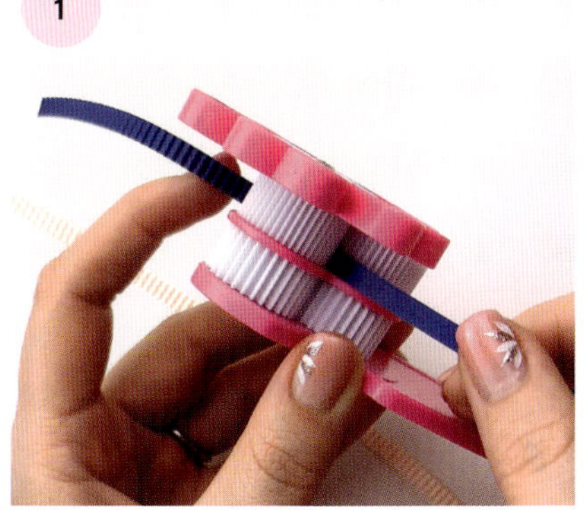

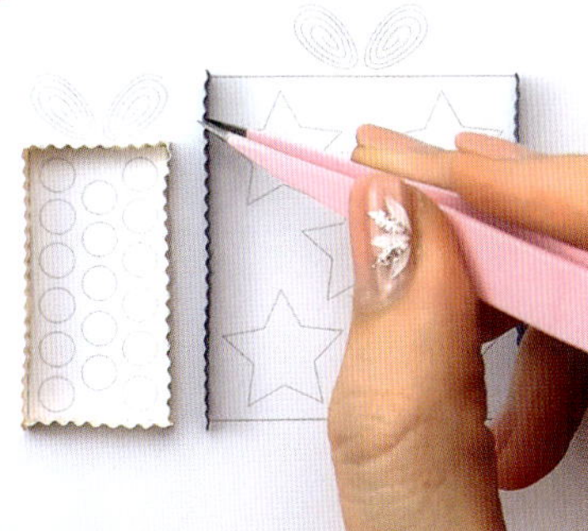

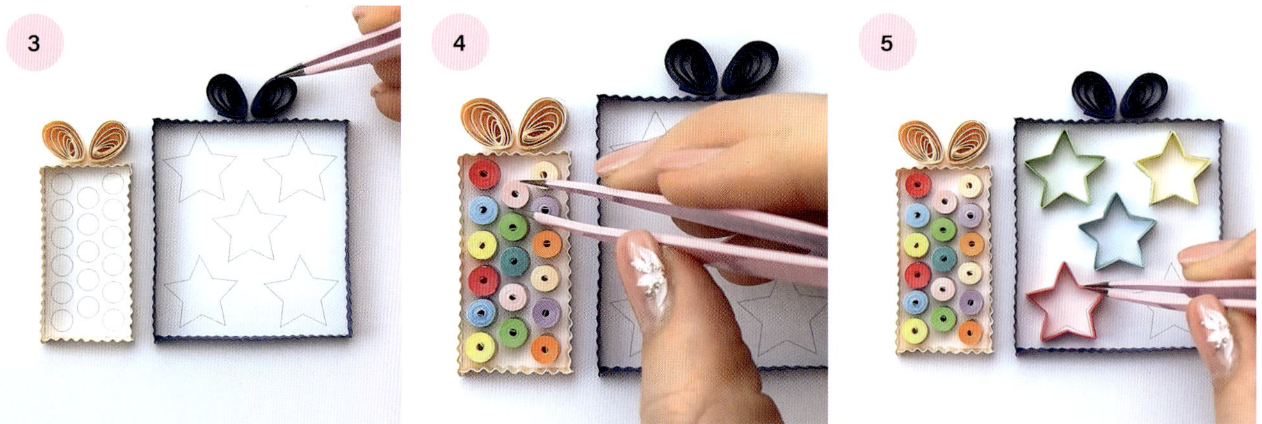

Bows

3 At the top of each gift sits a matching bow; each bow is made from two rounded teardrop shapes. Cut two strips measuring 13cm (5⅛in) for each bow and follow the instructions on page 98 to make the teardrop shapes. Use the 10mm (⅜in) hole on the quilling board. Once all teardrops are made, apply a little glue to the base of each element and stick down to the template.

Polka dots

4 The polka dots are made from tight coil shapes, there are 17 in total. Cut 17 strips in a variety of colours of your choice, each 13cm (5⅛in) long, and follow the instructions on page 100 to make. Add a little glue to the base of each tight coil and stick down.

Stars

5 There are five stars decorating the larger gift, one in each colour: magenta, sky blue, light yellow, viridity and orange. To make, cut 15cm (6in) strips and follow the instructions on the quilling shape pages to make. Once the stars are made, apply a little glue directly to the edge of the elements and stick down.

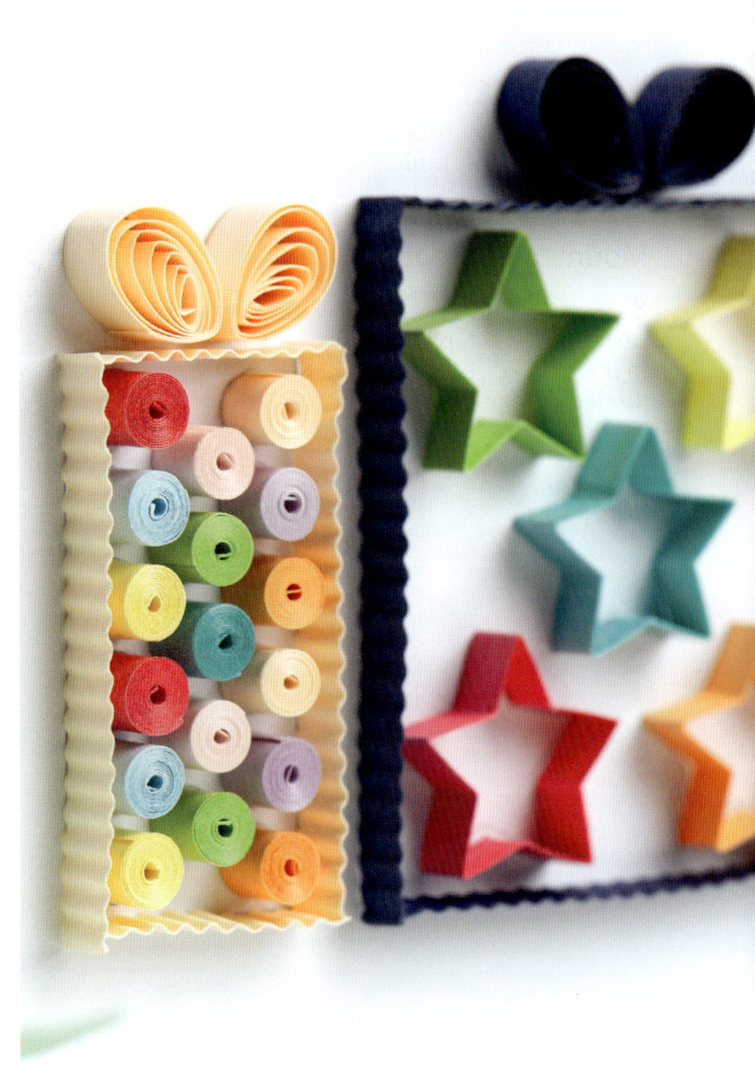

Bunting

6 Across the top of the card hangs a string of rainbow bunting. Make the bunting string first: cut two strips in indigo for the bunting string, one measuring 4.2cm (1⅝in) and one measuring 6cm (2⅜in). Slightly score the strips around your quilling tool to give them a curved shape.

7 Apply a little glue to the thin edge of the strips and use tweezers to guide them into place, holding to allow the glue to bond. To make the seven rainbow triangles, cut strips measuring 2.4cm (¹⁵⁄₁₆in) each, one in each of the following colours: turquoise, orange, viridity, magenta, sky blue and two in light yellow. Fold each strip in half, add a little glue to the base of each and fix down to the template.

Mounting the card

8 To make into a greetings card, cut the template down to the desired size, add a little double-sided tape or glue to the back of the template and mount onto a complementary coloured card base.

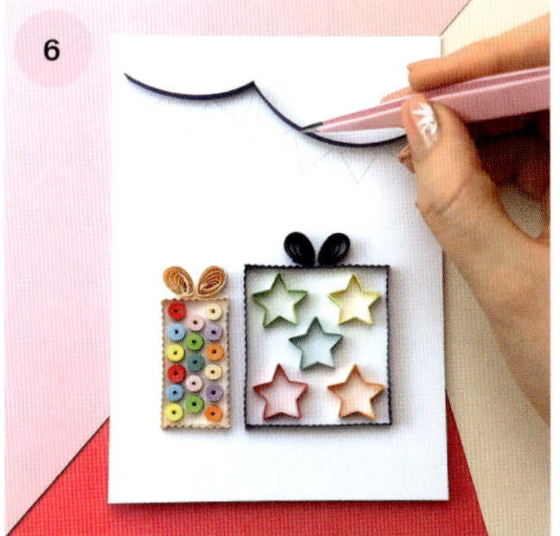

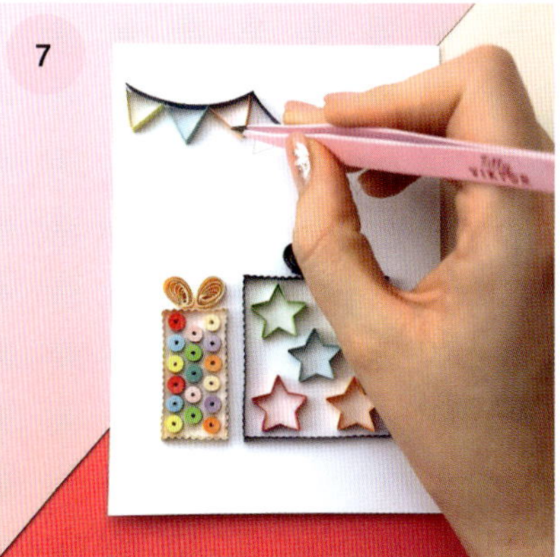

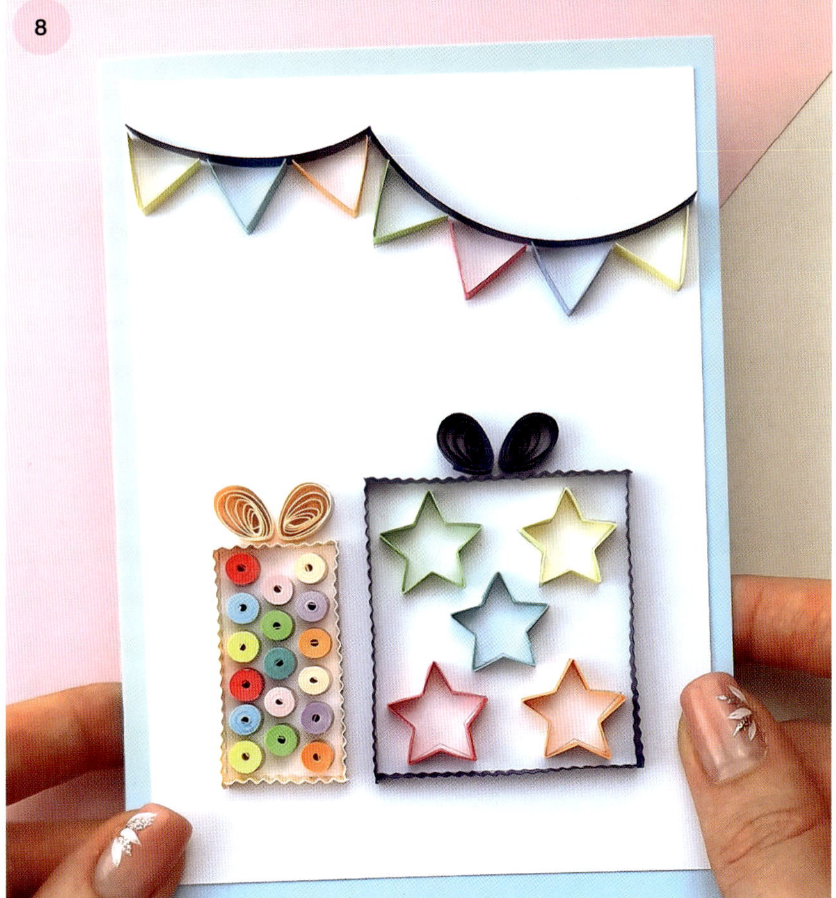

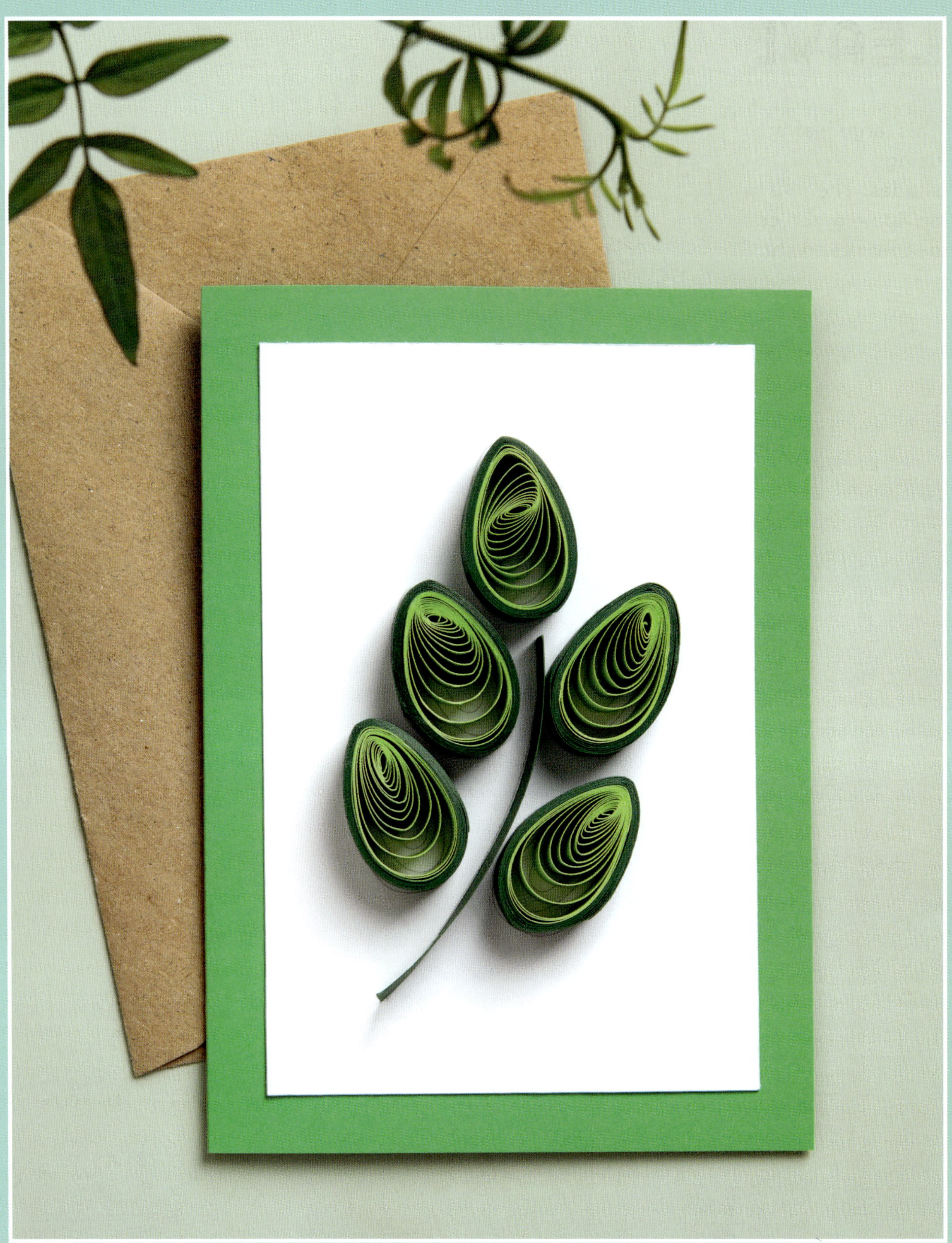

LEAVES

This large leaf artwork is so simple but elegant. It is made using just one simple quilled element using two green shades. The five leaves are made from teardrop shapes in an apple green colour, each teardrop is then wrapped in a deeper green shade to match the stem.

Stem

1 Cut a 7cm (2¾in) strip in forest green. Apply a little glue to the strip edge and stick to the template.

2 Hold in place with your tweezers for a moment to allow the glue to bond.

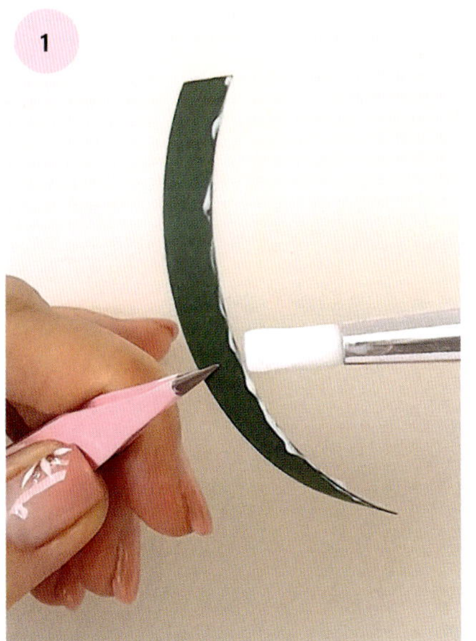

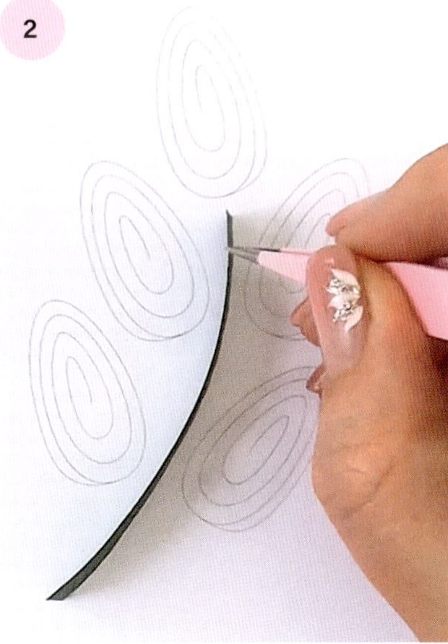

Leaves

3 To make the rounded teardrops, take five full strips in viridity, each measuring 54cm (21¼in) long. Follow the instructions on page 98 to make rounded teardrop shapes, using the 22mm (⅞in) hole on the quilling board.

4 Take a further five 54cm (21¼in) long strips in forest green, which you will wrap around the inner leaves. Apply a little glue to the end of one viridity teardrop.

5 Fix a forest green strip to a teardop shape. Hold in place to allow the glue to bond.

6 Once the glue has bonded, wind the strip around the teardrop, fixing in place when you reach the end of the strip.

7 Repeat steps 4 and 5 for the four remaining teardrops. Once your leaves are made, add a little glue to the template using a small brush, and fix the teardrops to the template.

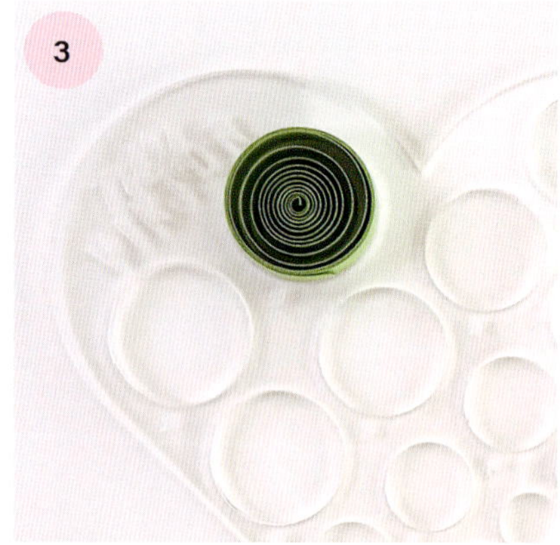

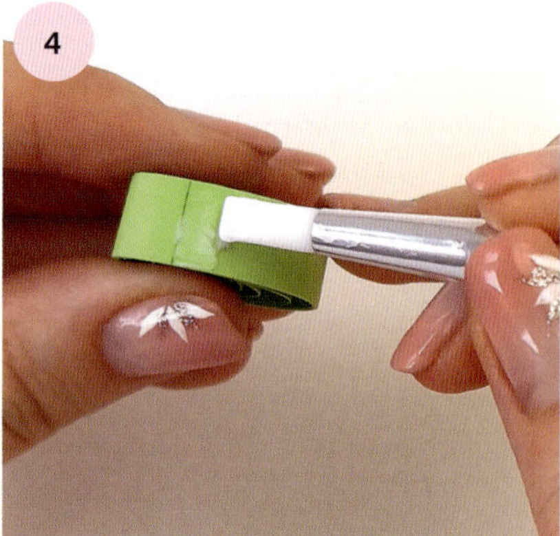

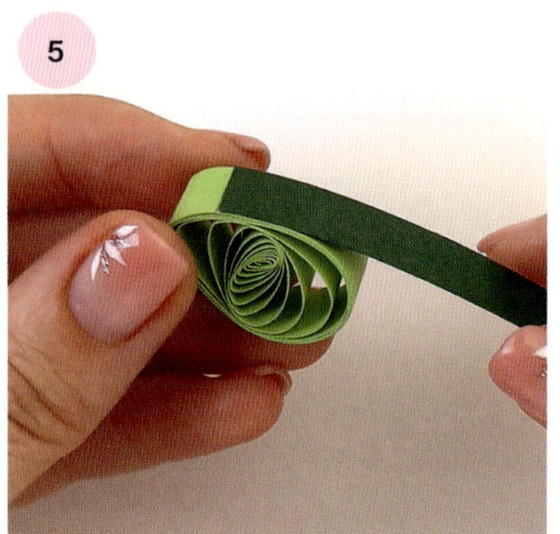

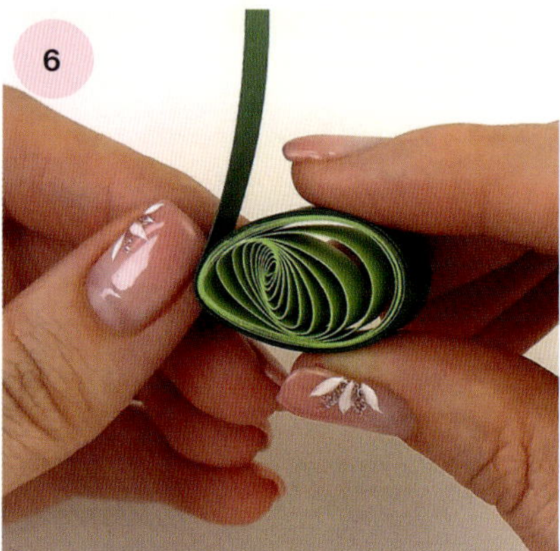

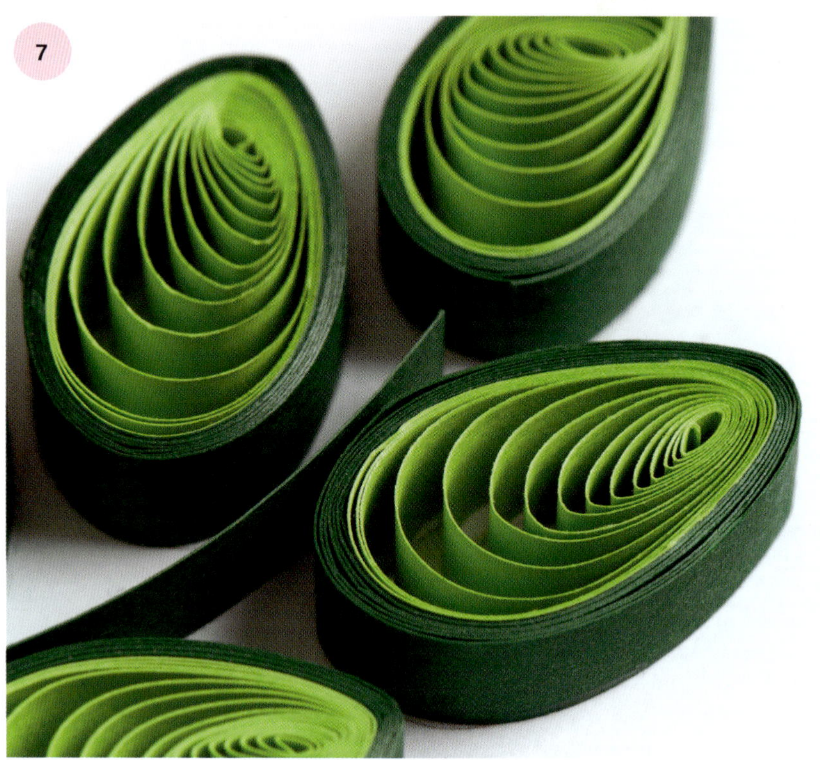

Mount

8 To finish this piece, trim the template and mount the artwork on to
a card base of your choice. I chose a green colour to complement the
shades within, and made this into a greetings card.

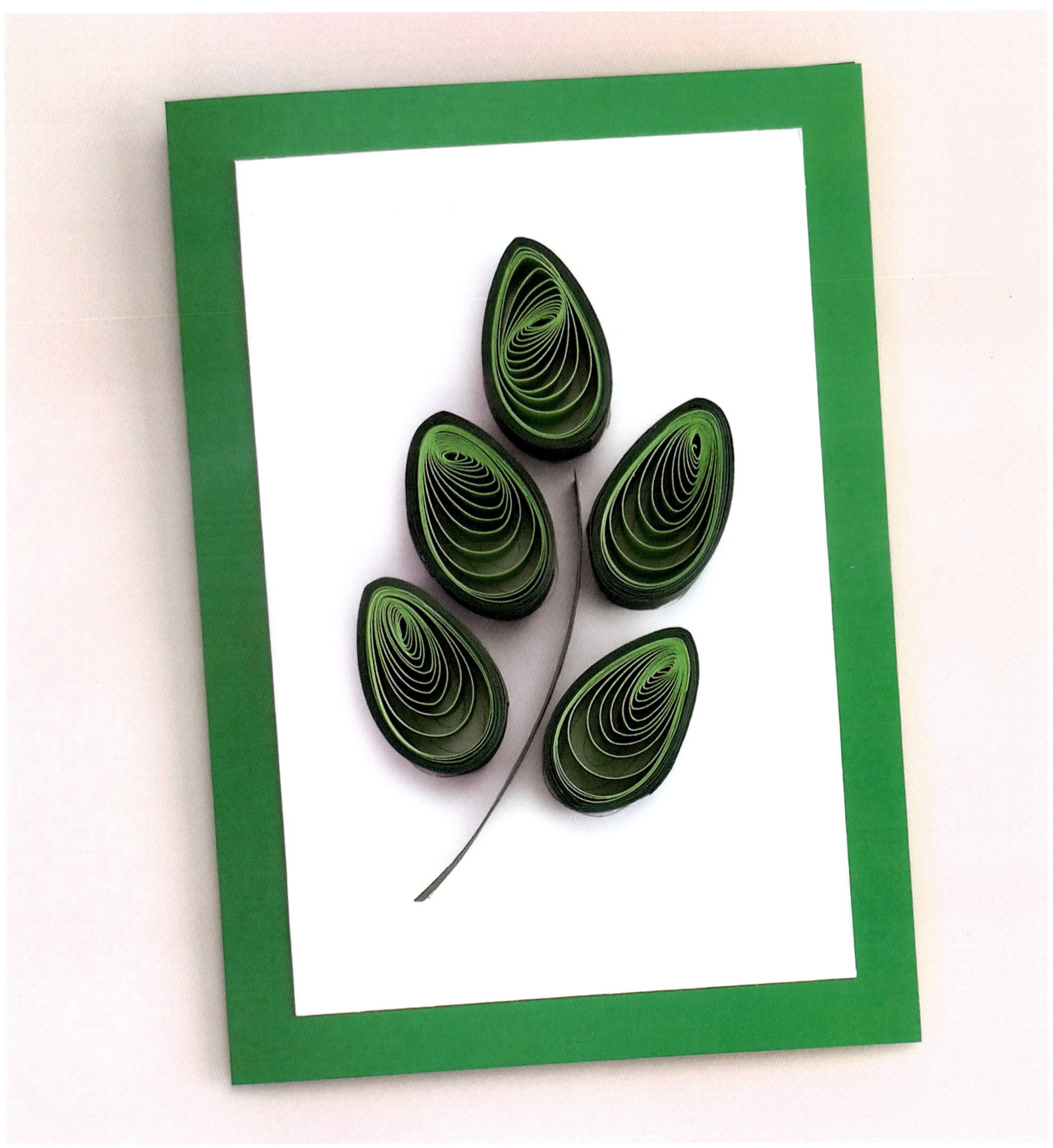

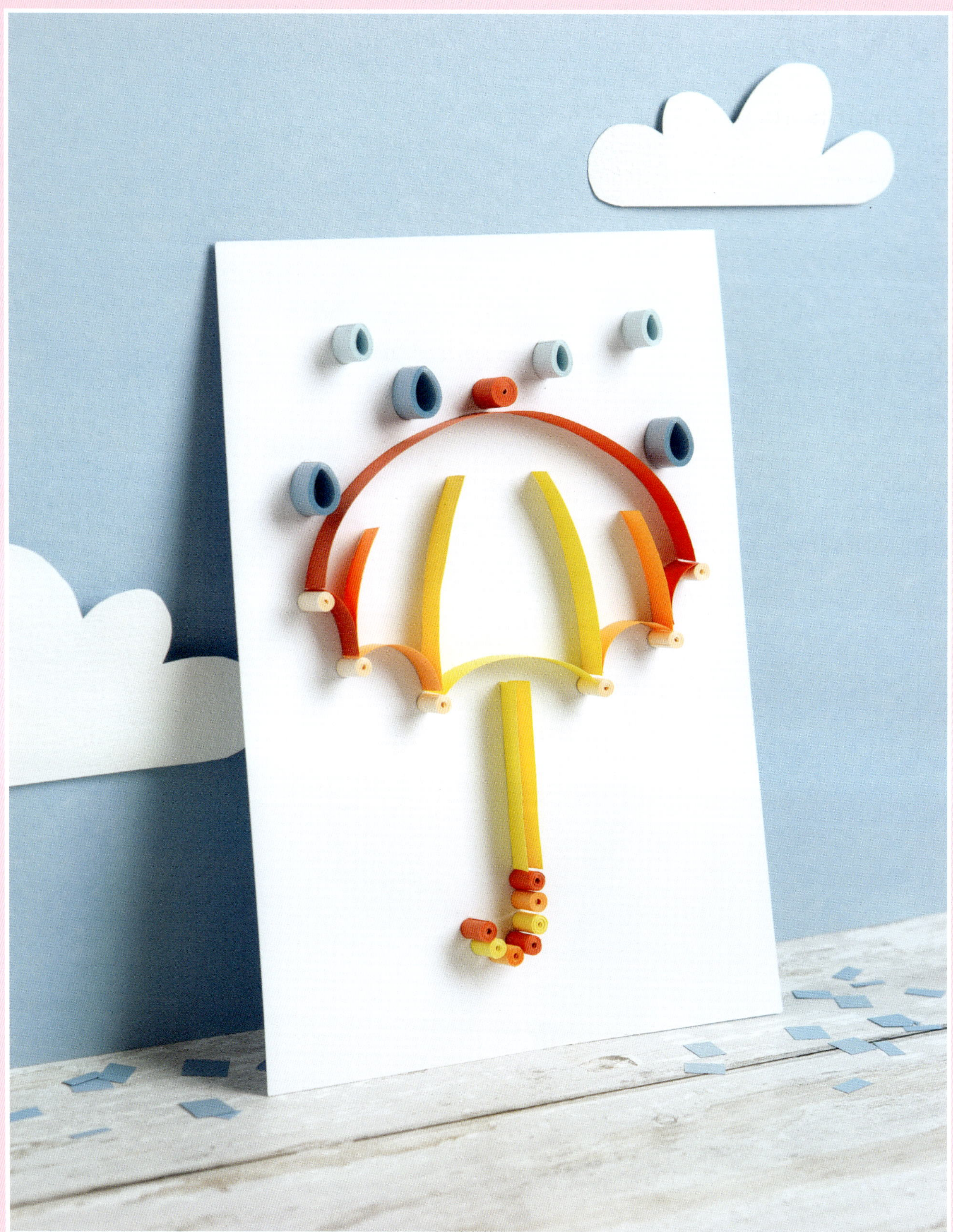

UMBRELLA

This umbrella artwork is so simple yet effective. Made in bright rainbow colours, it is definitely a statement piece for any wall.

Canopy

1 Cut a 18cm (7¹/₁₆in) strip in red for the top of the canopy. Score the strip lightly round your quilling tool to give a curved shape.

2 Apply a little glue to the first couple of centimetres (an inch) of the strip edge and stick to the template, using the tweezers to guide your rainbow arch in place. Hold in place with tweezers for a moment to allow the glue to bond.

3 Once the first section has stuck, apply a little glue to a thin glue brush and paint it directly onto the template as shown.

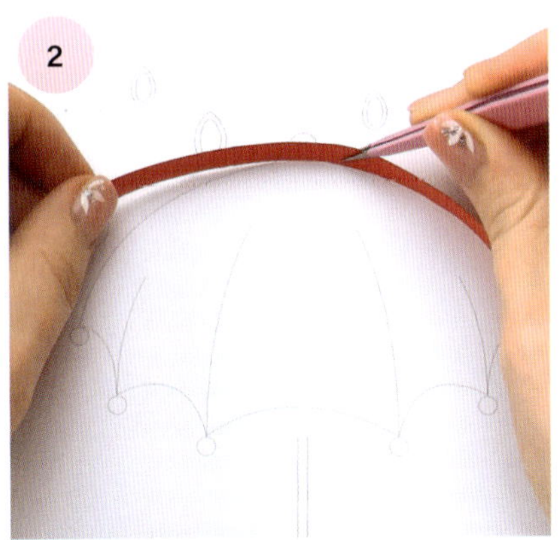

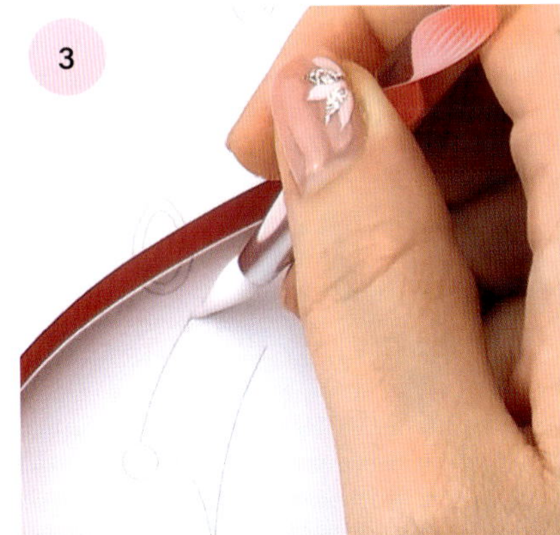

4 Use the tweezers to guide your strip into place sticking down as you go, trimming off any excess once you reach the end.

5 Cut two smaller 2cm (¾in) strips in red for the first set of curves for the umbrella top. Score around your tool to give a curved shape. Apply a little glue directly to the edges and stick down, as shown.

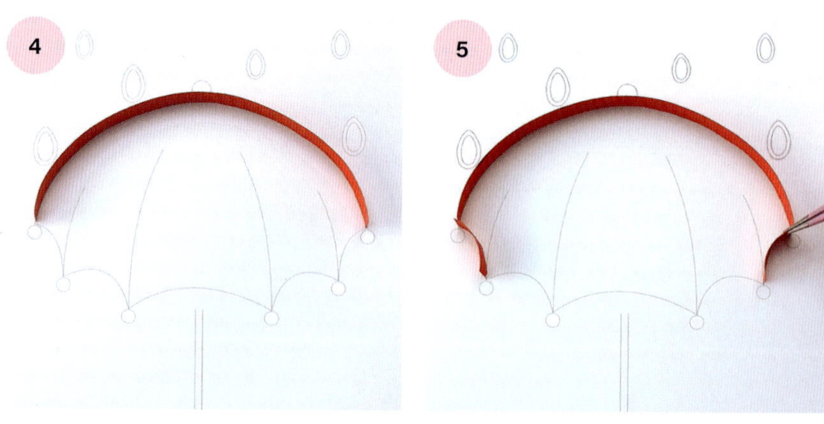

6 Cut two 2.9cm (1⅛in) strips in orange and one 4.8cm (1⅞in) strip in lemon. Follow the same process as above for scoring the strips and sticking them to the template.

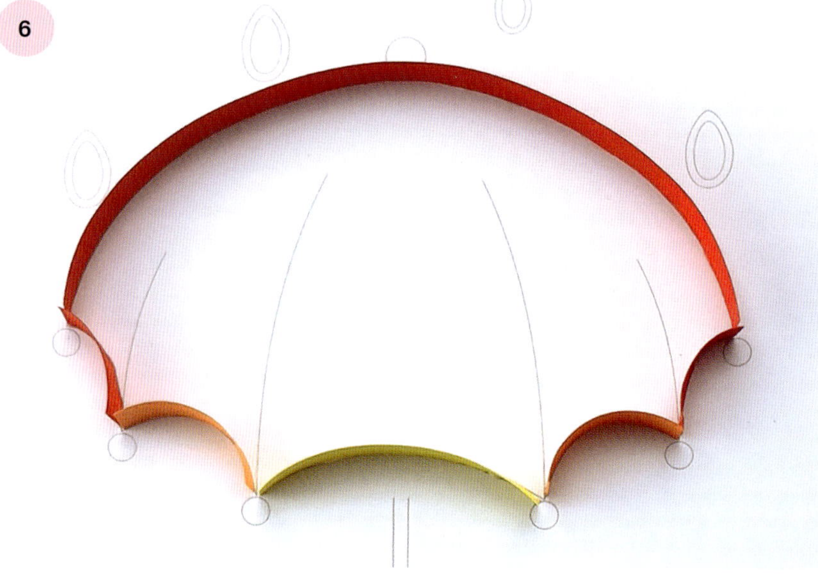

7 Cut two 3.3cm (1⁵⁄₁₆in) strips in orange for the smaller sections and two 5.5cm (2³⁄₁₆in) strips in lemon for the larger sections.

8 Add a little glue to the thin edge of the strips and fix down to the template.

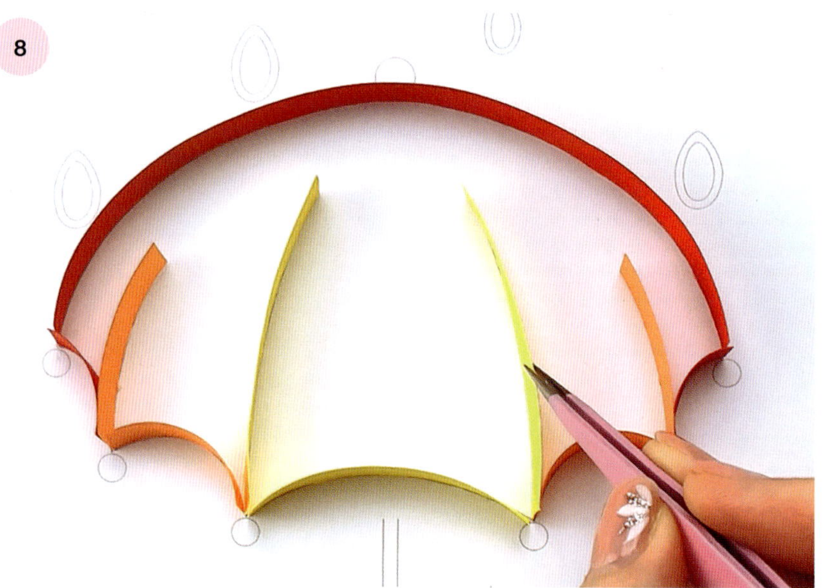

Handle

9 Cut two 4.7cm (1⅞in) strips in lemon. Apply glue to the thin edge of one strip and fix down to the template, using your tweezers to hold in place until the glue bonds. Repeat for the second yellow strip.

10 Cut three strips in red, two in orange and two in lemon, all measuring 12cm (4¾in). Follow the instructions on page 100 to make the tight coils.

11 Apply a little glue to the base of each tight coil shape and stick down to the template.

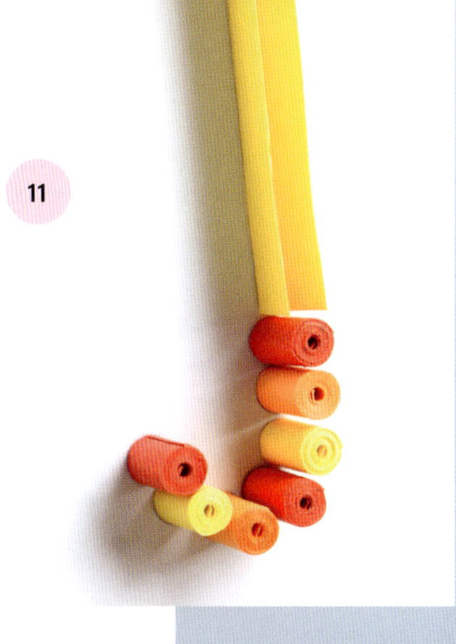

Raindrops

12 Cut three 30cm (12in) strips in grey blue for the larger raindrops, and three 19cm (7½in) strips in sky blue. Follow the instructions on page 113 to make the ring teardrops. Use the 11mm (⁷⁄₁₆in) hole on the quilling board to make the larger teardrops, and the 8mm (⁵⁄₁₆in) hole for the smaller teardrops.

13 Once all teardrops are made, apply a little glue to the base of the shapes and stick down to the template.

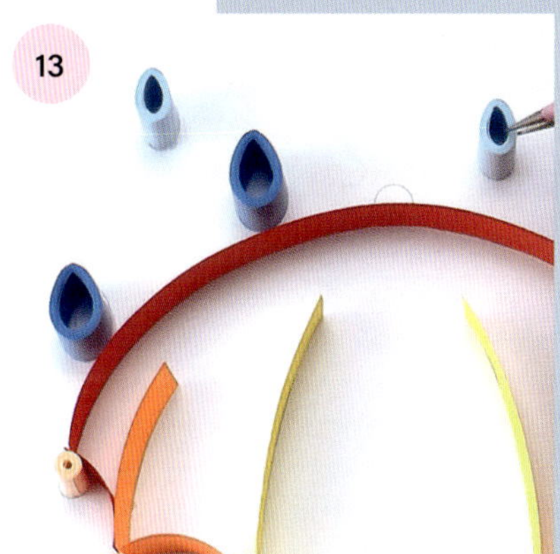

Finishing touches

14 Cut a 30cm (12in) strip of red and follow the instructions on page 100 to make the tight coil. Apply a little glue to the base of the shape and stick down to the template.

15 Cut six 12cm (4¾in) strips in apricot and make tight coils. Apply a little glue to the base of each shape and stick down to the template.

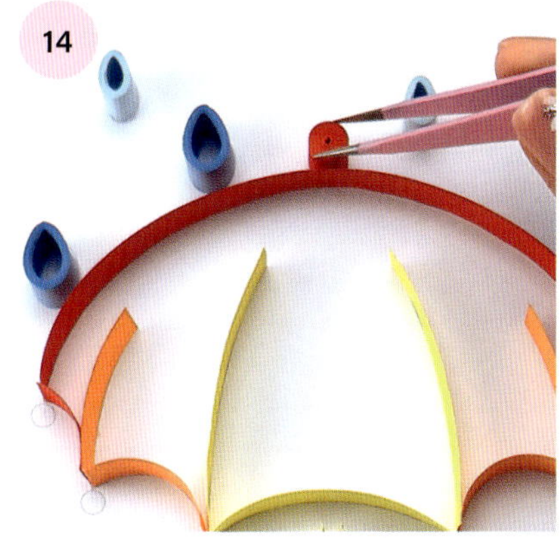

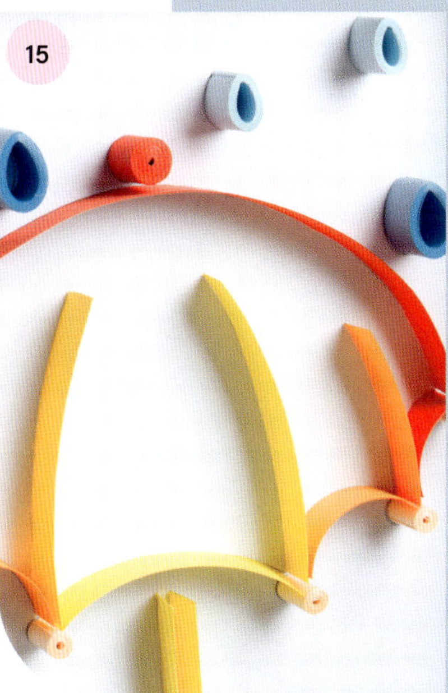

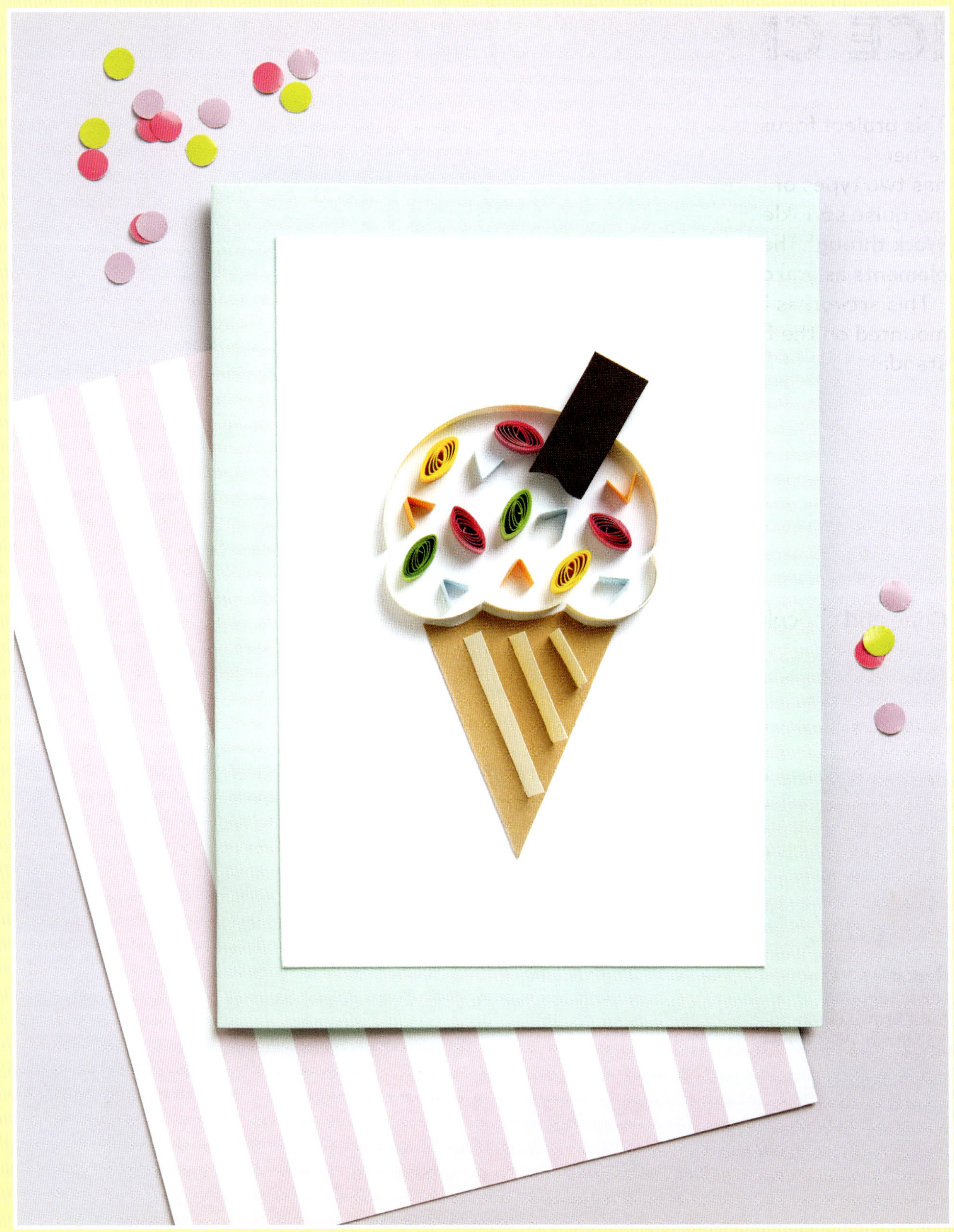

ICE CREAM CONE

This project focuses more on the art of edge quilling rather than on specific quilled elements. The ice cream has two types of sprinkles: triangle chips and mini marquise sprinkles, made in a fun rainbow palette. Work through the steps in order, sticking down the elements as you go.

   This artwork is ideal for a fun celebration, or perfect mounted on the front of a card or even framed as a standalone art piece.

Cone and chocolate flake

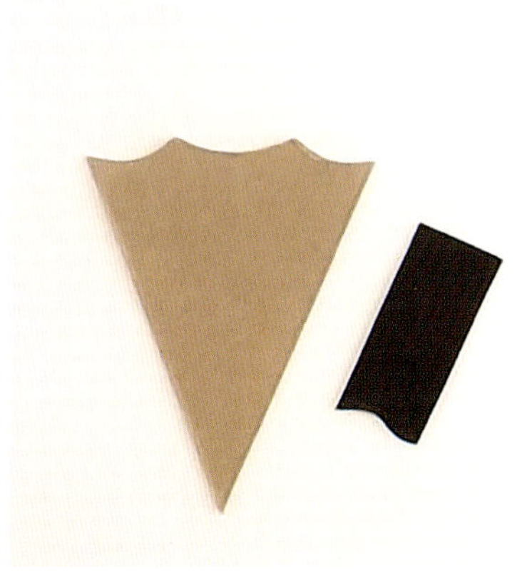

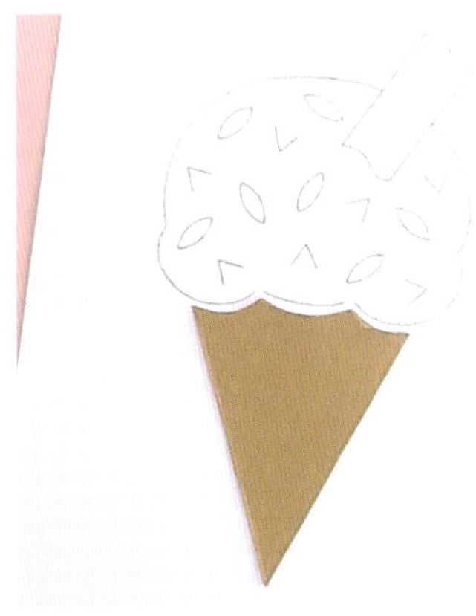

1 Start by tracing and cutting out the ice cream cone from a sheet of light brown card and the chocolate flake from dark brown card.

2 Add a little glue to base of the cone and fix down to the template. Set the flake aside for now.

Ice cream

3 Start with the arch at the top. Take a strip of cream quilling paper and apply a little glue to the first couple of centimetres (an inch) of the strip edge. Use tweezers to guide the strip in place on the template. Hold in place with your tweezers for a moment to allow the glue to bond.

4 Once the first section has stuck, apply a little glue to your glue brush and paint it directly onto the template as shown. Use tweezers to guide the strip in place, sticking down as you go.

5 Ignore the gap for the flake and stick the full strip down until you reach the end of the line on the template as shown. When you reach the end of the printed template use sharp scissors to trim the excess part of the strip.

6 Stick down the three bottom sections of the ice cream, following the same steps as above.

Sprinkles

7 There are seven mini marquise in total: three in magenta, two in lemon and two in viridity. Cut seven 10cm (4in) strips and follow the instructions on page 107 to make the elements, using the 7mm (¼in) hole on your quilling board.

8 There are nine triangle chips in total: four in orange and five in sky blue. Cut 1cm (⅜in) strips and fold them in half to make a triangle shape.

9 Apply a little glue to the base of each element and fix down to the template as shown, reserving one in each colour to mount the flake on.

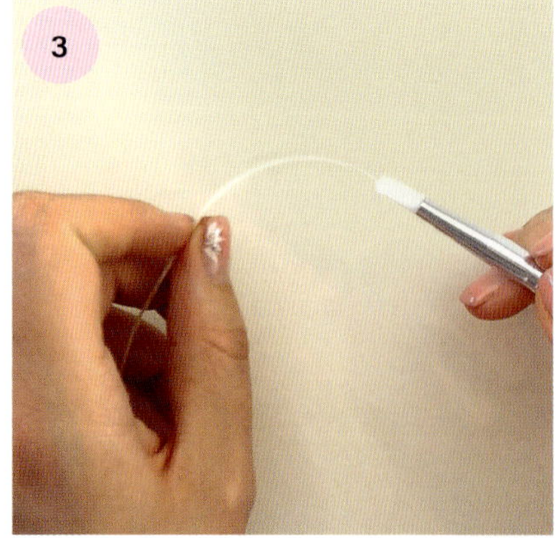

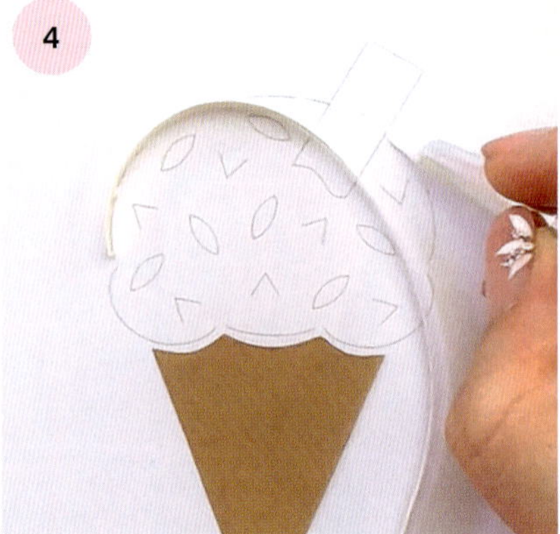

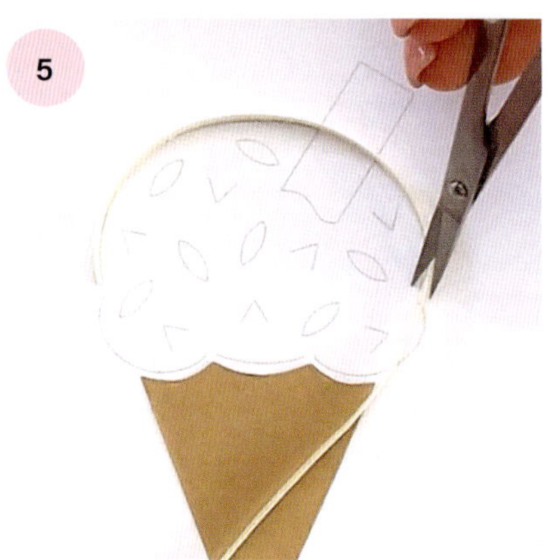

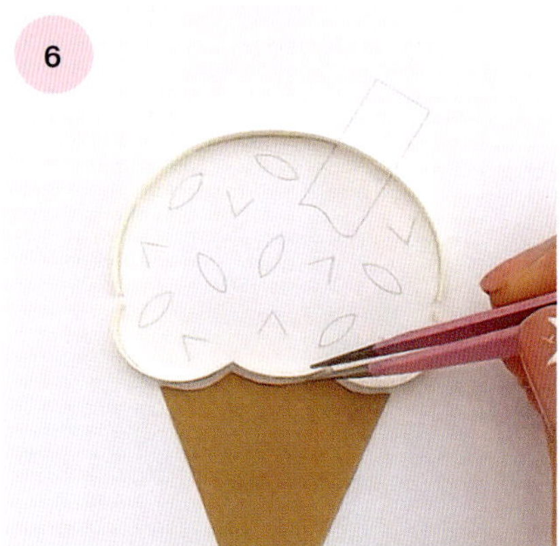

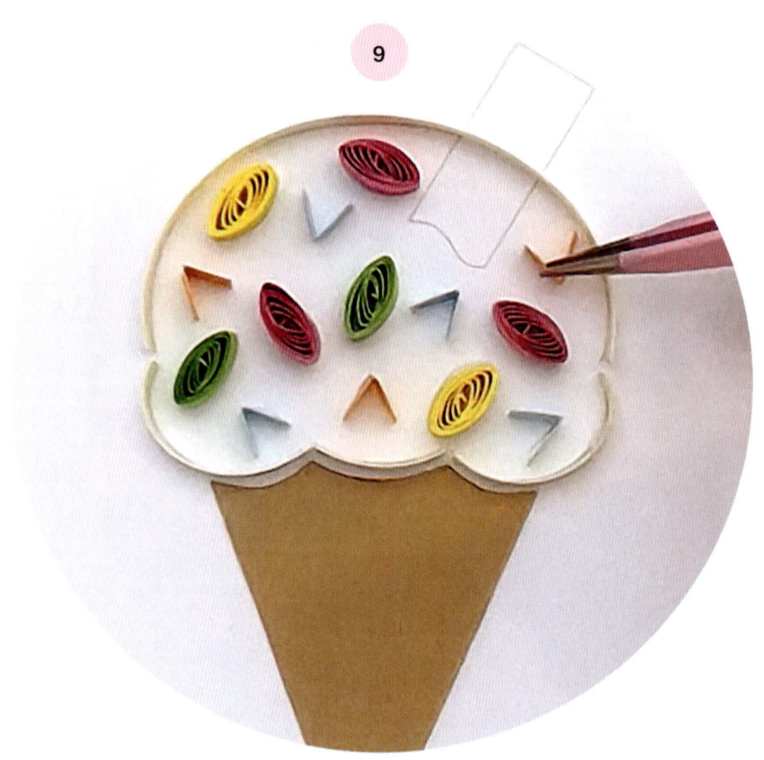

Flake

10 Stick down the last triangle elements to the template base where the flake will sit. Apply glue to both these shapes and the cream strip, and mount the flake on top.

Cone

11 To complete the ice cream, cut 3cm (1³⁄₁₆in), 2cm (¾in) and 1cm (³⁄₈in) strips in cream. Apply glue to the base of the strips and stick down as shown.

Mount

12 Mount the ice cream to the card base of your choice!

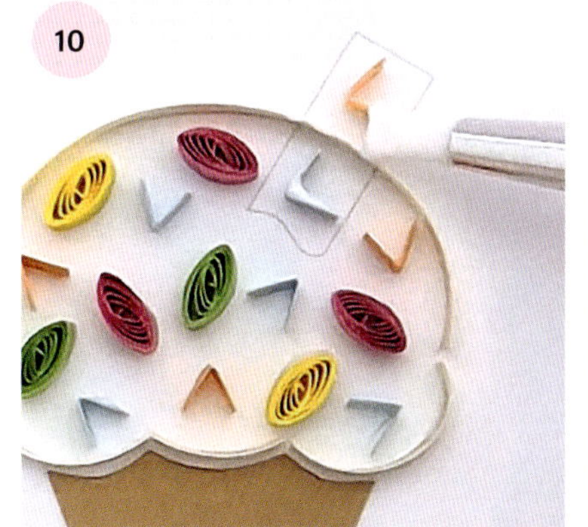
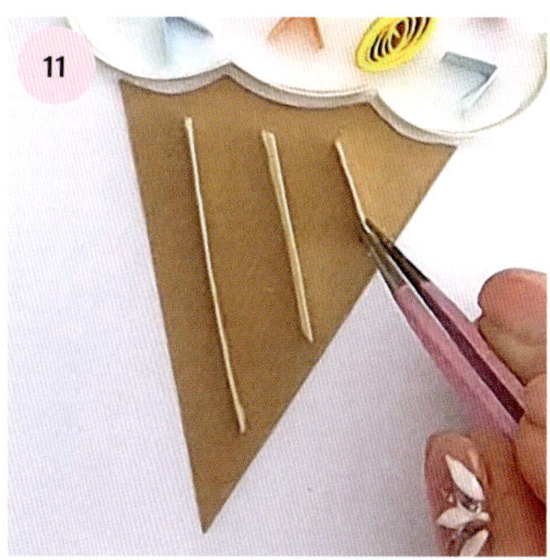

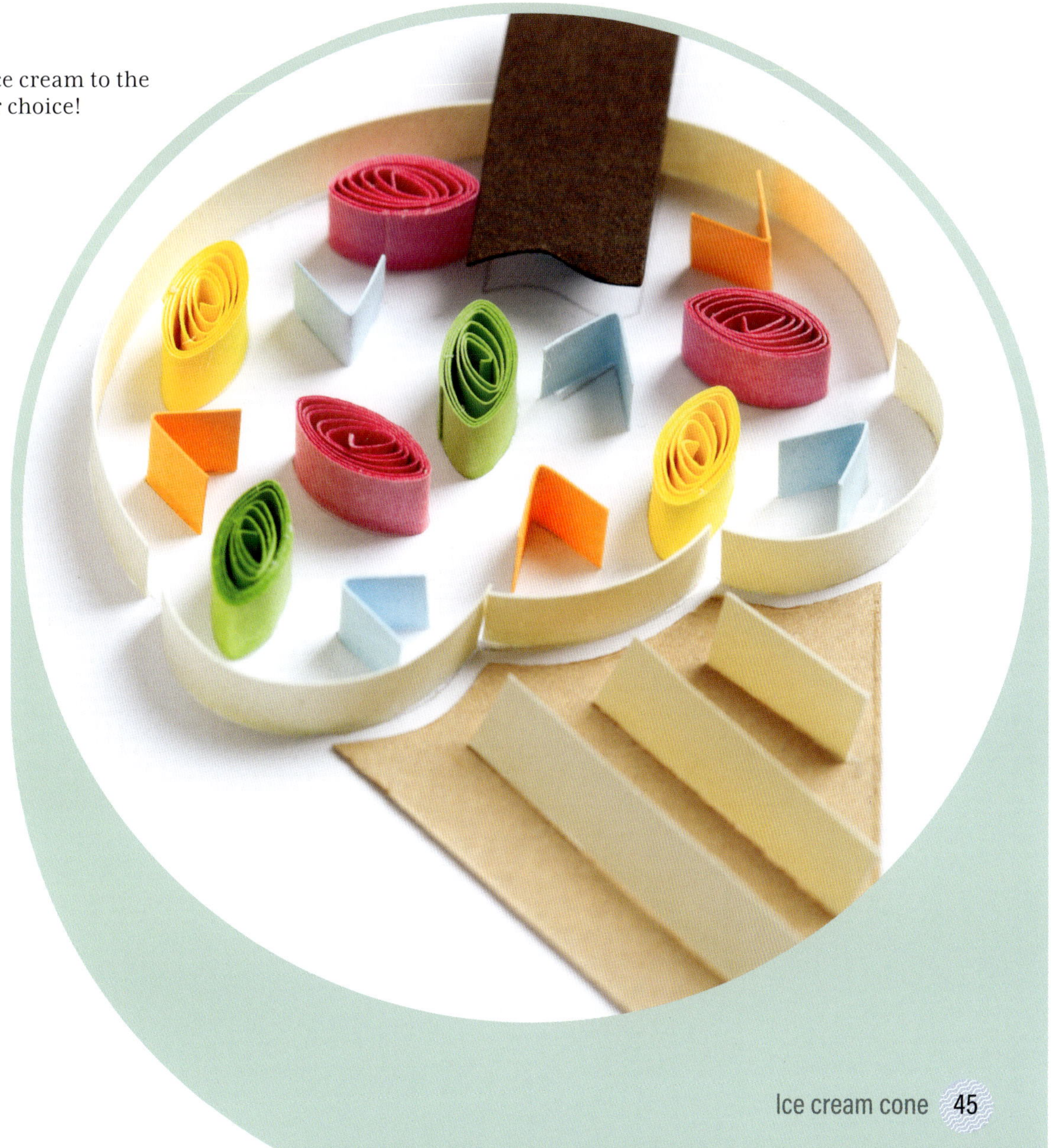

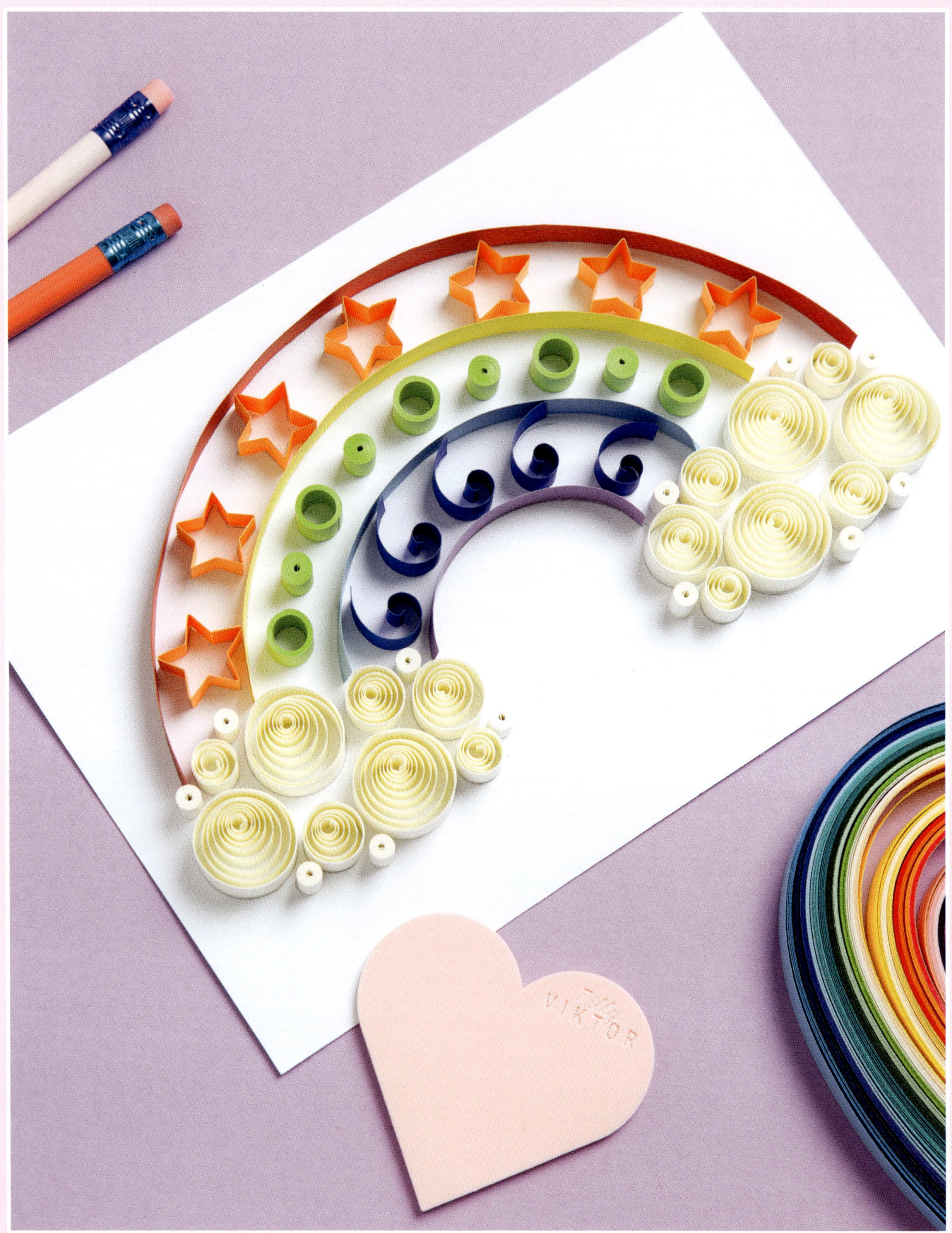

RAINBOW

This rainbow artwork is definitely a showstopper! Made in traditional rainbow colours, this piece is simple and fun to make. Use a more pastel colour palette if you prefer a lighter finish.

You will need

Rainbow template, page 122
Quilling papers, I used 5mm (³⁄₁₆in)
Quilling tool, 10mm (³⁄₈in)
Scissors
Tacky PVA glue
Glue brush
Quilling board
Tweezers

Quilling paper colours

Purple (6)
Grey blue (10)
Red (18)
Viridity (24)
Beige (36)
Lemon (39)
Orange (41)
Royal blue (48)

Quilled elements

Arch
Star
Loose swirl/Open scroll
Ring coil
Tight coil
Loose coil

Rainbow arches

1 Start your rainbow by making and sticking down all four arches. Take a full strip in red, lemon, grey blue and purple and score them slightly using the metal end of your quilling tool – for guidance on this follow the arch instructions on page 109.

2 Starting with the red, apply a little glue to the first couple of centimetres (an inch) of the strip edge and stick to the template, using your tweezers to guide your rainbow arch in place. Hold in position with your tweezers for a moment to allow the glue to bond. Once the first section has stuck, apply a little glue to your glue brush and paint it directly onto the template as shown. Use the tweezers to guide your strip into place, sticking down as you go. Trim away the excess paper with sharp scissors.

3 Repeat step 2 with the remaining three coloured arches.

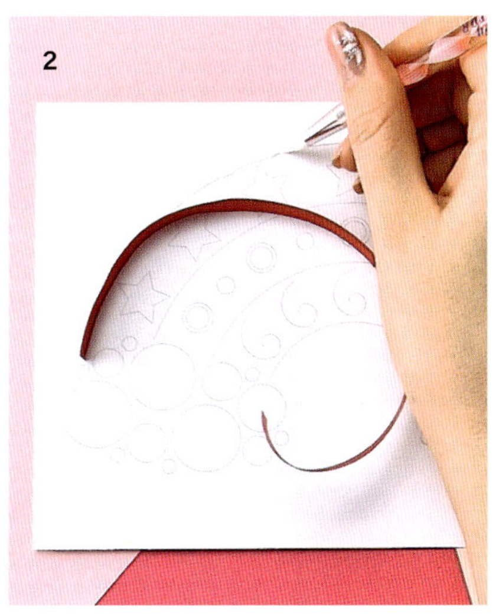

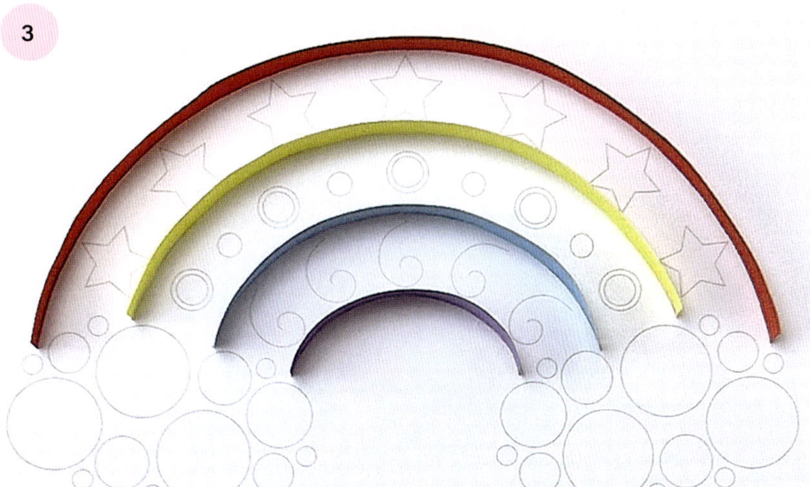

Stars

4 There are seven stars to make in orange. Cut seven 15cm (6in) strips and follow the instructions on page 111 to make. Once the stars are made, apply a little glue directly to the edges and stick down.

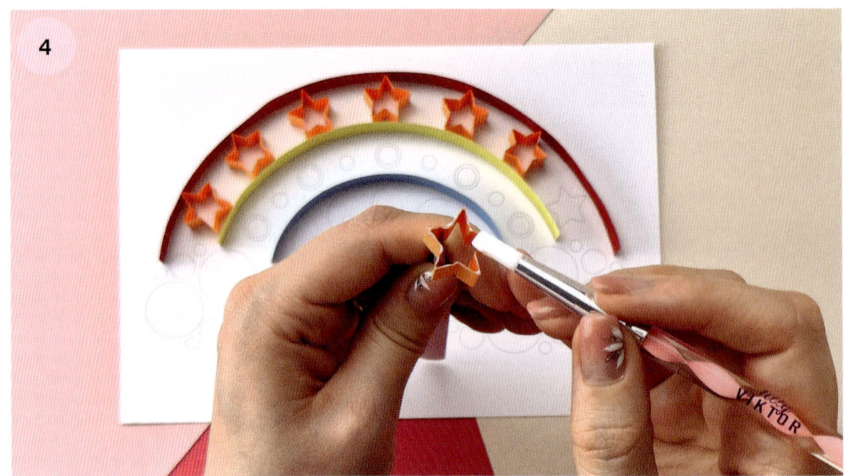

Tight and ring coils

5 For the tight coils cut four 24.5cm (9⅝in) strips, for the ring coils cut five 22cm (8¹¹⁄₁₆in) strips, all in viridity, using the 10mm (⅜in) hole on the quilling board for this shape. Follow the instructions on page 100 and 102 to make both elements. Once all are made, apply a little glue to the base of the shapes and stick down to the template.

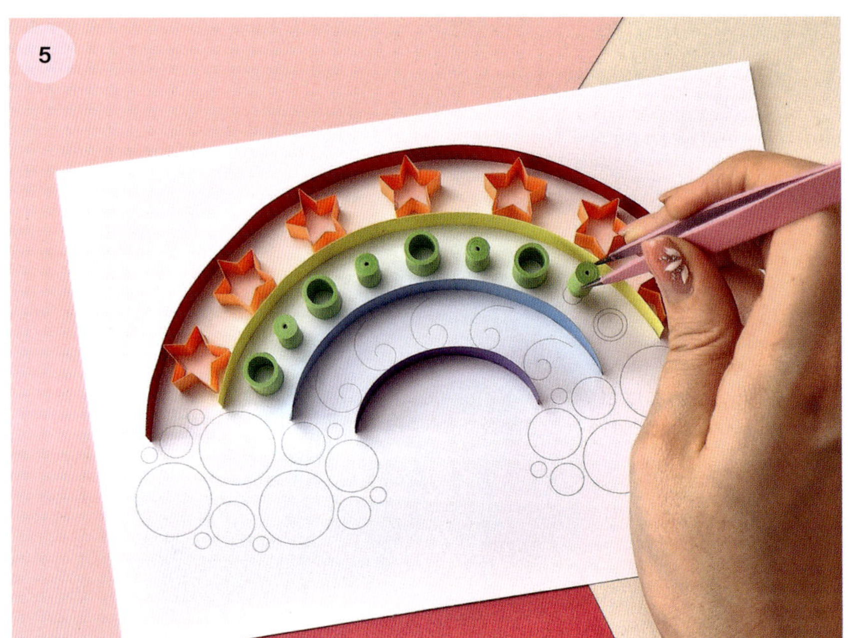

Loose swirls

6 The next elements to decorate the rainbow are loose swirls. There are five in total, all in royal blue. Cut five strips of 4.2cm (1⅝in) and follow the instructions on page 108.

7 Once all scrolls are made, apply a little glue to the base of each one, and stick down to the template.

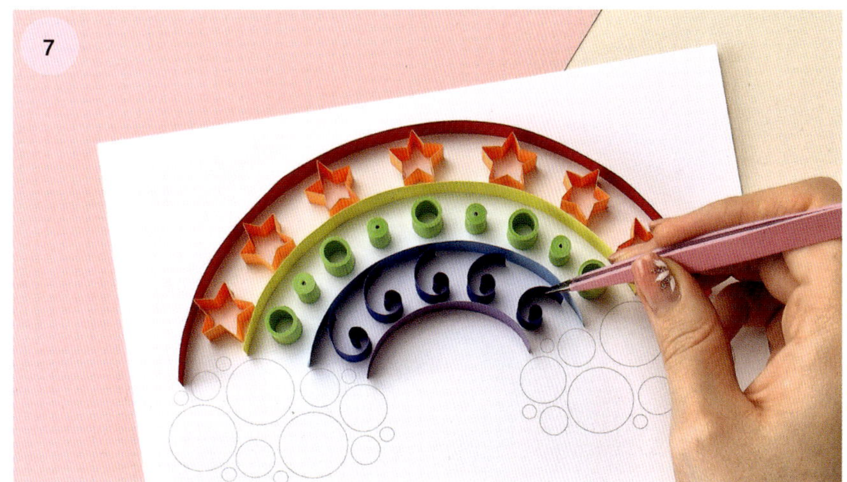

Fluffy clouds

8 To finish your rainbow in style you need to add the fluffy clouds! These are made from a mix of tight coils and loose coils. Cut 12 beige strips, each measuring 14cm (5½in), and follow the instructions on page 100 to make 12 tight coils. Once made, apply glue to the base of each coil and fix down to the template.

9 Cut six 38cm (14¹⁵⁄₁₆in) strips in beige for the largest loose coils. using the 22mm (⅞in) hole on your quilling board. Then cut two 21cm (8¼in) strips also in beige, using the 16mm (⅝in) hole on your quilling board. Cut a further four beige strips measuring 18cm (7¹⁄₁₆in) each, using the 13mm (½in) hole on the quilling board. Finally, cut two beige strips measuring 11cm (4⁵⁄₁₆in) each, using the 10mm (⅜in) hole on the quilling board to. Follow the instructions on page 104 to make all the above sized loose coils. Once all are made apply glue to the base of each element and stick down to the template.

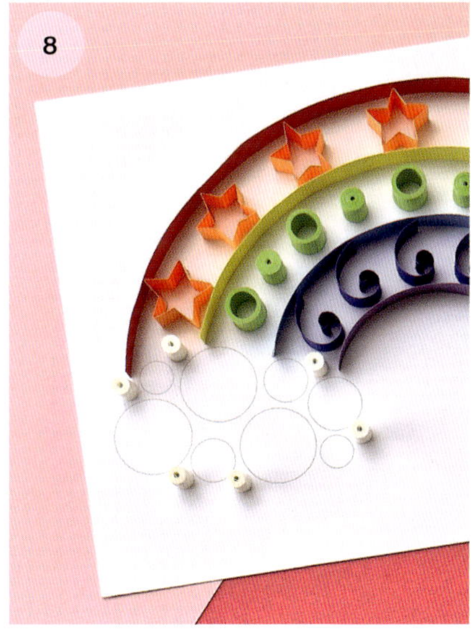

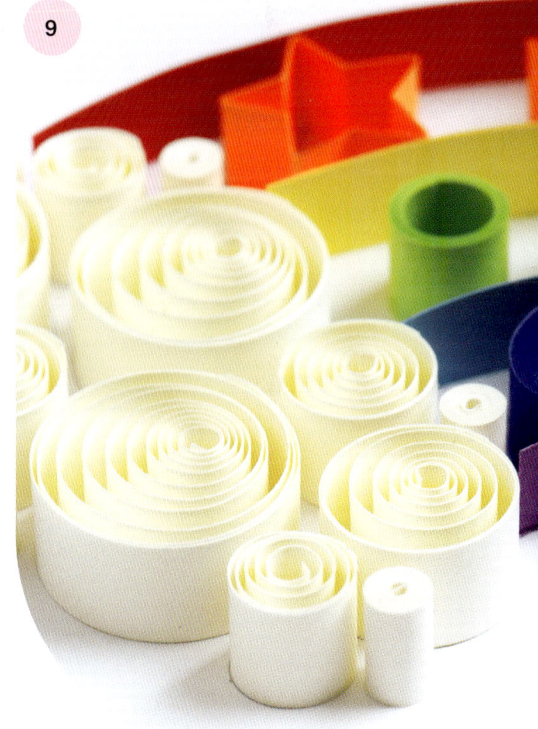

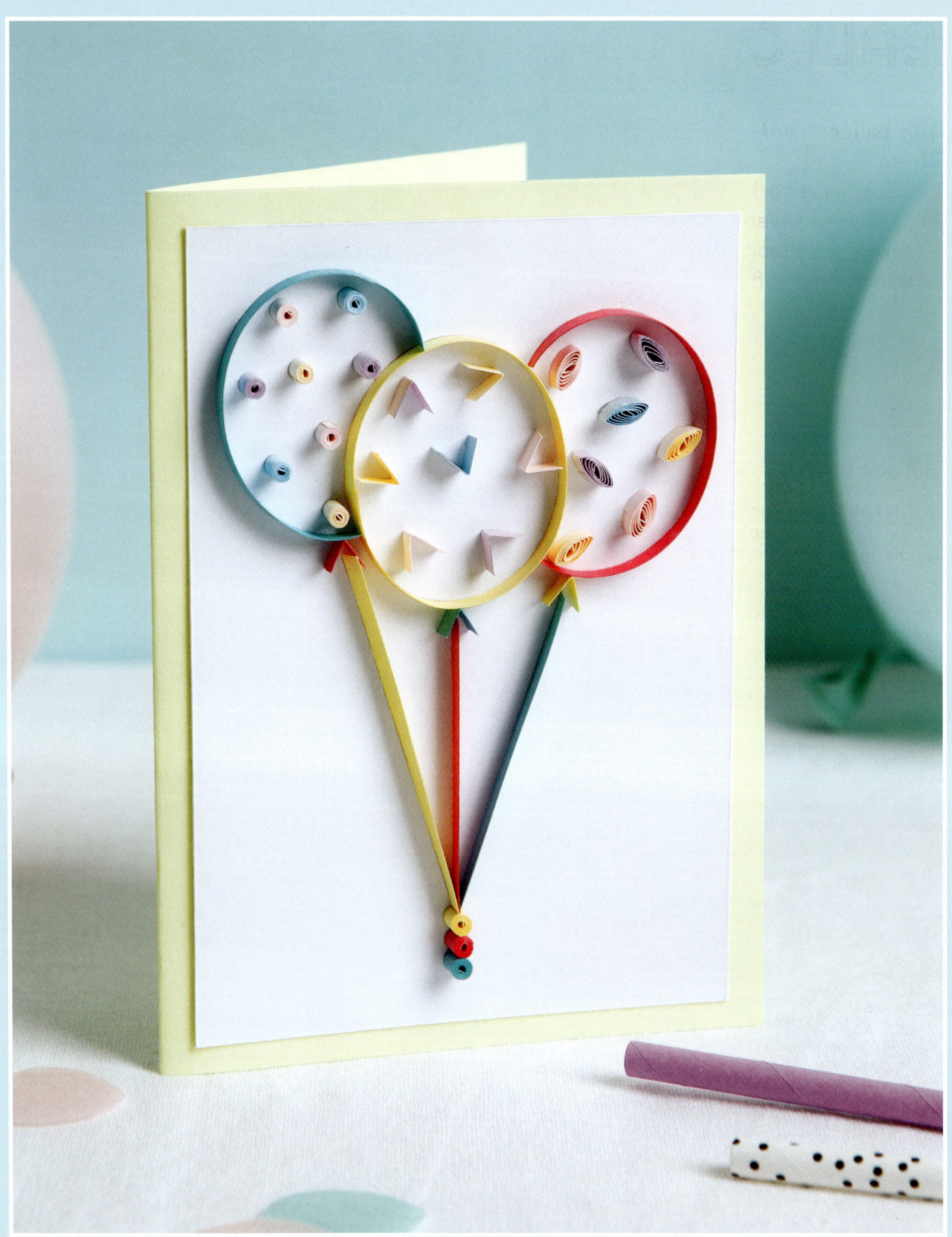

BALLOONS

This balloon card is perfect for all celebratory occasions! These balloons decorated in pastel tones are simple to make. The artwork requires four different quilled shapes in a range of seven colours.

Make the balloon outlines first, followed by the strings and then finish off by adding the quilled decorations.

Quilling paper colours

Baby pink (2)
Light purple (7)
Sky blue (9)
Light yellow (38)
Magenta (51)
Apricot (52)
Turquoise (56)

Quilled elements used

Arch
Triangle
Tight coil
Marquise

Balloon outlines

1 The balloon outlines are made from one strip, stuck down to the template on its thin edge. Cut three 15cm (6in) strips, one each in light yellow, hot pink and turquoise.

2 Run the metal tip of the quilling tool across the length of the paper strips to give them a nice curved shape as shown.

3 Begin with the turquoise balloon. Apply a little glue to the first couple of centimetres (an inch) of the strip edge and stick to the template, using the tweezers to guide your balloon outline in to place. Hold in place with your tweezers for a moment to allow the glue to bond. Once the first section has stuck, apply a little glue to a thin paintbrush and paint it directly onto the template as shown. Use the tweezers to guide your strip into place, sticking down as you go.

4 Once you complete the balloon shape there will be a little excess paper. Using sharp scissors, trim away the excess.

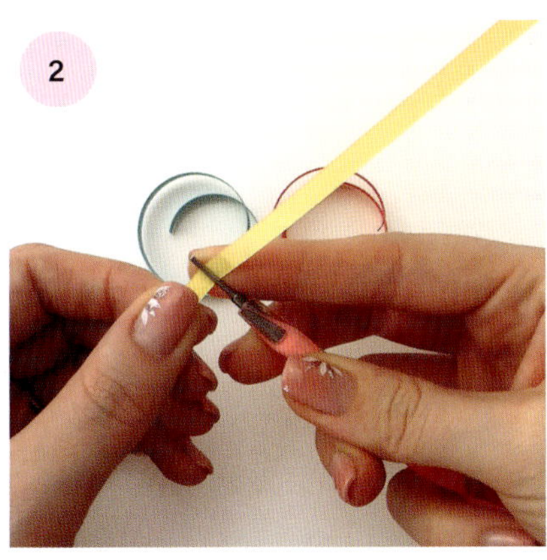

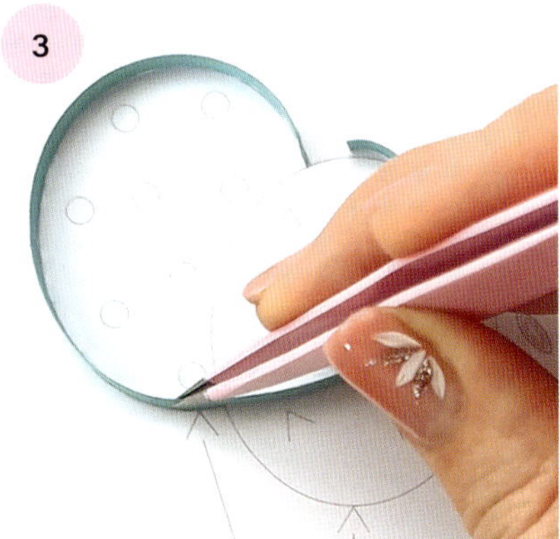

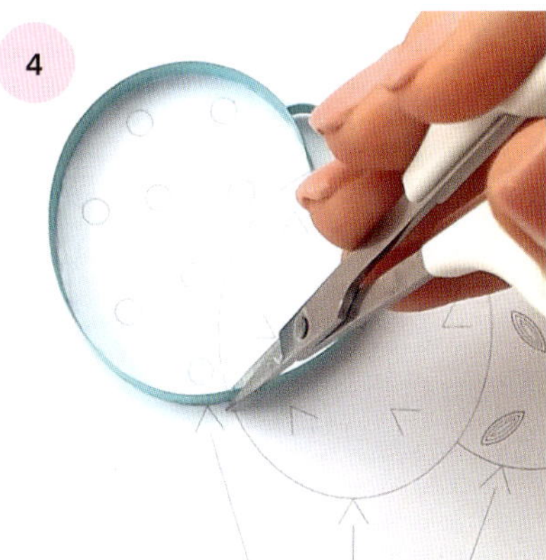

5 Repeat steps 3 and 4 for the other two balloon shapes, using the tweezers to manipulate the strips into place.

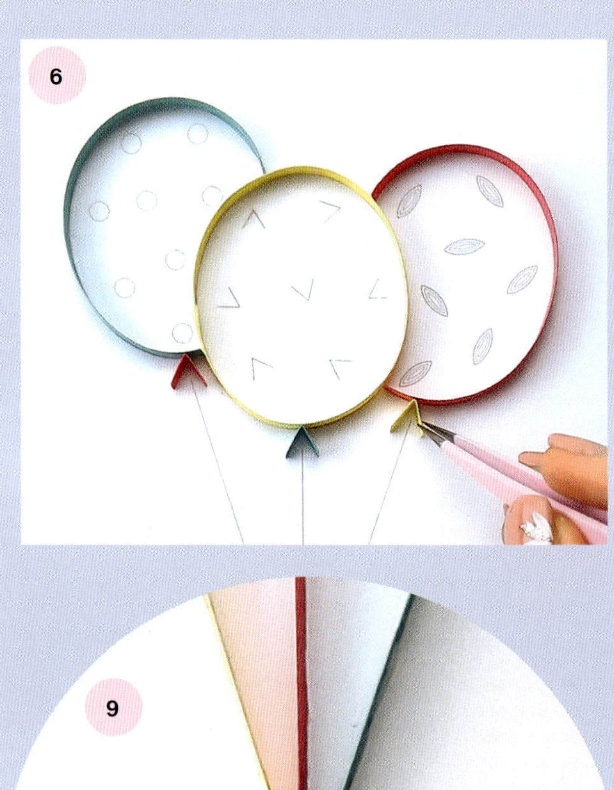

Balloon base

6 Cut three 1cm (⅜in) strips, one each in light yellow, magenta and turquoise, and fold them in half. Add a little glue to the edge and stick down at the base of each balloon. I have mixed up the colours, but you could match the bases to the balloons if preferred.

String

7 The balloon strings are made from one strip, stuck down to the template on its thin edge. The left string measures 6.4cm (2½in), the middle string measures 5cm (2in) and the right string measures 5.5cm (2³⁄₁₆in). Cut all three strips in light yellow, magenta and turquoise using the measurements listed above.

8 Apply a little glue to the strip edge and stick to the template, holding in place with your tweezers for a moment to allow the glue to bond.

9 Cut three 6cm (2⅜in) strips, one in each balloon colour, for the circles at the base of the balloon strings. Follow the instructions for making tight coils on page 100, add a little glue to the base and stick down.

Decorations

10 Each balloon has different elements decorating the interior, these elements are made up in four different colours: I used apricot, sky blue, baby pink and light purple. The left balloon has tight coils, these strips measure 6cm (2⅜in) each. The middle balloon has triangle confetti, these strips measure 1cm (⅜in) each. The right balloon has mini marquise shapes, these strips measure 7cm (2¾in) each and require the use of the 6mm (¼in) hole on the quilling board. Cut all strips as indicated above, referring the image below for the colours, and follow the instructions on pages 100, 107 and 109 to make the elements. Once they are made, apply glue to the base and fix down to the template.

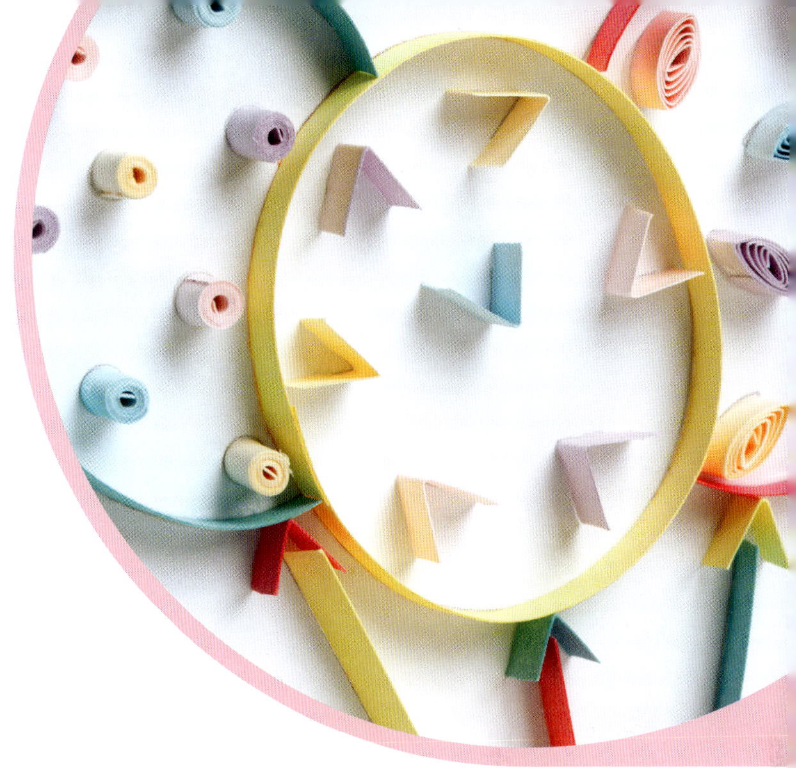

Mount the card

11 To make the design into a card, cut the balloon template down to the desired size. Add a little double-sided tape or glue to the back of the template and mount onto a card base of your choice.

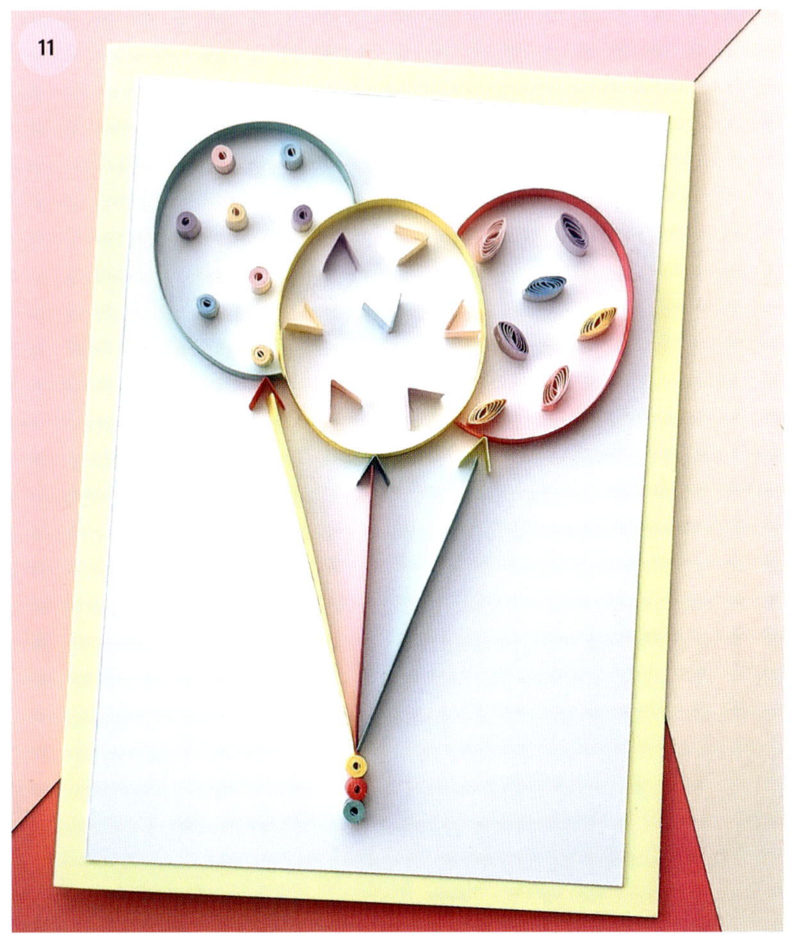

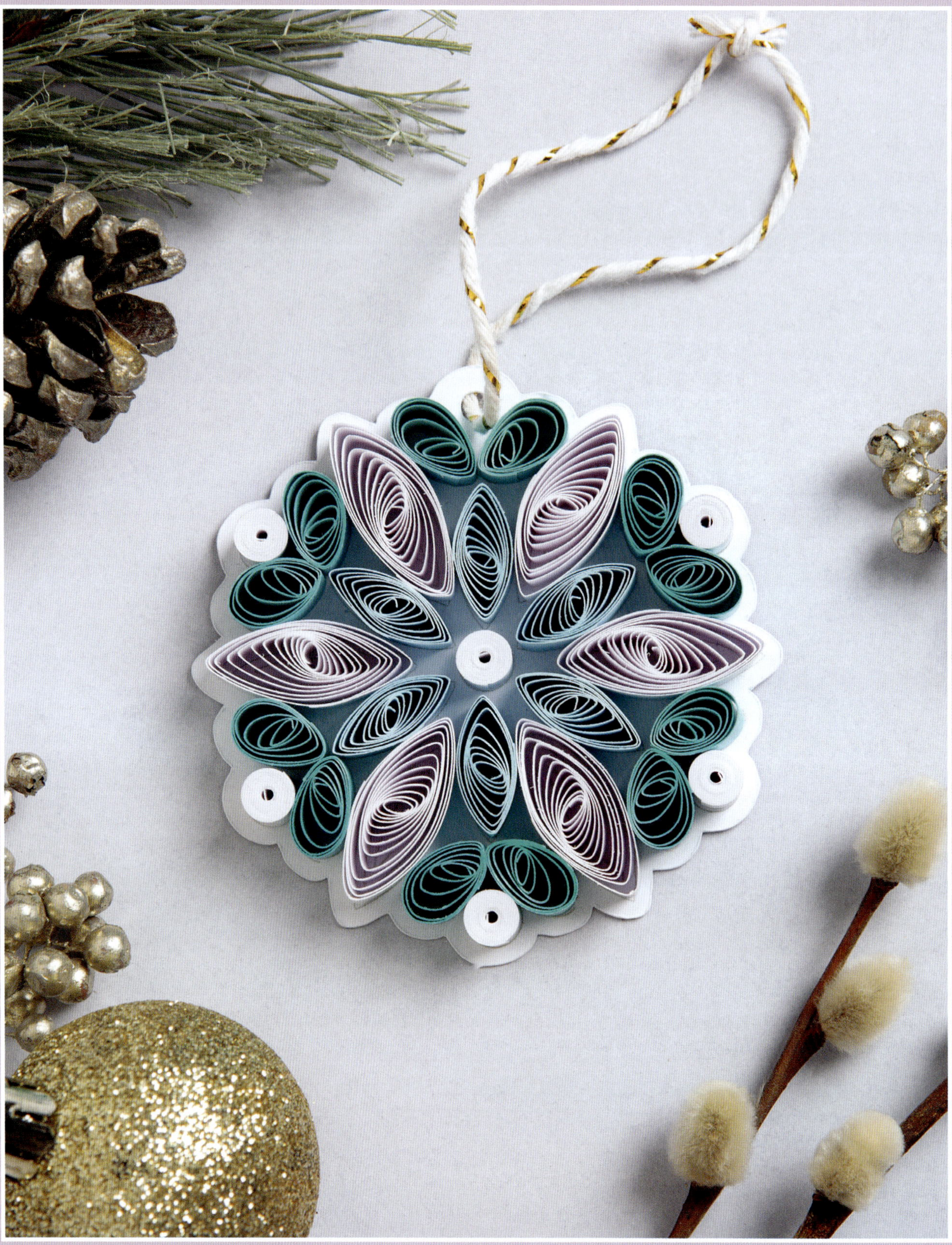

SNOWFLAKE

This snowflake is the perfect decoration for your winter wonderland Christmas tree or as a beautifully thoughtful greeting card. Made from just three quilled elements in icy shades, this snowflake is simple to make but is stunning once completed.

Template

1 Cut around the dotted outer line of the template.

2 At the top of the snowflake is the marker where we will thread the string once the snowflake is completed. Pierce through the mark on the template with sharp scissors.

Snowflake centre

3 The snowflake centre is made up of a simple tight coil shape. To make the coil, cut one strip in bleach measuring 22cm (8^{11}⁄$_{16}$in) and follow the instructions on page 100. Add a dab of glue to the base of the element and fix down to the template.

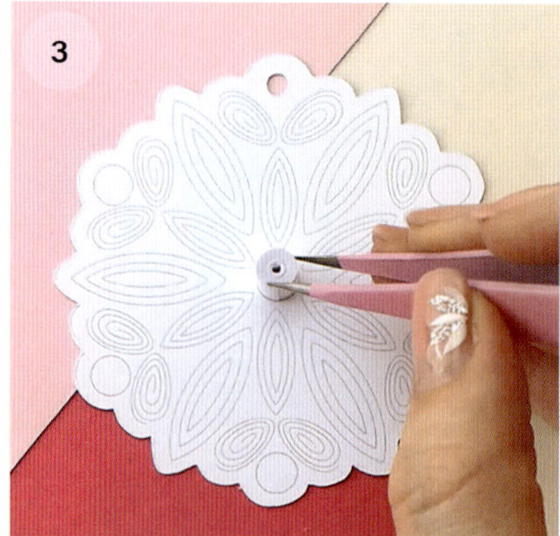

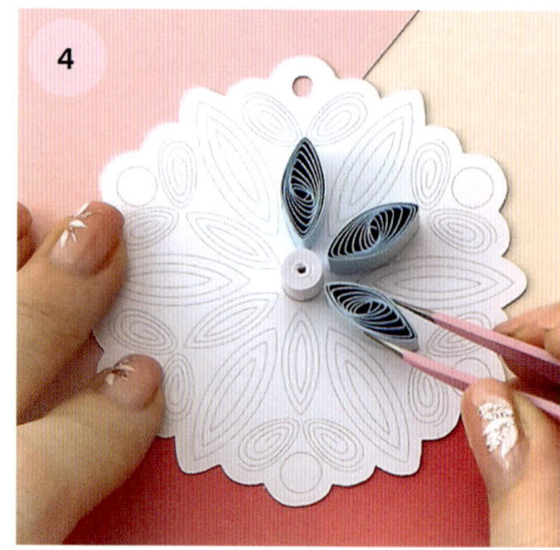

Small marquise

4 The first elements surrounding the centre tight coil are small marquise shapes: there are six in total, all in sky blue. Cut six strips measuring 19cm (7½in) and follow the instructions on page 107 to make the marquise shapes, using the 12mm (½in) hole on your quilling board. Once all six shapes are made, add a little glue to the base of each and fix them down to the template base.

Large marquise

5 Between the small blue marquise shapes are six larger light purple ones. Cut all six strips measuring 39cm (15½in) and make the large marquise shapes in the same way, but using the 18mm (¹¹⁄₁₆in) hole on your quilling board.

6 Once all six are made, add a little glue to the base of each element and fix down to the template base.

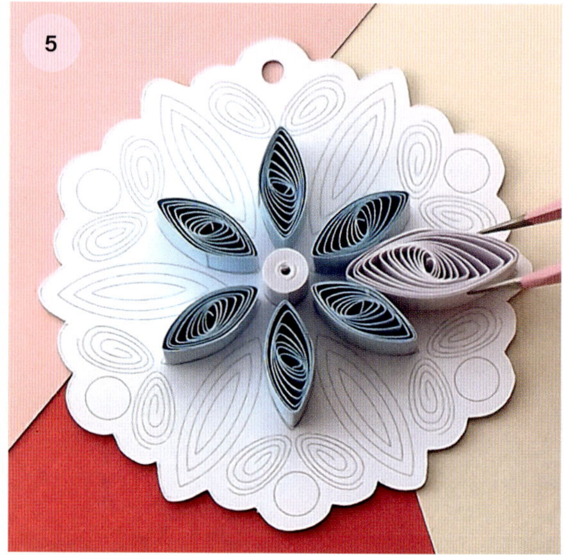

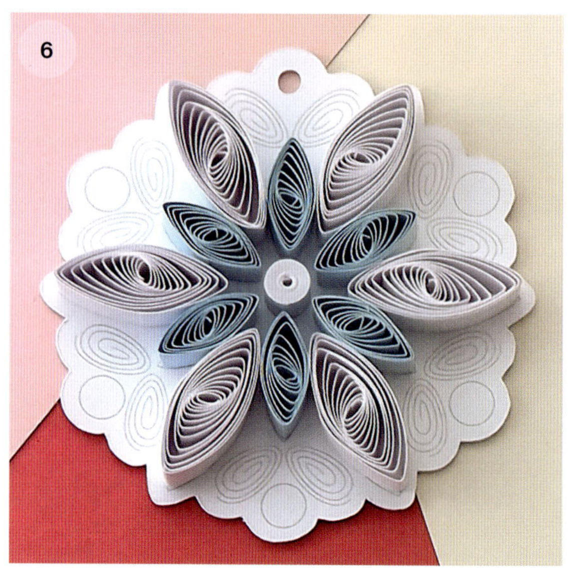

Teardrops

7 Between each large purple marquise sits a pair of rounded teardrops in emerald. There are 12 of these in total. Cut all 12 strips measuring 13cm (5⅛in) and follow the instructions on page 98 to make the teardrop shapes. Use the 10mm (⅜in) hole on the quilling board.

8 Once all 12 are made, add a little glue onto the base of each shape and fix down to the template.

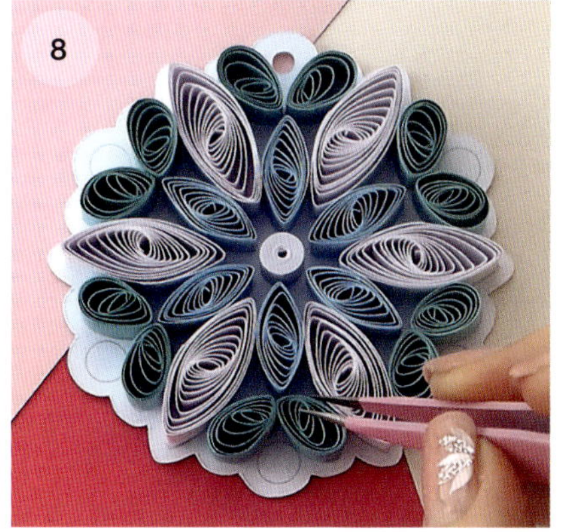
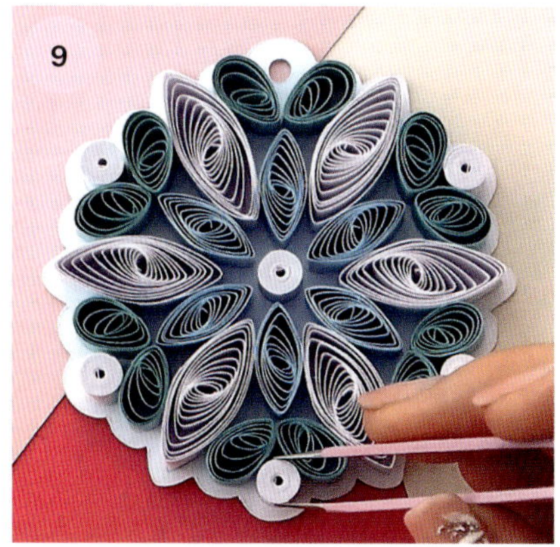

Tight coils

9 The final elements to add are five tight coils in bleach, which sit at the very edge of the snowflake. Cut six strips measuring 22cm (8¹¹⁄₁₆in) and follow the instructions on page 100 to make five tight coils. Once they are all made, add a dab of glue to the base of each one, and fix down to the template.

To finish

10 Cut a 30cm (12in) piece of string or ribbon and thread through the hanging hole. Tie a knot in one end and hang your decoration for all to see!

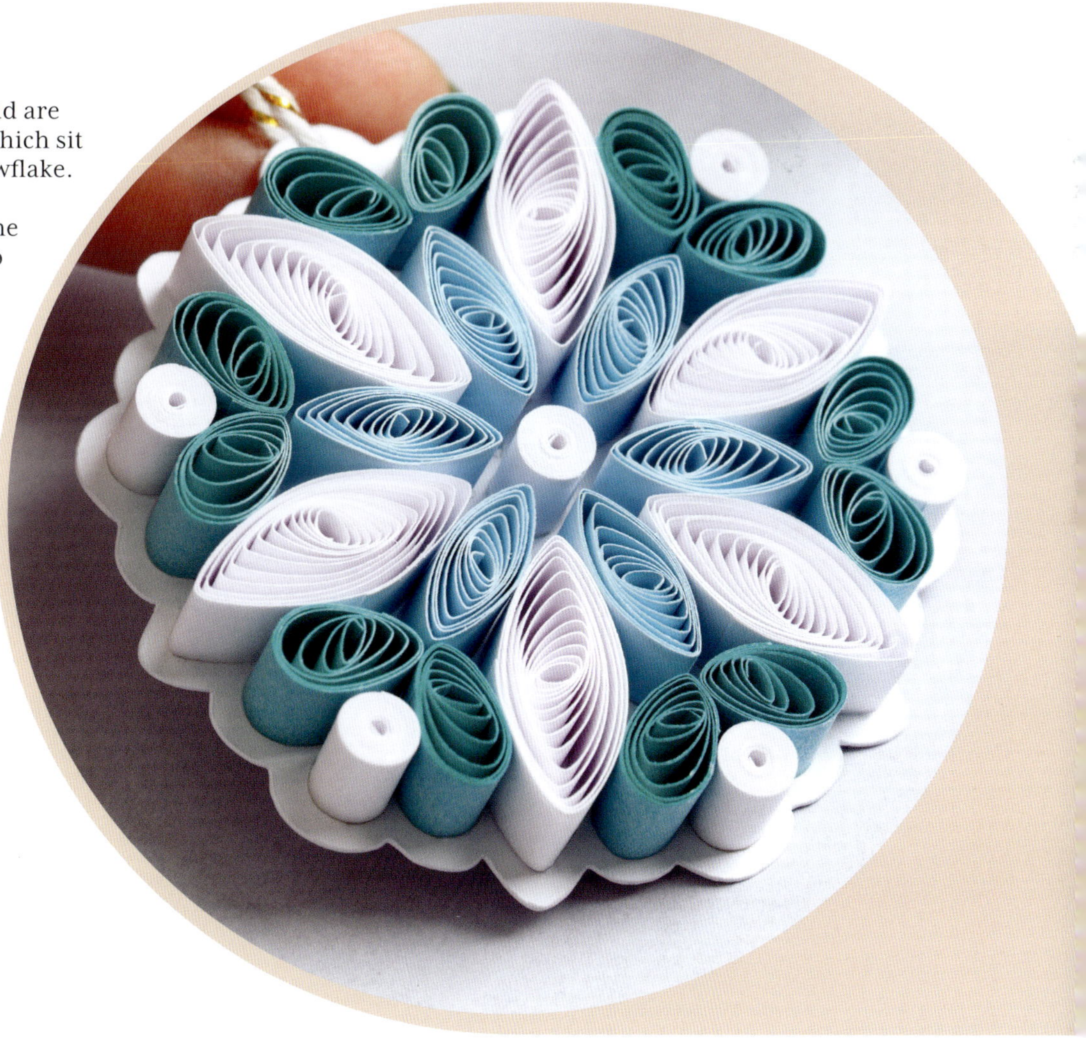

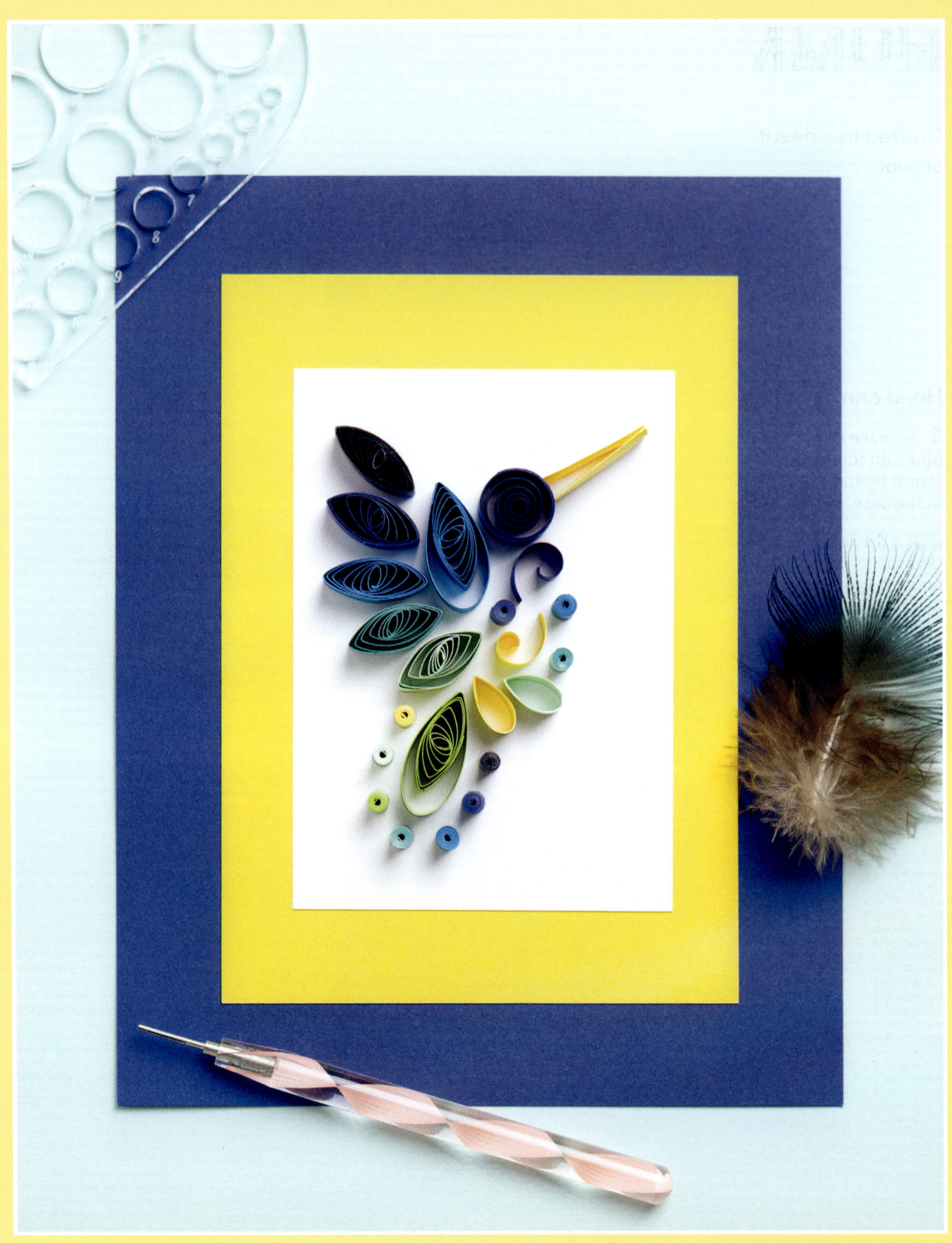

HUMMINGBIRD

Crafted in a beautiful blue colour palette, this hummingbird artwork practically buzzes with personality!

Head and beak

1 To make the hummingbird's head, cut a 30cm (12in) strip in royal blue and follow the loose coil instructions on page 104, using the 15mm (⁹⁄₁₆in) hole on the quilling board. Once made, apply a little glue to the base of the coil and stick down to the template.

2 For the beak, cut a 4.6cm (1¹³⁄₁₆in) strip in lemon and fold in half. Using a glue brush, apply a little glue to the base and stick down, holding in place to allow the glue to bond.

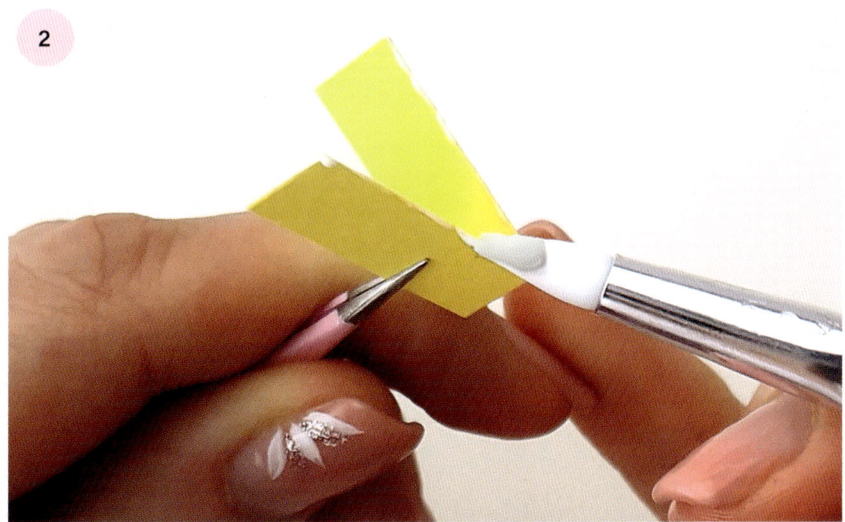

You will need

Hummingbird template, page 125
Quilling papers, I used 10mm (³⁄₈in)
Quilling tool, 10mm (³⁄₈in)
Scissors
Tacky PVA glue
Glue brush
Quilling board
Tweezers
Plain card in royal blue and
bright yellow for the mount
(optional: mine measures
19 x 15cm/7½ x 6in in blue and
15 x 10.5cm/6 x 4⅛in in yellow)

Quilling paper colours

Sapphire (12)
Indigo (13)
Light green (22)
Viridity (24)
Lemon (39)
Royal blue (48)
Turquoise (56)

Quilled elements

Triangle
Loose swirl/Open scroll
Tight coil
Loose scroll
Hollow teardrop
Marquise

Body and chest

3 The body and chest of the hummingbird are made up of four different elements, the first of which are the loose swirls, one in lemon and one in royal blue. Cut a 3cm (1³⁄₁₆in) strip in each colour and follow the instructions on page 108 to make the swirls. Add a little glue to the base of both swirls and fix down to the template.

4 At the centre of the body sit three tight coil shapes. Cut a 8cm (3⅛in) strip in sapphire, royal blue and turquoise, then follow the instructions on page 100 to make. Apply glue to the base and fix down.

5 Next, make both large and small hollow teardrops: there are two in each size in two different colours. For the large size cut a 6.5cm (2⁹⁄₁₆in) strip in sapphire and viridity. For the small size cut a 3.5cm (1³⁄₈in) strip in both lemon and light green, then follow the instructions on page 112 to make. Dab a little glue on the base of each element and fix down to the template.

6 Inside the larger hollow teardrops are marquise shapes in matching colours. Cut a 30cm (12in) strip in viridity and sapphire, using the 15mm (⁹⁄₁₆in) hole on the quilling board and follow the instructions on page 107 to make.

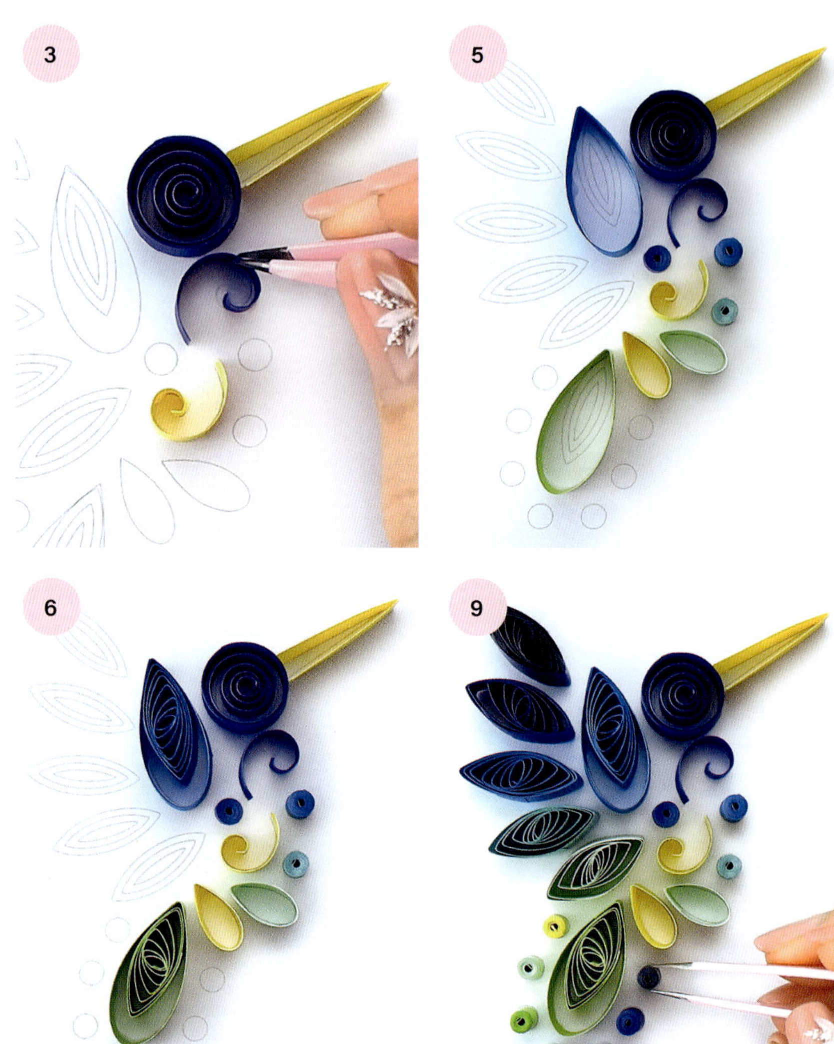

Wings

7 The wings on this magnificent bird are made with five different shades of marquise shapes. Cut one 30cm (12in) strip each in indigo, royal blue, sapphire, turquoise and light green, and make the marquise shapes using the 15mm ($^9/_{16}$in) hole on the quilling board. Once all the marquise shapes are made, apply a little glue to the base of each shape and fix down to the template.

Tail

8 At the base of the body sits a ring of tight coils in seven different shades: lemon, light green, viridity, turquoise, royal blue, sapphire and indigo. Cut an 8cm ($3^1/_8$in) strip in each colour and make the tight coils.

9 Once all elements are made, apply a little glue to the base of each shape and fix down to the template.

Mount and frame

10 To finish this piece cut and mount the artwork on to a base card of your choice and frame. I chose a bright yellow and deep blue shade to complement the shades within.

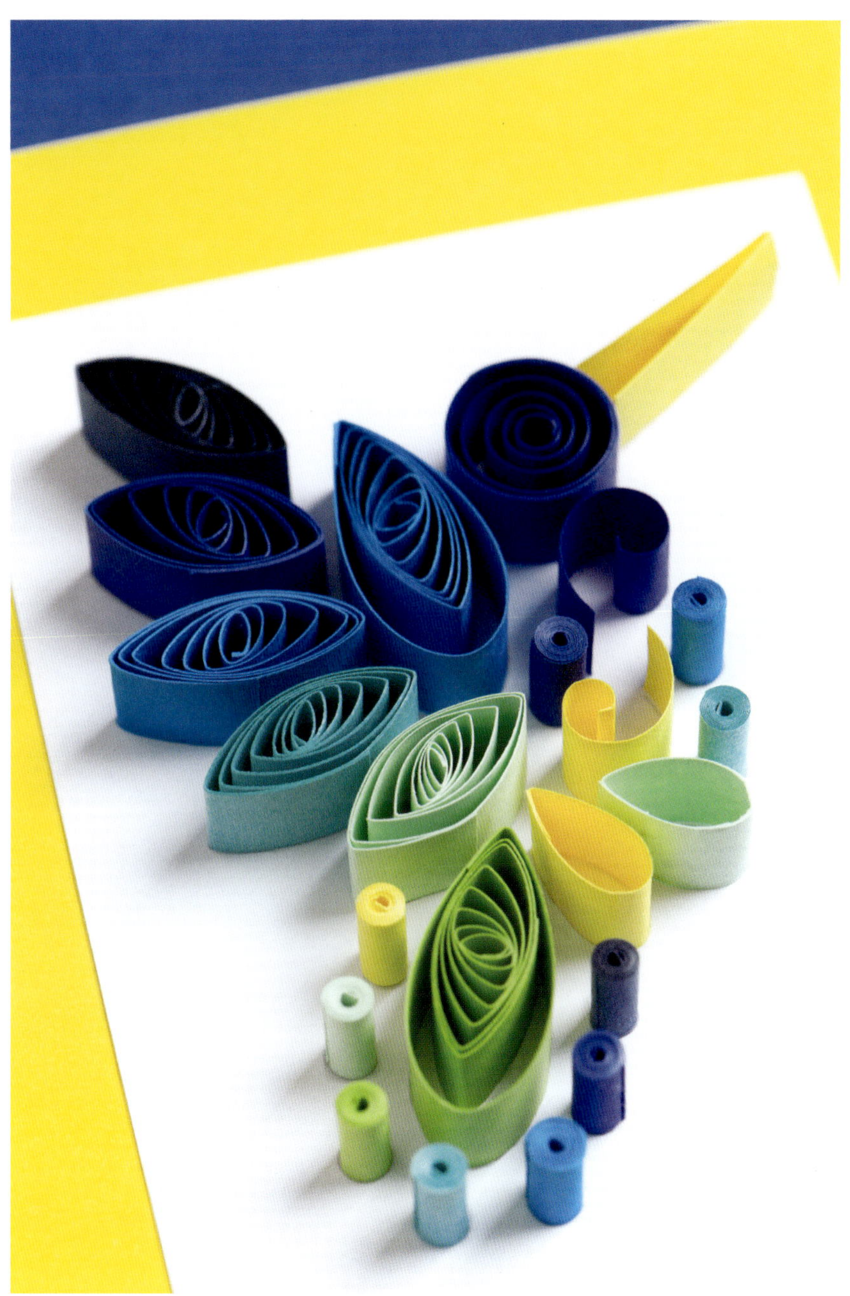

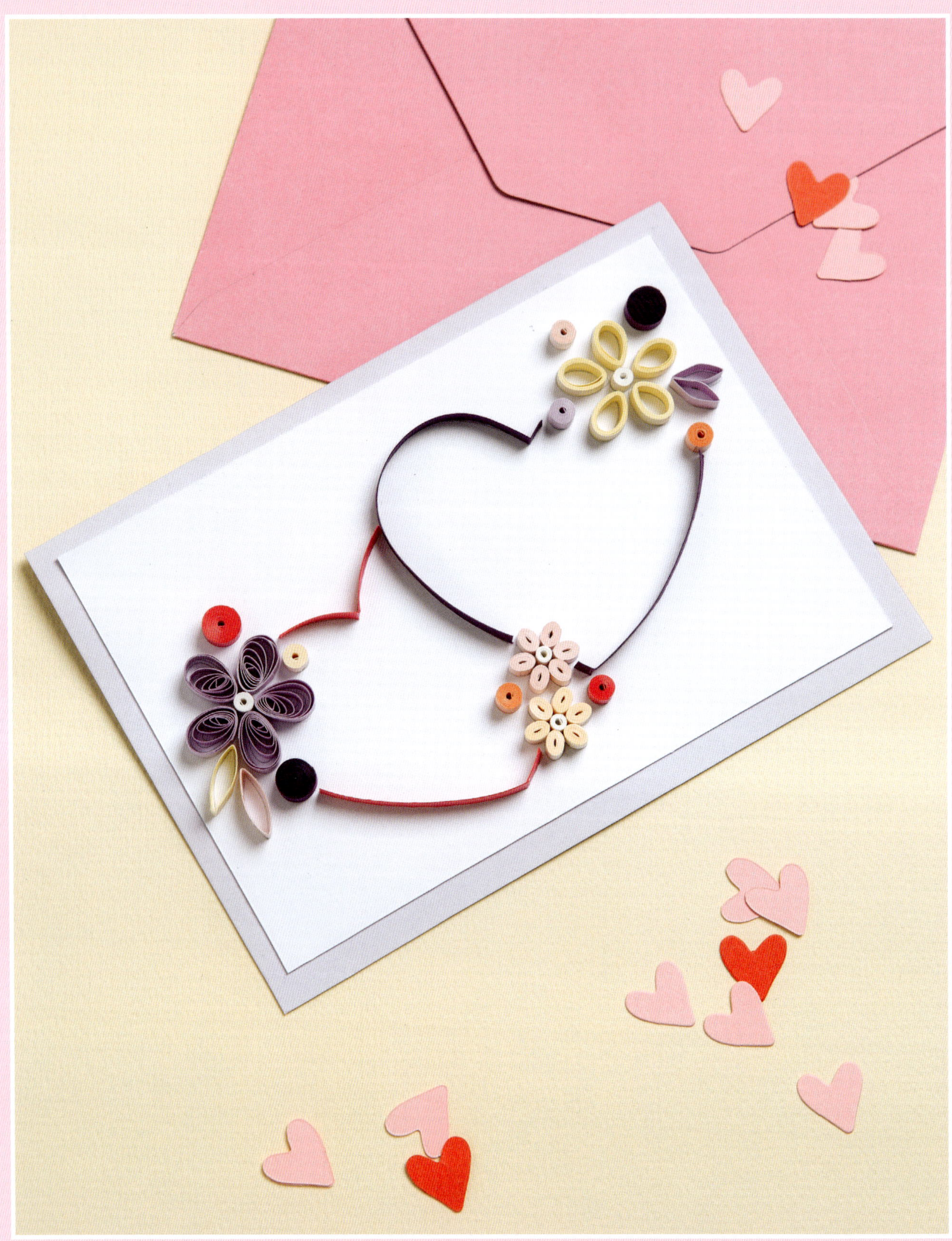

HEART DUO

This pair of hearts is a sweet way to let that special person in your life know exactly how you feel. Perfect for any occasion, the colours can be changed to suit the recipient. This particular piece uses seven different quilled elements in eight different colours.

Heart shapes

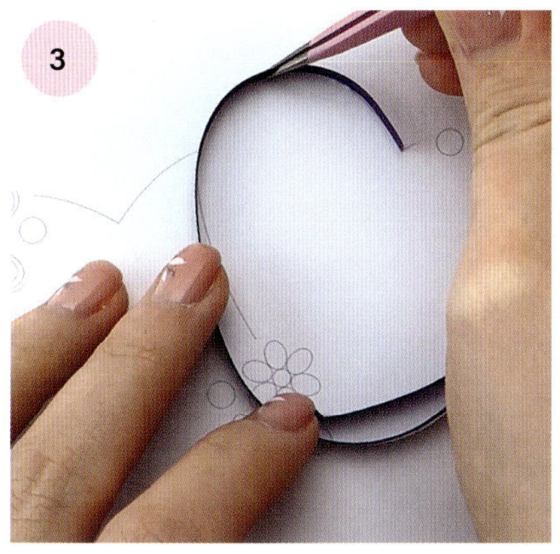 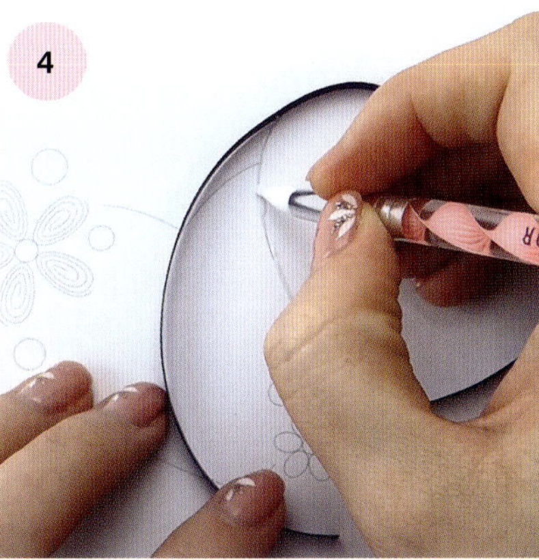

1 Take a full strip of magenta and dark purple and cut in half. Take one of the halves of each and slightly score the edge with your quilling tool for a curved finish.

2 Take the dark purple strip and apply a little glue to about 2cm (¾in) of the strip edge. Stick it to the template to form the bottom right of the heart, using the tweezers to guide your strip in place.

3 Hold in place with your tweezers for a moment to allow the glue to bond. Take the rest of the dark purple strip and, following the instructions above, craft the top left part of the heart.

4 Once the first section has stuck, apply a little glue to your paintbrush and paint it directly onto the template as shown.

5 Use the tweezers to guide your strip into place, sticking down as you go. When you reach the end of the printed template, use sharp scissors to trim the excess.

6 Repeat steps 1–5 to create the outline of the hot pink heart.

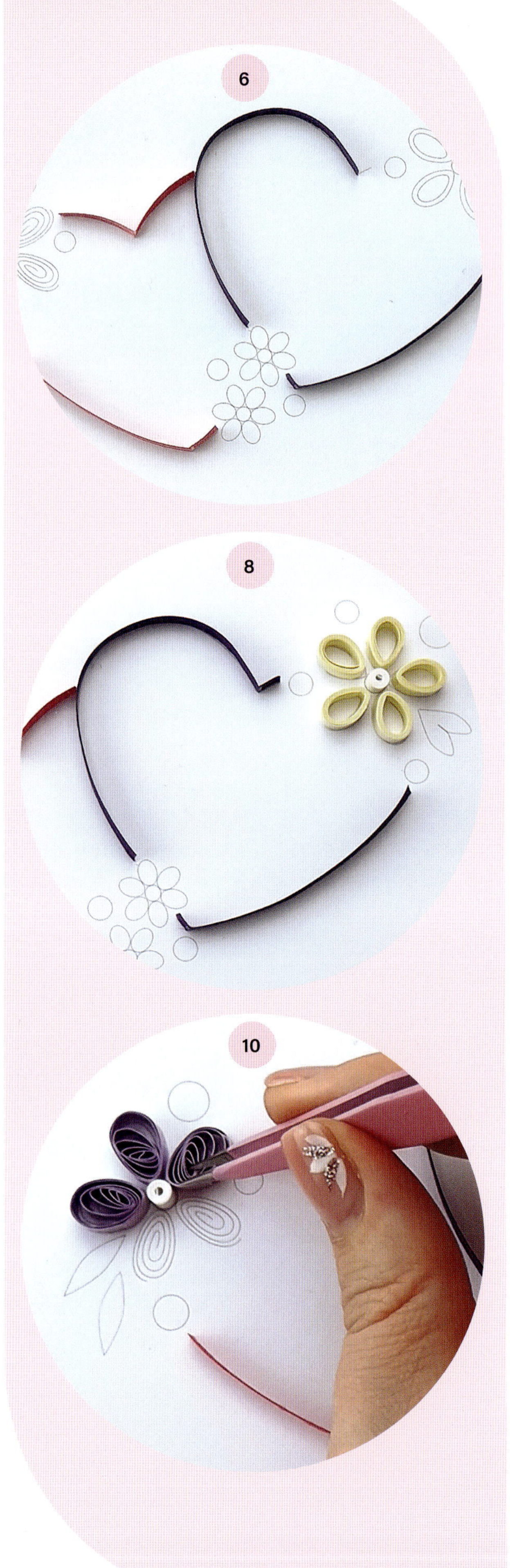

Ring teardrop flower

7 Cut five 13cm (5⅛in) strips in cream for the petals and one 8cm (3⅛in) strip in beige for the centre of the flower. Follow the instructions on pages 113 and 100 to make the ring teardrops and tight coil. Use the 8mm (⁵⁄₁₆in) hole on the quilling board for the ring teardrops.

8 Add a little glue to the base of each element and fix them down to the template, starting with the tight coil centre.

Teardrop flower

9 Cut five 13cm (5⅛in) strips in light purple for the petals and one 8cm (3⅛in) strip in beige for the centre of the flower. Follow the instructions on pages 98 and 100 to make the teardrops and tight coil. Use the 10mm (³⁄₈in) hole on the quilling board to make the teardrops.

10 Once all elements are made, add a little glue to the base of each element and fix down to the template starting with the tight coil centre.

Mini daisies

11 Cut six 10cm (4in) strips of each colour and follow the instructions on page 103 to make ellipse coils. Cut a 5cm (2in) strip in beige for each flower and follow the instructions on page 100 to make two tight coils.

12 Add a little glue to the base of each shape and fix down to the template.

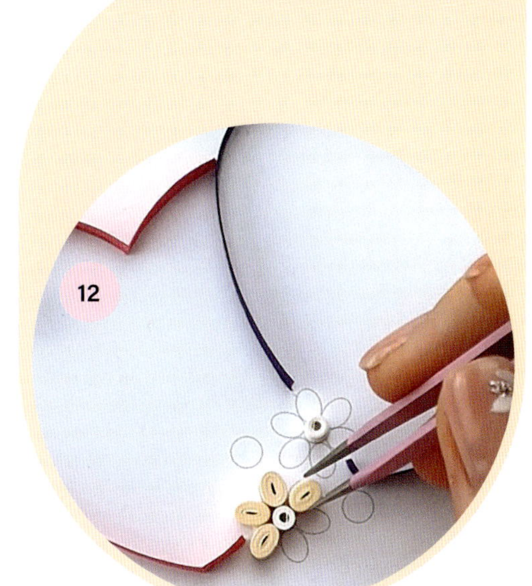

Tight coils

13 Cut one 13cm (5⅛in) strip in the following colours for the small tight coils: magenta, pink, light purple, dark purple, peach and apricot. Cut one 27cm (10⅝in) in the magenta and two 27cm (10⅝in) strips in the dark purple, for the large tight coils. Follow the instructions on page 100 to make tight coils.

14 Add a little glue to the base of each shape, and fix down to the template.

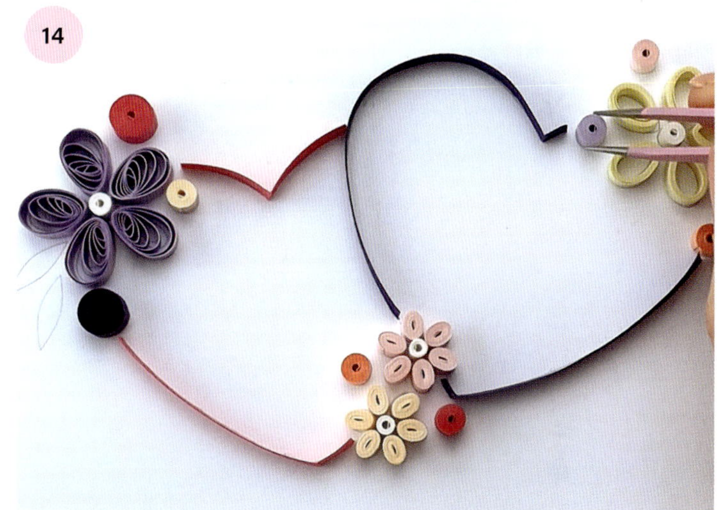

Leaves

15 Cut a 3.5cm (1⅜in) strip of cream and pink, and follow the instructions on page 106 to make the hollow marquise shapes. Using your glue brush, dab a little glue to the bottom and fix down.

Pointed heart

16 Finally, add a cute pointed heart to the hollow teardrop flower. Cut a 4.5cm (1¾in) strip in light purple and follow the instructions on page 110 to make. Using your glue brush, dab a little glue to the bottom and fix down.

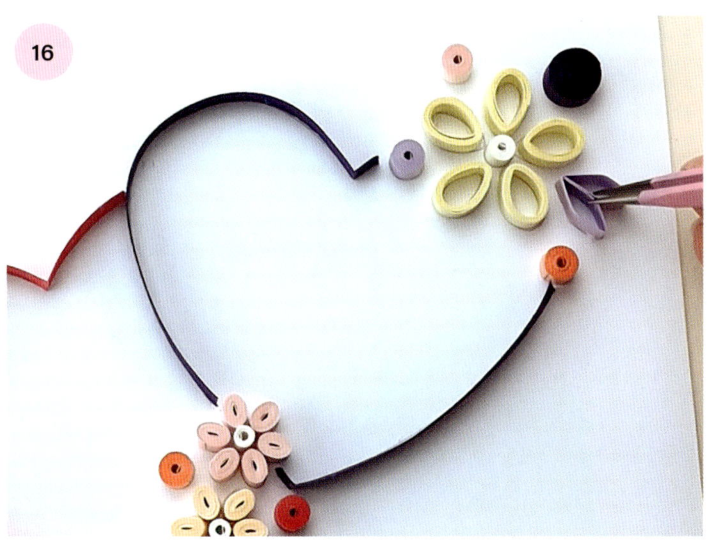

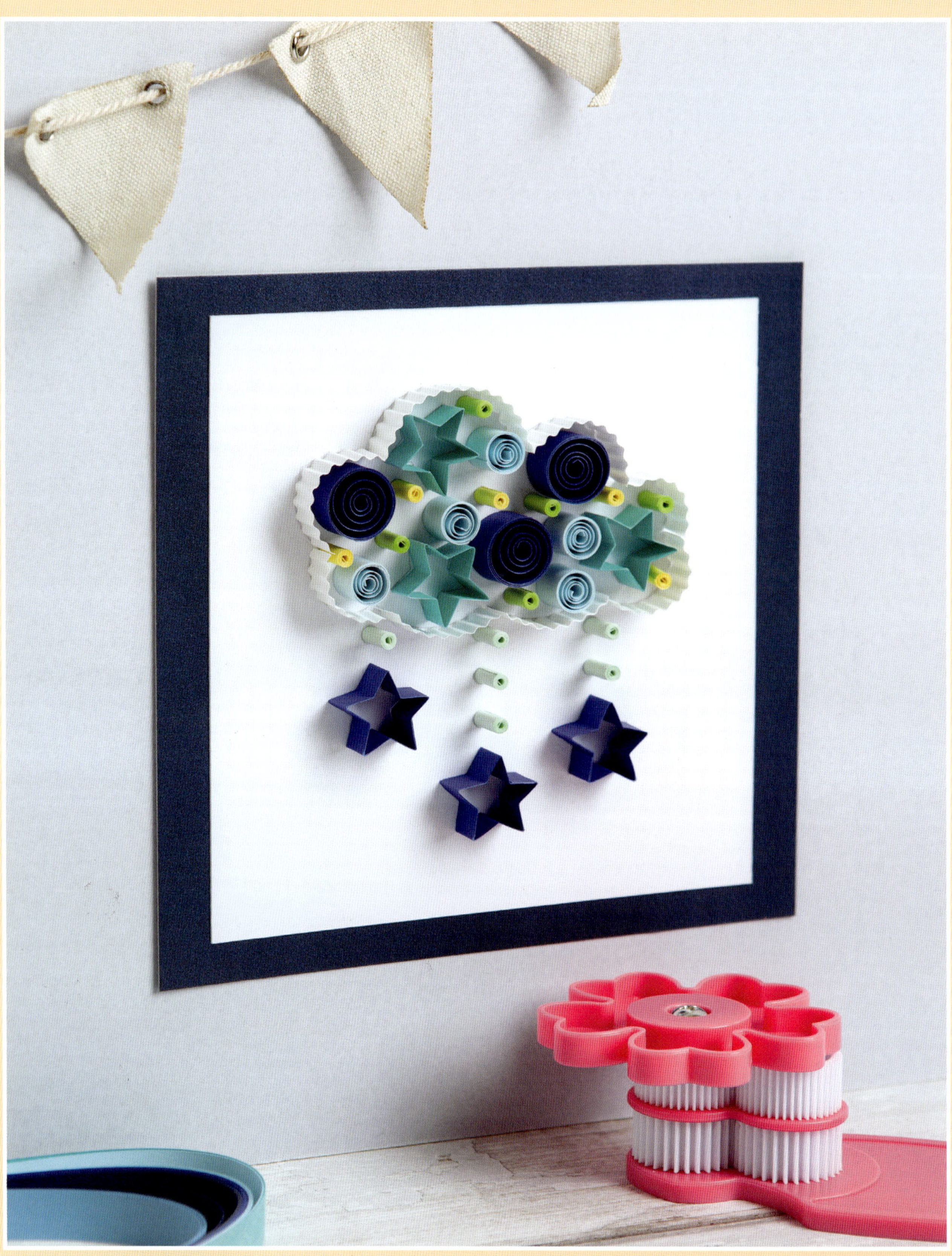

DREAMY CLOUD

Crafted in a dreamy blue palette, this fluffy cloud artwork is the perfect addition to any bedroom or a beautiful framed gift to hang in a newborn's nursery!

TIP

You can make this piece without the use of a paper crimper; the crimped paper simply adds a little interest to the finished piece.

Cloud outline

1 Take a full strip in bleach and run it through a quilling crimper (this step is optional).

2 The cloud is made up of eight arch shapes. Starting with the very top of the cloud, apply a little glue to the first couple of centimetres (an inch) of the strip's thin edge and use tweezers to guide your strip into place. Hold down with your tweezers for a moment to allow the glue to bond. Once the first section has stuck, apply a little glue to your glue brush and paint it directly onto the template. Use your tweezers to guide the strip into place, sticking down as you go. When you reach the end of the printed template use sharp scissors to trim the excess part of the strip. Follow these steps for the seven remaining cloud arches.

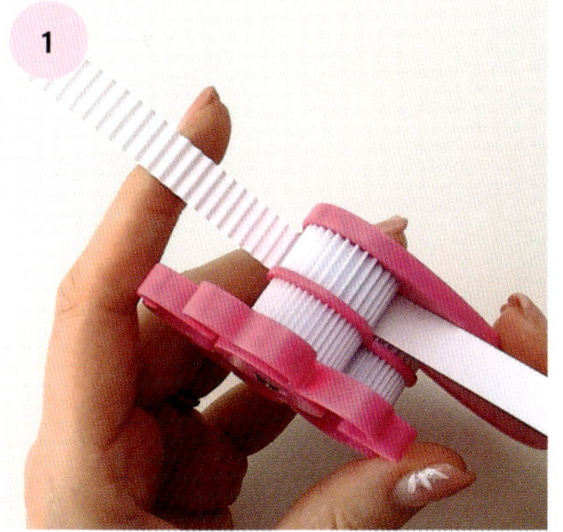

Loose coils

3 The first elements to decorate the inside of the cloud are the large loose coils. Cut three 30cm (12in) strips of royal blue and follow the instructions on page 104 to make, using the 15mm (⁹⁄₁₆in) hole on the quilling board.

4 The next elements are the small loose coils, five in total, all in sky blue. Cut five 13cm (5⅛in) strips and use the 9mm (⅜in) hole on the quilling board to make. Once all the loose coils are made, apply a little glue to the base of the coils and stick down to the template.

Stars

5 To make the stars, cut three 15cm (6in) strips in royal blue, three 15cm (6in) strips in turquoise and follow the instructions on page 111 to make. Once the stars are made, apply a little glue directly to the edge of the elements and stick down.

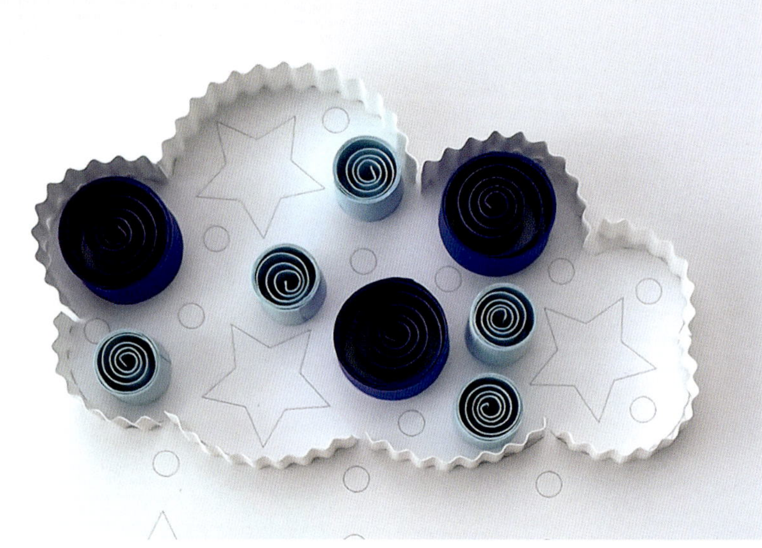

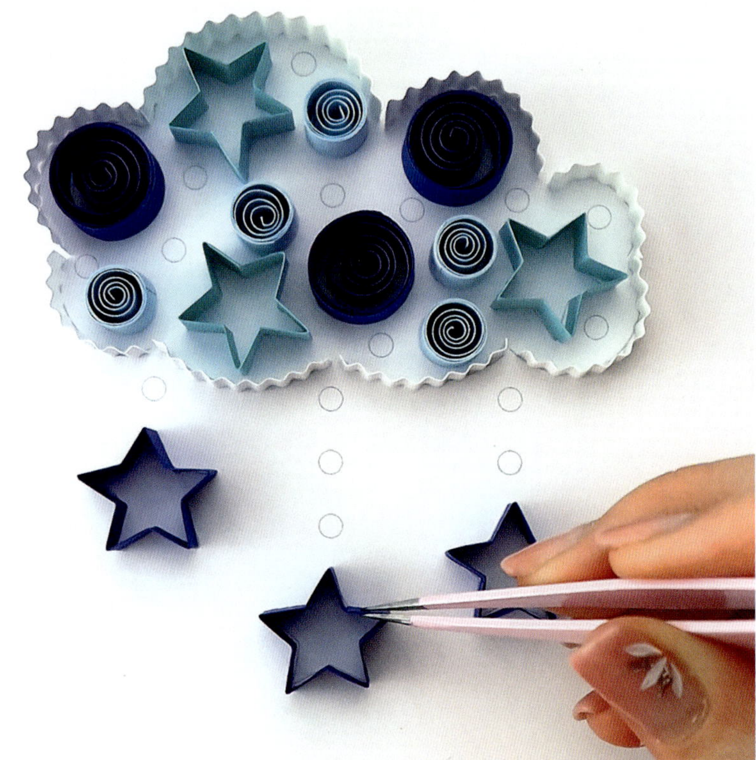

Tight coils

6 The final elements to decorate this artwork are tight coils, 16 in total. The 10 tight coils inside the cloud are a mix of lemon and viridity, the six tight coils hanging down are all light green.

7 For all the tight coils, cut 6cm (2⅜in) strips and follow the instructions on page 100 to make the elements. Once all are made, apply a little glue to the base of the shapes and stick down to the template.

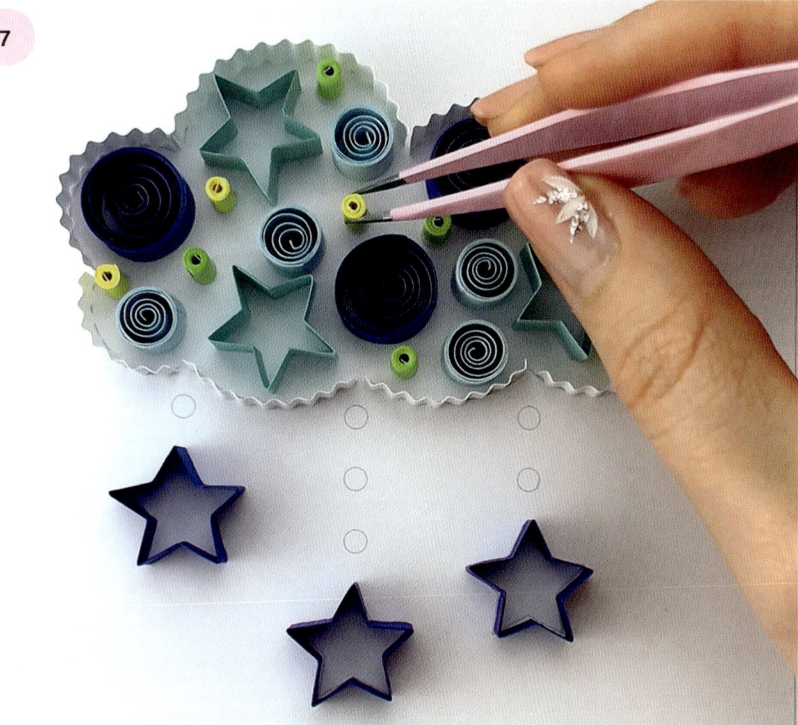

Mount and frame

8 To finish this piece, trim around the template and use double-sided tape or glue to mount the artwork on to a base card of your choice then frame. I have chosen indigo to complement the shades within.

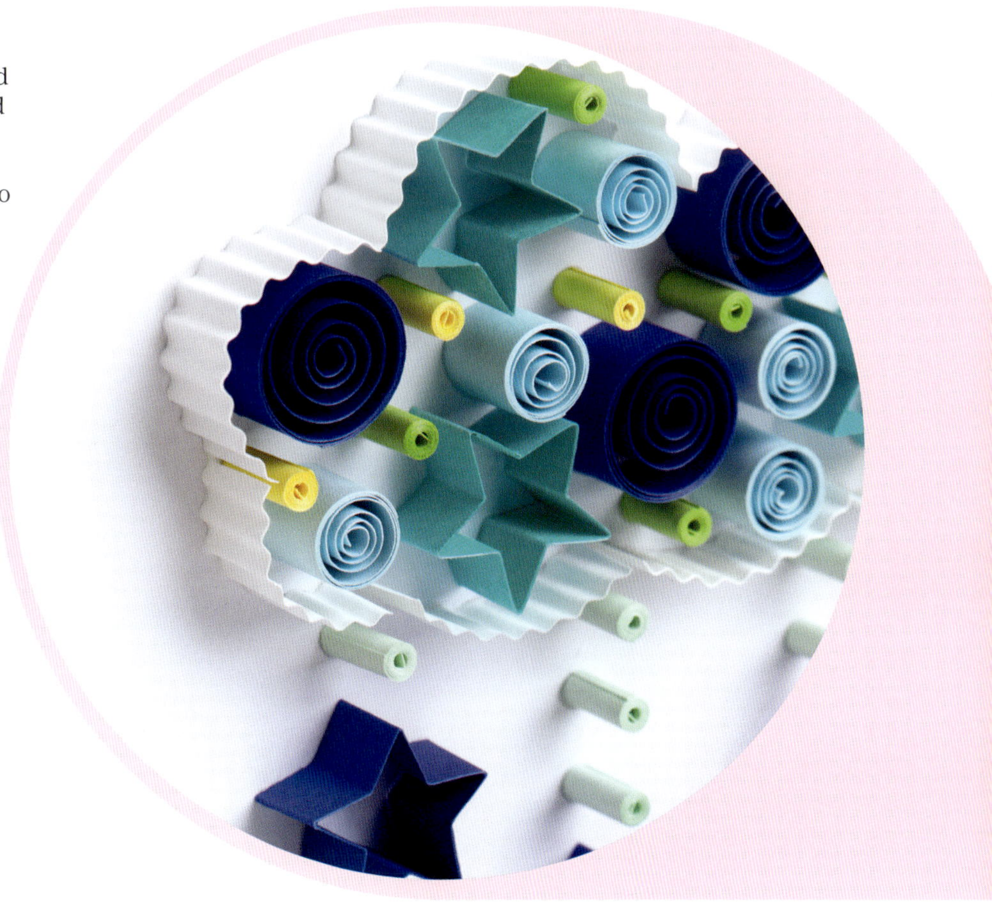

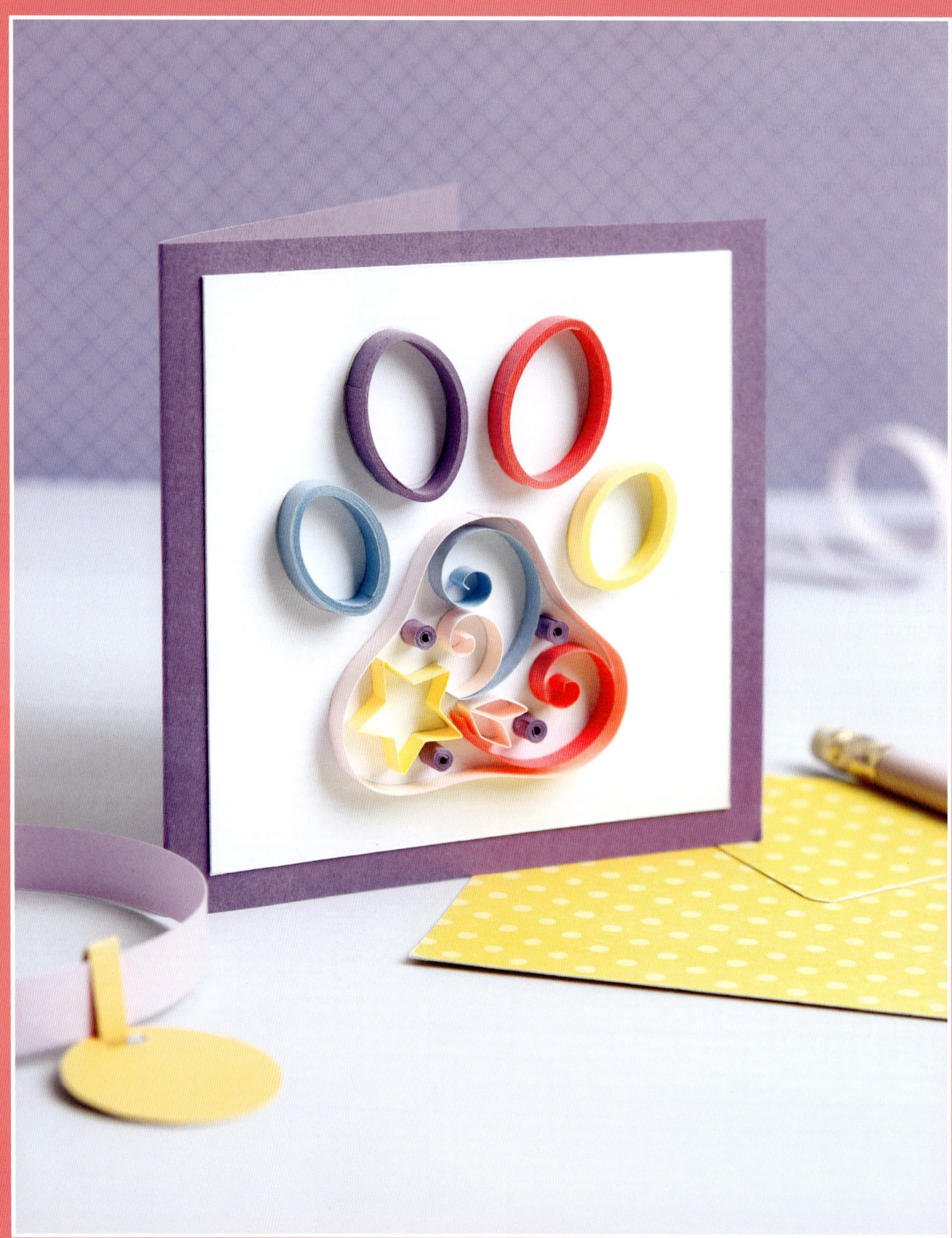

PAW PRINT

This paw print card is perfect for all pet lovers! Designed in pretty pastel tones, this design is a simple make, using five different quilled elements.

You will need

Paw print template, page 117
Quilling papers, I used 5mm (³⁄₁₆in)
Quilling tool, 10mm (³⁄₈in)
Scissors
Tacky PVA glue
Glue brush
Quilling board
Tweezers
Plain card in purple for the mount (optional: mine is 10 x 10cm/4 x 4in)

Quilling paper colours

Baby pink (2)
Purple (6)
Grey blue (10)
Light yellow (38)
Magenta (51)

Quilled elements

Loose swirl/Open scroll
Star
Hollow ellipse
Tight coil
Pointed heart

Paw outline

1 The paw outline is made from one long strip, sticking it down to the template on its thin edge. Take a baby pink strip, apply a little glue to the first couple of centimetres (an inch) of the strip edge and stick to the template, using the tweezers to guide your paw outline into place. Hold in place with your tweezers for a moment to allow the glue to bond. Once the first section has stuck, apply a little glue to a glue brush and paint it directly onto the template. Use the tweezers to guide your strip into place, sticking down as you go.

2 Once you complete the paw shape there will be excess paper. Use sharp scissors to trim away the excess, leaving a 5mm (³⁄₁₆in) tab. Apply glue to this tab and stick it to the start of the paw as shown.

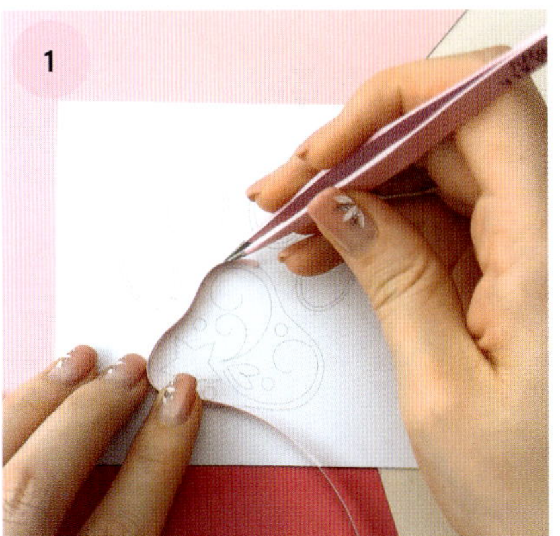
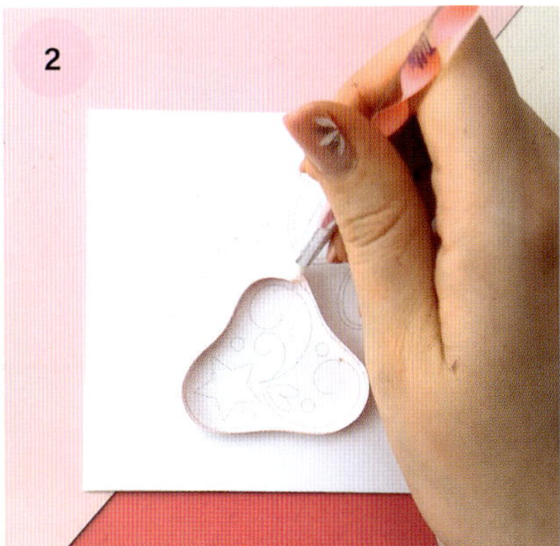

Paw pads

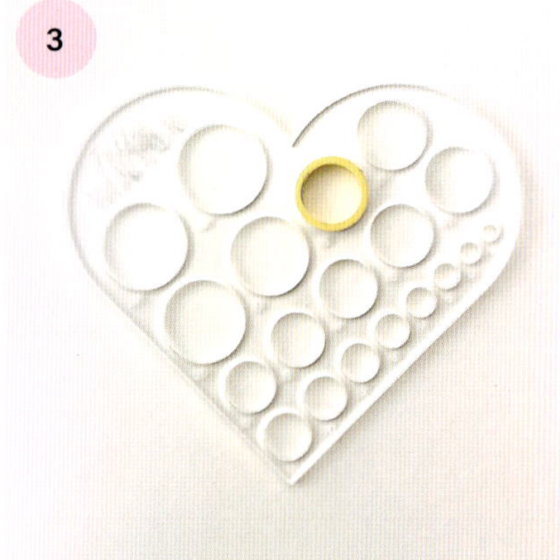

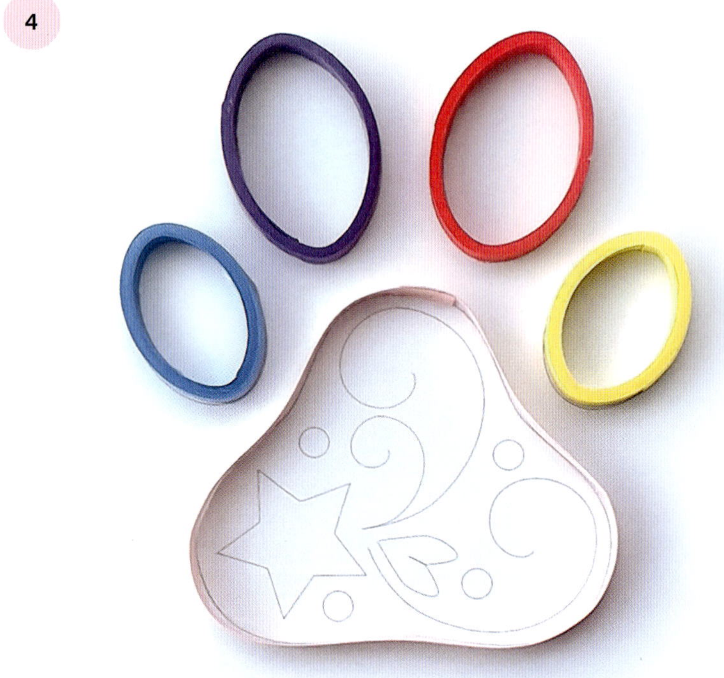

3 There are four pads in two different sizes in this artwork. Take a full 54cm (21¼in) strip in grey blue, magenta, purple and light yellow and follow the instructions on page 114 to make hollow ellipse elements. For the larger pads use the 22mm (⅞in) hole and for the smaller pads use the 18mm (¹¹⁄₁₆in) hole on the quilling board, as shown.

4 Once all are made, apply a little glue to the base of the shapes and stick down to the template.

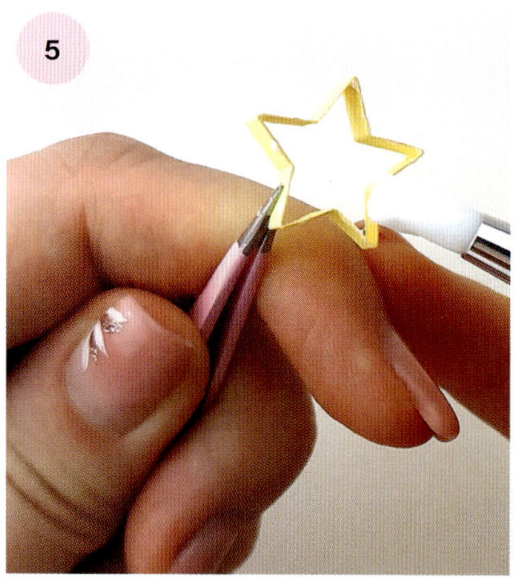

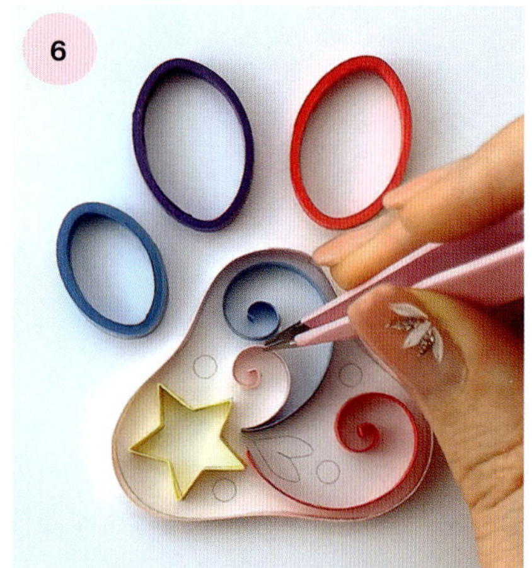

Paw elements

5 The paw has four different elements decorating the interior, each in a different colour, the first of which is the star. To make the star, cut a 15cm (6in) strip in light yellow and follow the instructions on page 111 to make. Once the star is finished, apply a little glue directly to the edge of the elements and stick down.

6 The next elements are three loose swirls, two large and one small. Cut one 7cm (2¾in) strip each of grey blue and magenta (these are for the larger swirls), and cut one 3.5cm (1⅜in) strip in baby pink for the small swirl. Follow the instructions on page 103 to make the swirls. Apply a little glue to the base of the shapes and stick down to the template.

7 The last elements are the pointed heart and the tight coils. Cut a 4cm (1⁹⁄₁₆in) strip in baby pink for the pointed heart and four 6cm (2⅜in) strips in purple for the tight coils. Follow the instructions on pages 100 and 110 to make both elements, then apply a little glue to the base and fix down to the template.

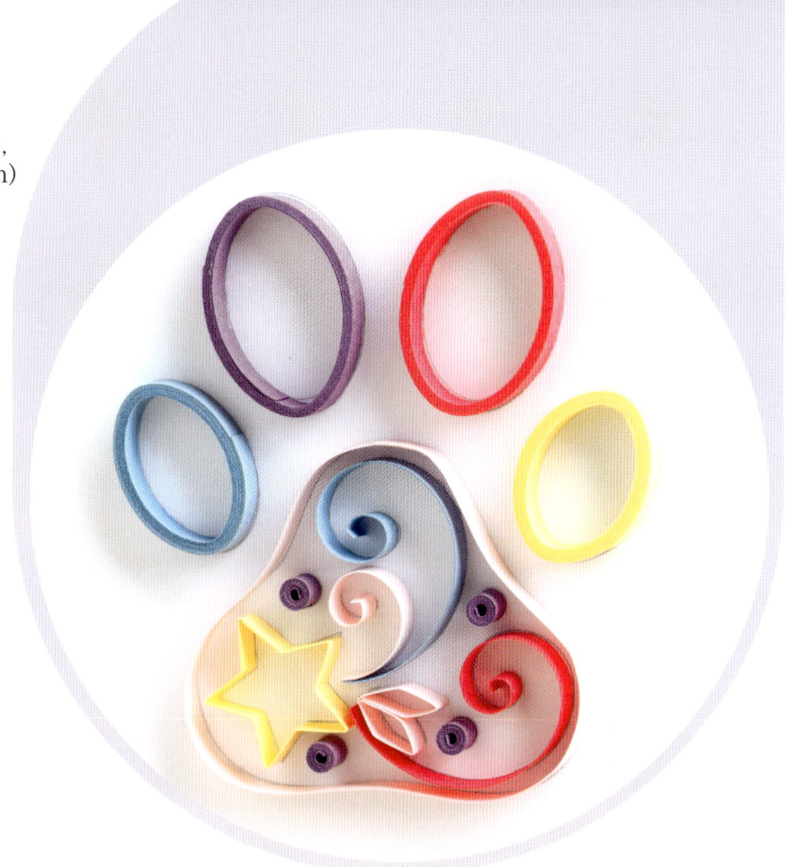

Mounting the card

8 Apply a little double-sided tape or glue to the back of the template and mount onto a complementary coloured card base.

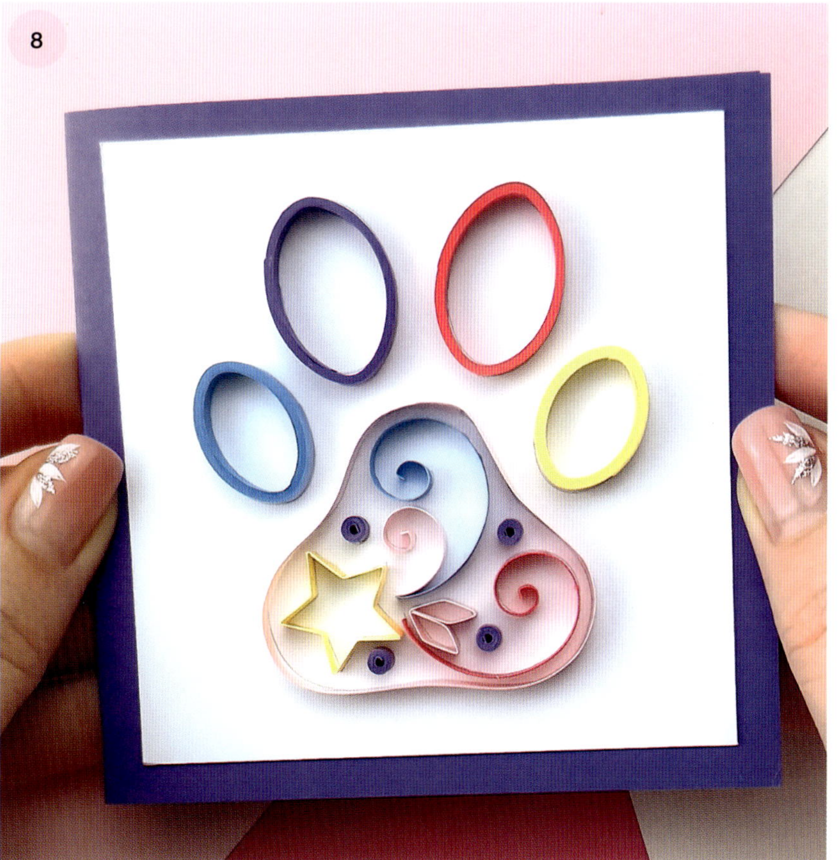

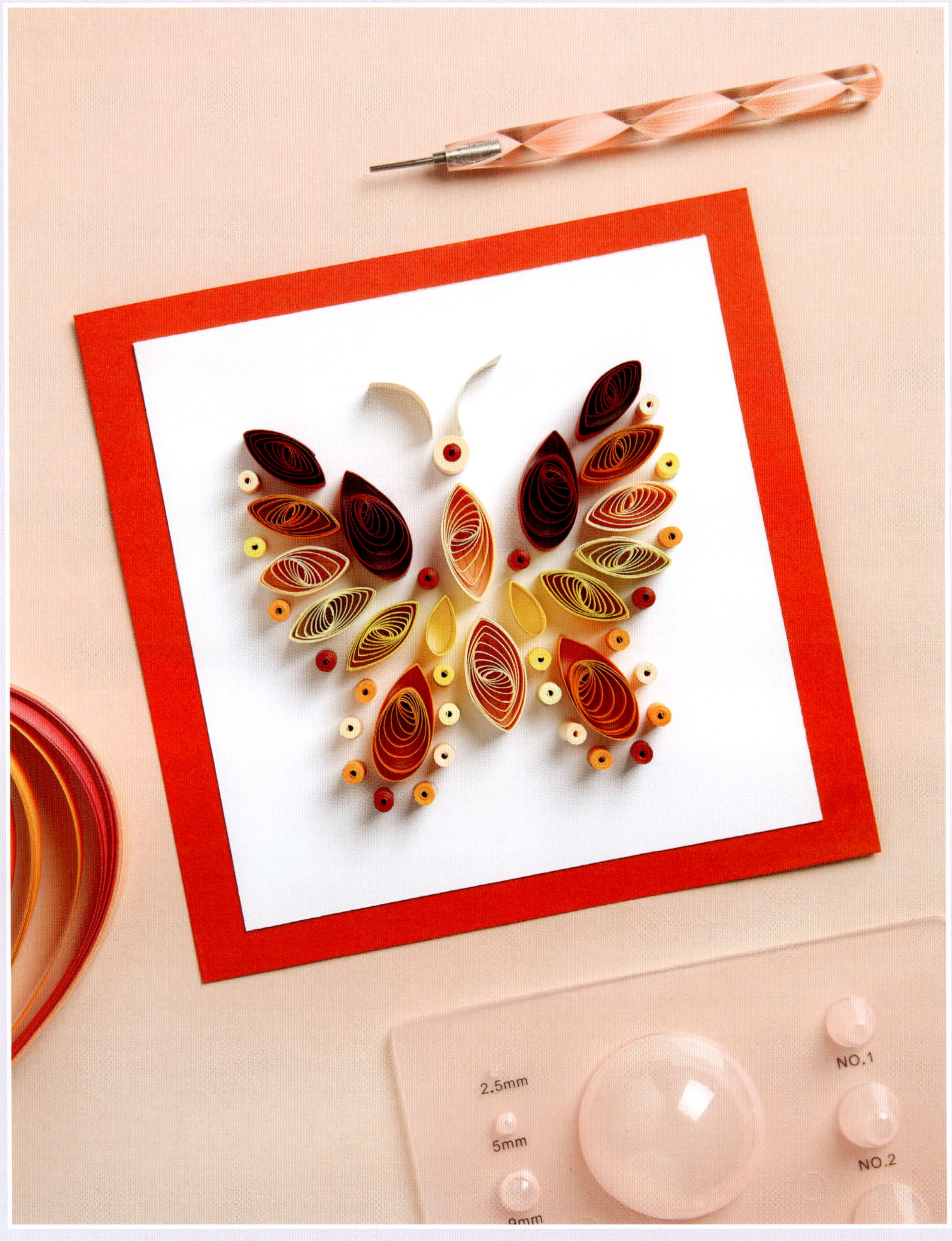
2.5mm
5mm
9mm
NO.1
NO.2

BUTTERFLY

Crafted in a fiery red and yellow ombre colour palette, this butterfly artwork is ablaze with personality! To make your design, cut all strips to the lengths indicated below. Work through the elements one by one, sticking them down as you go.

Butterfly head

1 The butterfly head is made from a multi-coloured tight coil. Cut one 10cm (4in) strip in xmas red for the inner colour and one 23cm (9¹⁄₁₆in) strip in apricot for the outer colour. Follow the multi-coloured tight coil instructions on page 101.

2 Apply a little glue to the base of the coil and fix down to the template for the head.

3 Cut two 2cm (¾in) strips in apricot and follow the instructions on page 104 to make the arch shapes. Using a glue brush, apply a small amount of glue to the base and stick down. Hold in place to allow the glue to bond.

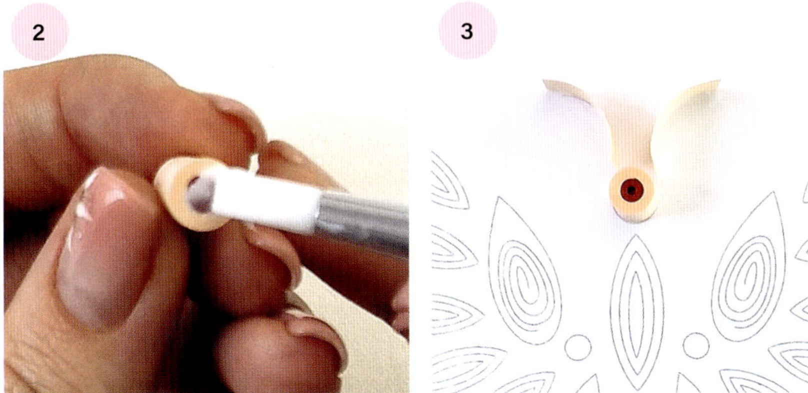

Body

4 Cut two 40cm (15¾in) strips in apricot, and follow the instructions on page 107 to make two large marquise shapes, using the 19mm (¾in) hole on your quilling board.

5 Use a glue brush to apply a small amount of glue to the base of each element and stick down to the template.

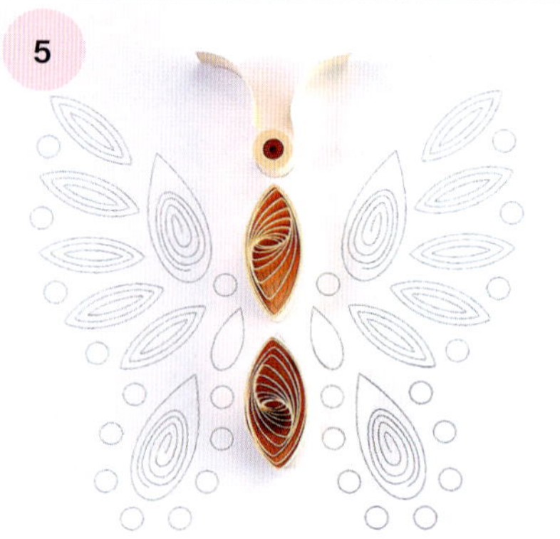

Wings

6 The butterfly wings are made up of four different elements, the first of which are four large hollow teardrops, two xmas red and two orange red. Cut two strips in each colour, each measuring 6.5cm (2⁹⁄₁₆in) long, and follow the instructions on page 112 to make the teardrop shapes.

7 Once made, apply a little glue to the base of each element and stick down.

8 Inside each of the hollow teardrops sits a quilled teardrop in a matching shade. Cut two strips of 25cm (9¾in) in each colour, and follow the instructions on page 98 to make teardrop shapes, using the 14mm (⁹⁄₁₆in) hole on the quilling board. Once made, fix down to the template base inside the hollow shapes.

9 Cut two 3.5cm (1⅜in) strips in lemon and make two hollow teardrops, then fix down to the template.

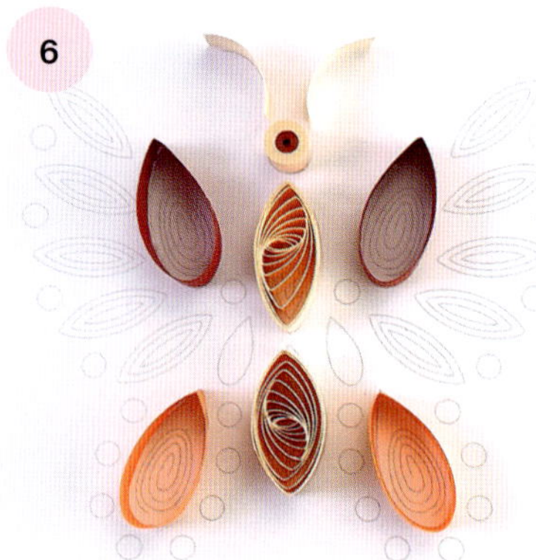

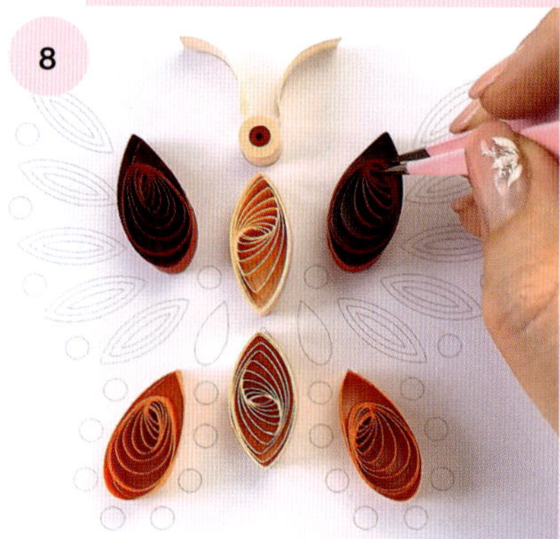

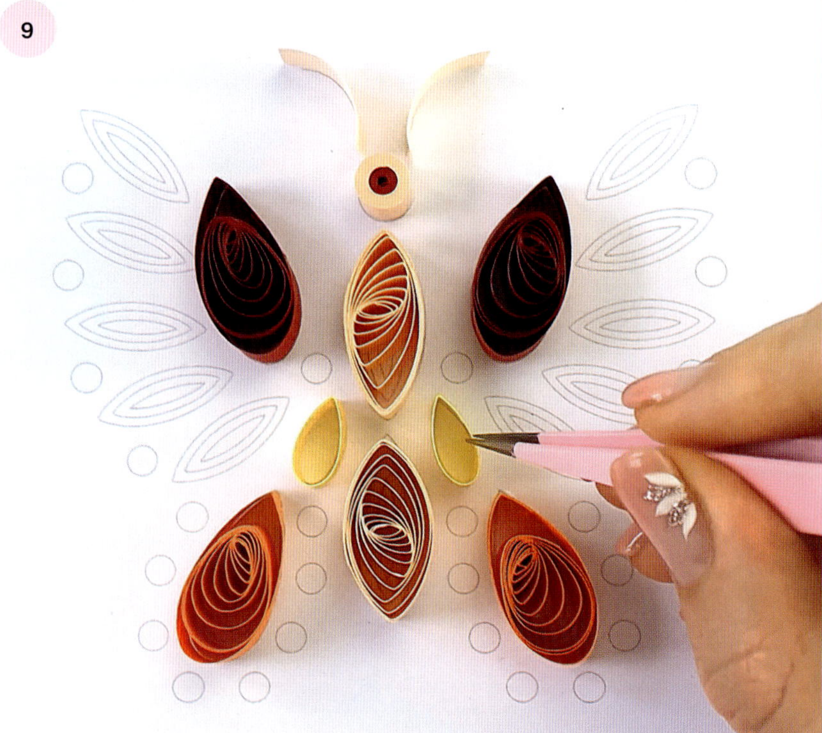

10 Cut two 30cm (12in) strips in each of the following colours: xmas red, orange red, apricot, lemon and light yellow. Follow the instructions to make marquise shapes using the 15mm (⁹⁄₁₆in) hole on your quilling board.

11 Apply glue to the back of each shape and stick down to the template.

12 The final elements to add are the tight coils: 26 in total, 13 on each wing. Cut six strips in apricot, four in lemon, eight in orange red, six in xmas red and two in light yellow, all measuring 10cm (4in). Follow the instructions on page 100 to make tight coils. Once made, apply a little glue to the base of each element and carefully stick down to the template.

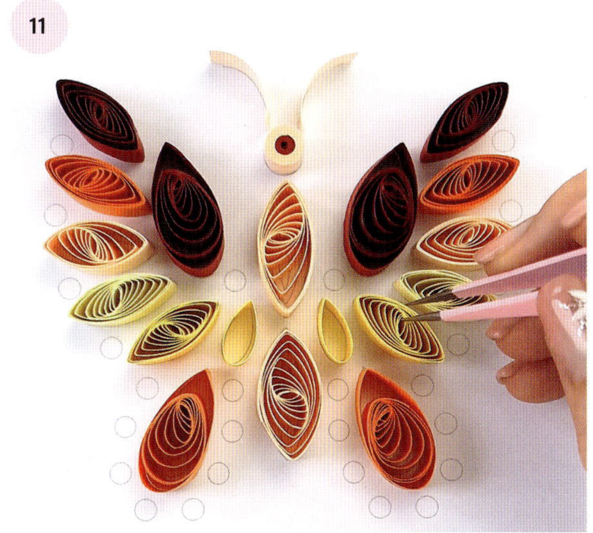

Mount and frame

13 To finish this piece, cut and mount the artwork onto a base card of your choice and frame. I have chosen a deep red colour to complement the shades within.

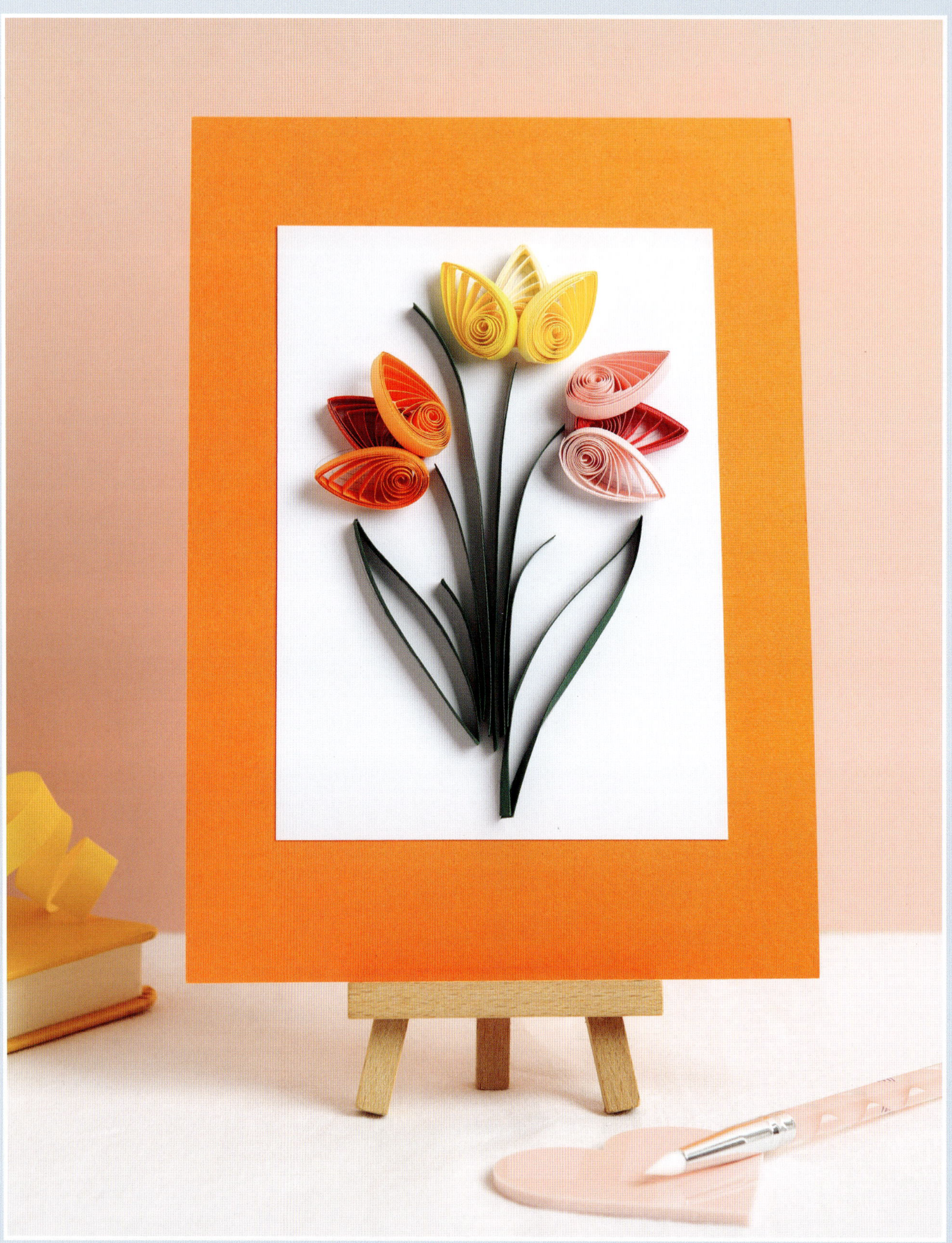

TULIPS

This bunch of tulips simply oozes springtime joy! It is simple to create yet so eye-catching once completed. It is made using just one simple quilled element with the addition of edge quilling for the stems and the leaf shapes.

Stems

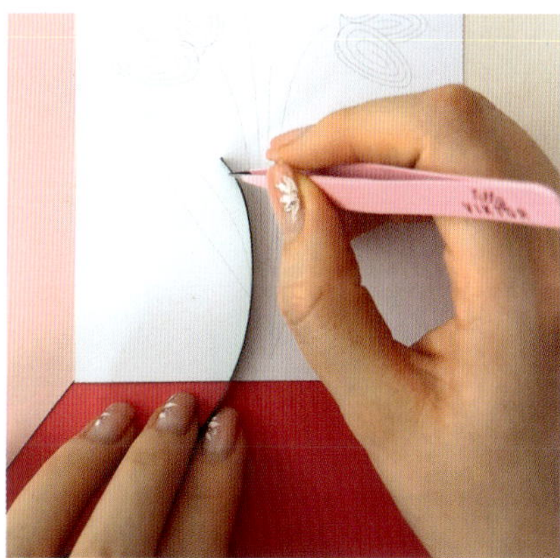

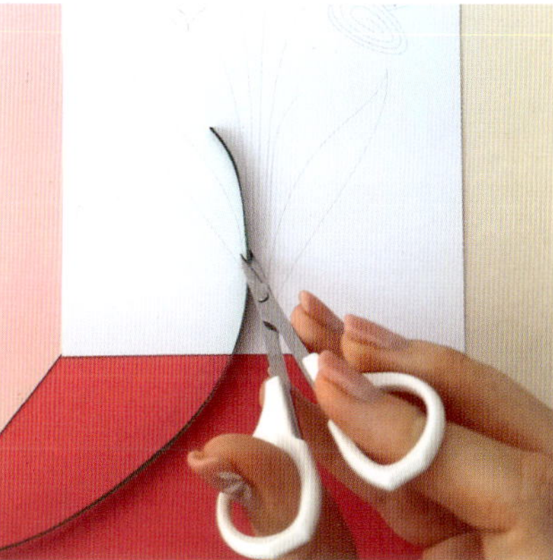

1 Start with the smallest stem on the left-hand side. Take a piece of forest green quilling paper and apply glue to the first few centimetres (an inch) of the base of the strip as shown. Stick to the template holding in place with your tweezers for a moment to allow the glue to bond.

2 Once the first section has stuck, apply a little glue to your glue brush and paint it directly onto the template. Use the tweezers to guide your strip into place, sticking down as you go. When you reach the end of the printed line, use sharp scissors to trim the excess part of the strip.

3 Follow these steps for the five remaining stems and the two leaf shapes.

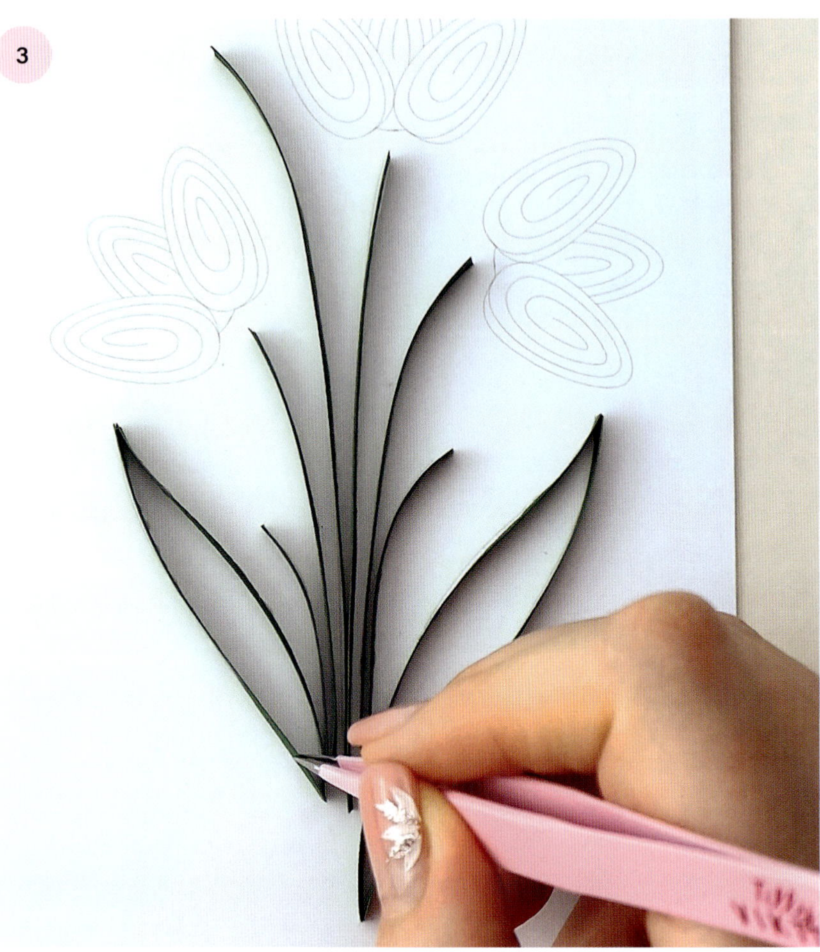

Tulip flowers

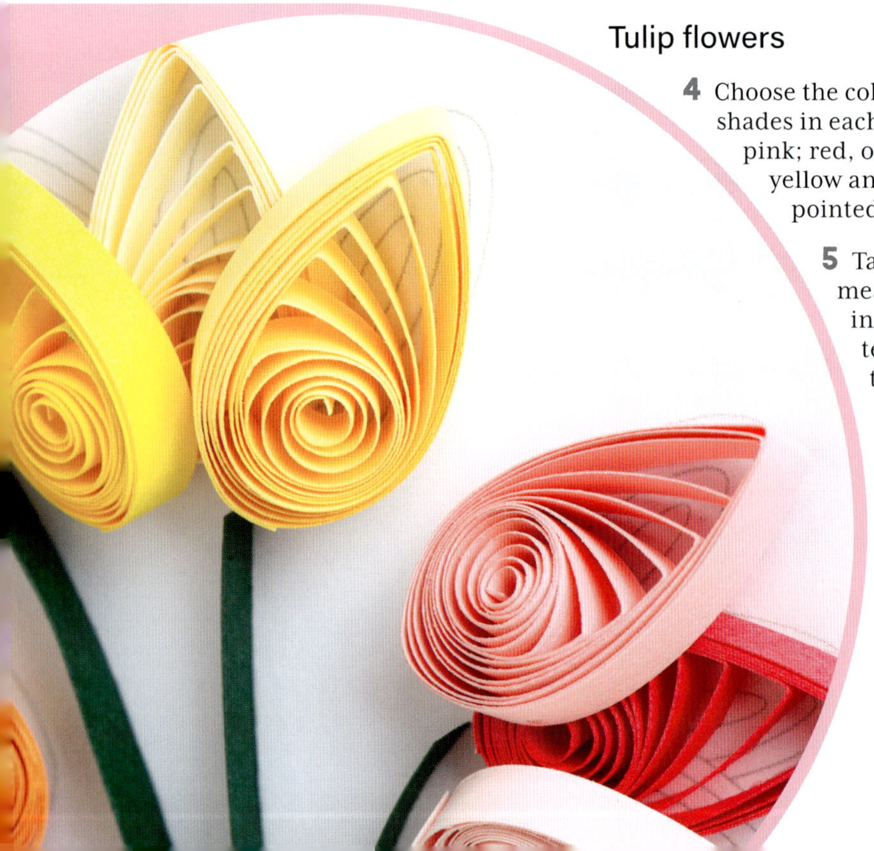

4 Choose the colours for your flowers, selecting three varying shades in each colour. I chose: magenta, pink and baby pink; red, orange and orange red; and lemon, light yellow and cream. The petals are made from nine pointed teardrop shapes, one in each shade.

5 Take a full strip in each of the nine colours measuring 39cm (15⅜in), and follow the instructions on page 99 to make the pointed teardrop shapes. Use the 19mm (¾in) hole on the quilling board.

6 Take a pointed teardrop for the central petal of the middle tulip, apply a little glue to the base of the petal and fix down to the template.

7 Apply a generous dab of glue to both the left-hand side of the quilled teardrop and also to the template itself. Press the second teardrop onto the glue. The petal will sit at an angle with the left side touching the base of the template and the right side leaning on the centre petal. Wait a couple of minutes to allow the glue to bond and repeat the same process for the right petal.

8 Repeat the process for the two remaining tulips.

Mount and frame

9 To finish this piece, apply some double-sided tape to the back of the tulip artwork and mount it onto a base card of your choice then frame. I have chosen a bright orange shade to complement the tulip colours.

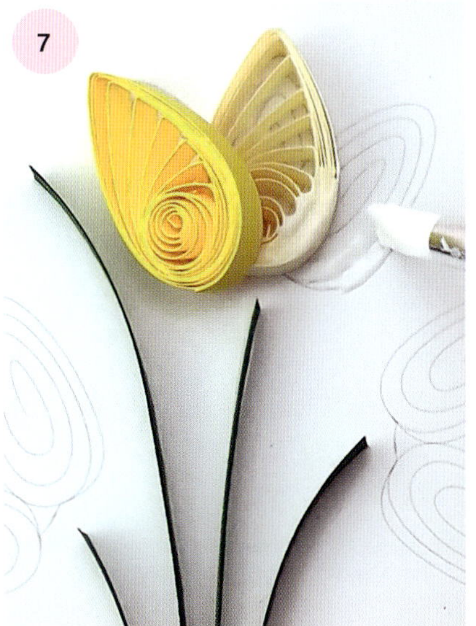
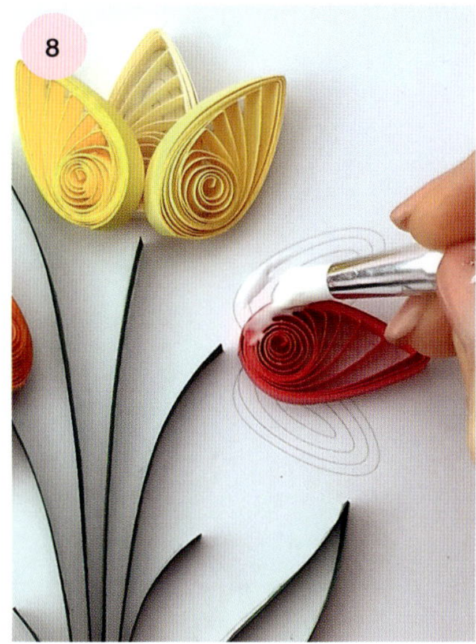
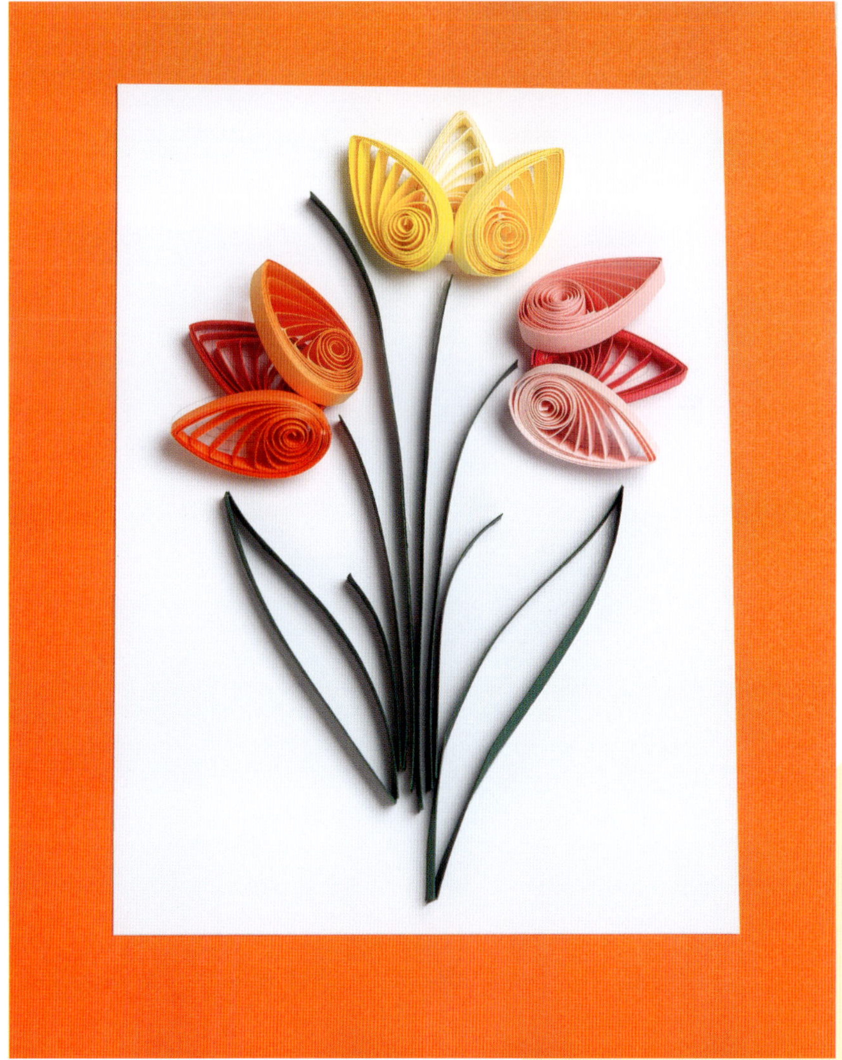

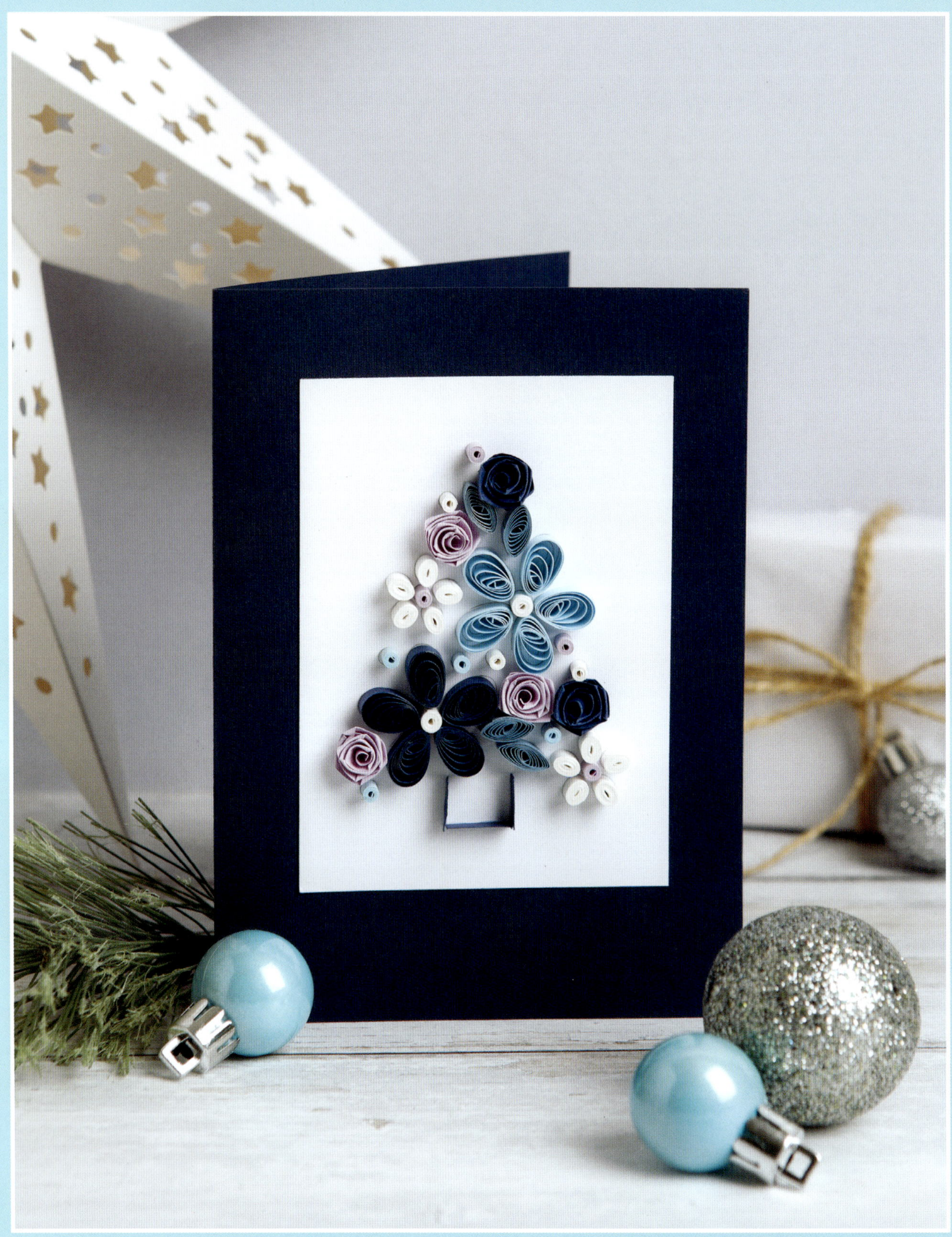

WINTER WONDERLAND TREE

Made in a stunning winter wonderland colour palette, this mini tree is the perfect greetings card to send at Christmas time. Encompassing five different quilled elements, this tree is relatively simple to make yet radiates festive spirit once finished!

Teardrop flowers

1 There are two large teardrop flowers in this piece, one in indigo and one in sky blue. There are five petals in each flower, each mounted around a tight coil shape. Cut ten 15cm (6in) strips for the petals, five in indigo and five in sky blue. Cut two 8cm (3⅛in) strips in white for the centre of the flowers.

2 Follow the instructions on pages 98 and 100 to make the rounded teardrop and tight coil shapes. Use the 10mm (⅜in) hole on the quilling board when making the teardrop shapes.

3 Once all elements are made, add a little glue to the base of each element and fix down to the template, starting with the tight coil centres.

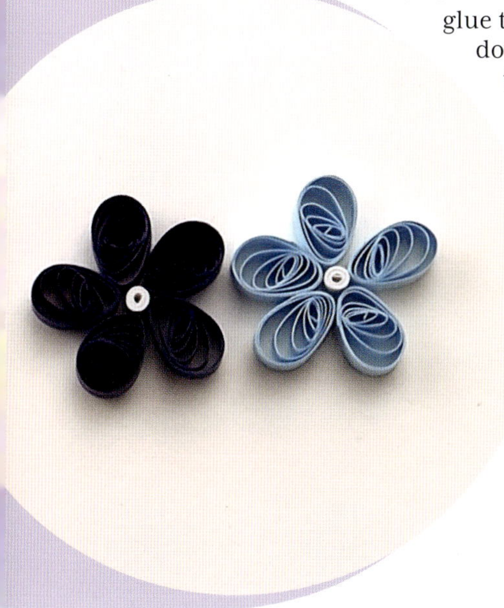

Mini daisies

4 There are two white mini daisies, with five petals in each flower. Cut ten 10cm (4in) strips in white and follow the instructions on page 103 to make the ellipse coils.

5 Each daisy has a tight coil centre. Cut a 5cm (2in) strip in light purple for each flower and follow the instructions on page 100 to make tight coils.

6 Once all elements are made, add a little glue to the base of the shapes and fix down to the template.

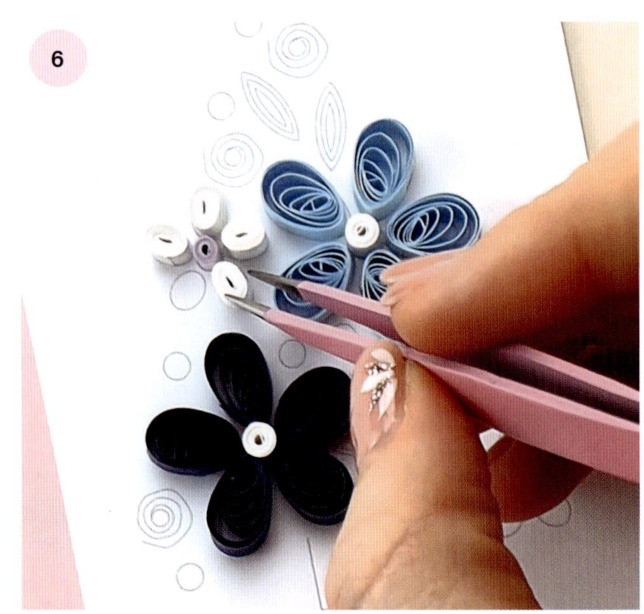

Marquise

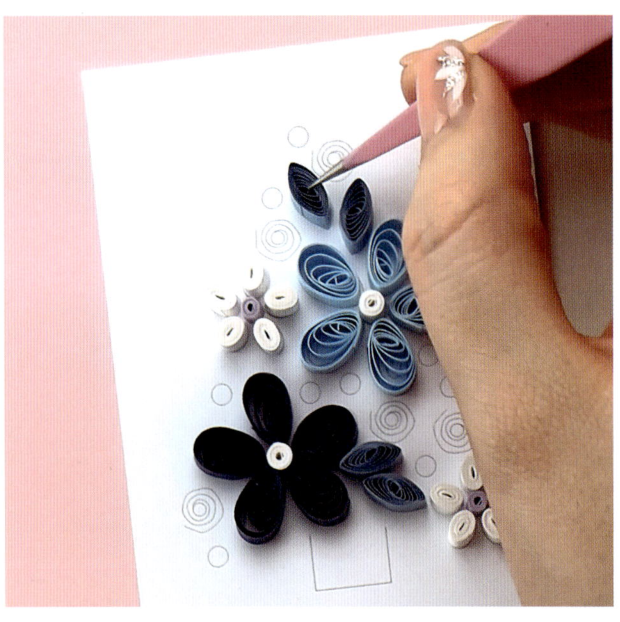

7 There are four marquise shapes, all in grey blue. Cut four strips measuring 13cm (3⅛in) and follow the instructions on page 107 to make the elements, using the 8mm (⁵⁄₁₆in) hole on your quilling board. Once all elements are made, add a little glue to the base of each shape and fix down to the template.

Tight coils

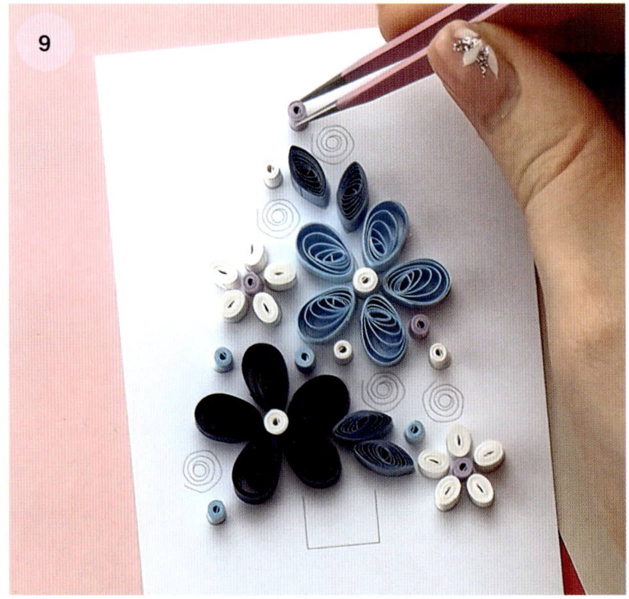

8 There are nine tight coils decorating this piece. Cut four strips in sky blue, two in light purple and three in white, all measuring 5cm (2in).

9 Follow the instructions on page 100 to make tight coils. Once all elements are made, add a little glue to the base of each shape and fix down to the template.

Roses

10 There are five quilled roses decorating this tree, two in indigo and three in light purple. Cut all strips measuring 10cm (4in) and follow the instructions on page 115 to make.

11 Once all five roses are made, add a generous amount of glue to the base of the roses and fix down to the template. Hold each rose in place to allow the glue to bond before moving on to the next rose.

Tree base

12 To finish your tree you just need to add its base, made from three small strips in indigo. Cut two strips measuring 1cm (⅜in) each for the sides and one 1.3cm (½in) strip for the base. Using your glue brush, apply a little glue to the thin edge of each strip and fix down to the template using your tweezers to hold in place to allow the glue to bond.

Mount your card

13 Fold a piece of dark blue A5 (14 x 21cm/5½ x 8¼in) card in half. Add either double-sided tape or glue to the back of your quilled tree design and fix down to the front of the card.

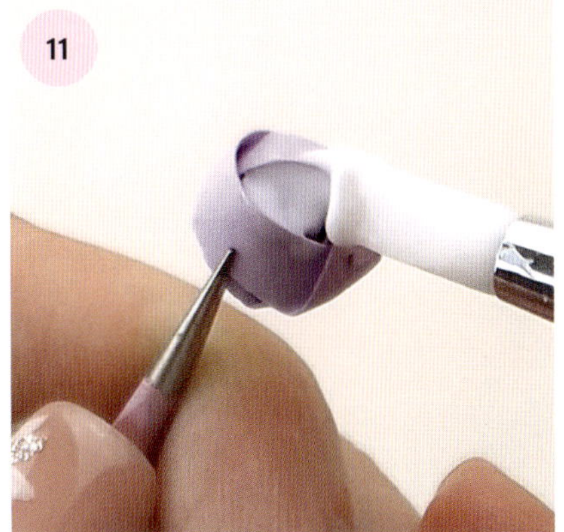

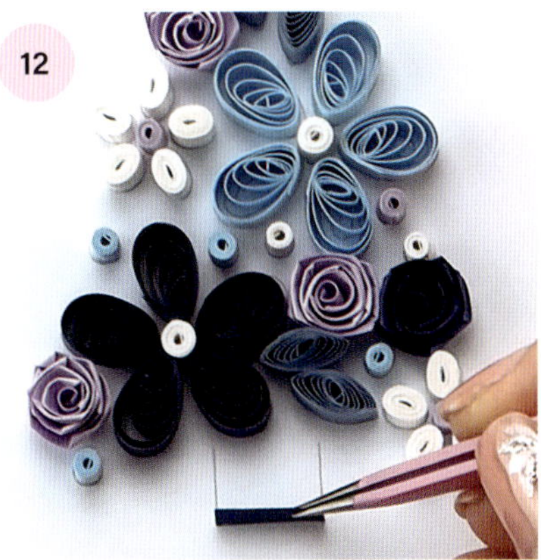

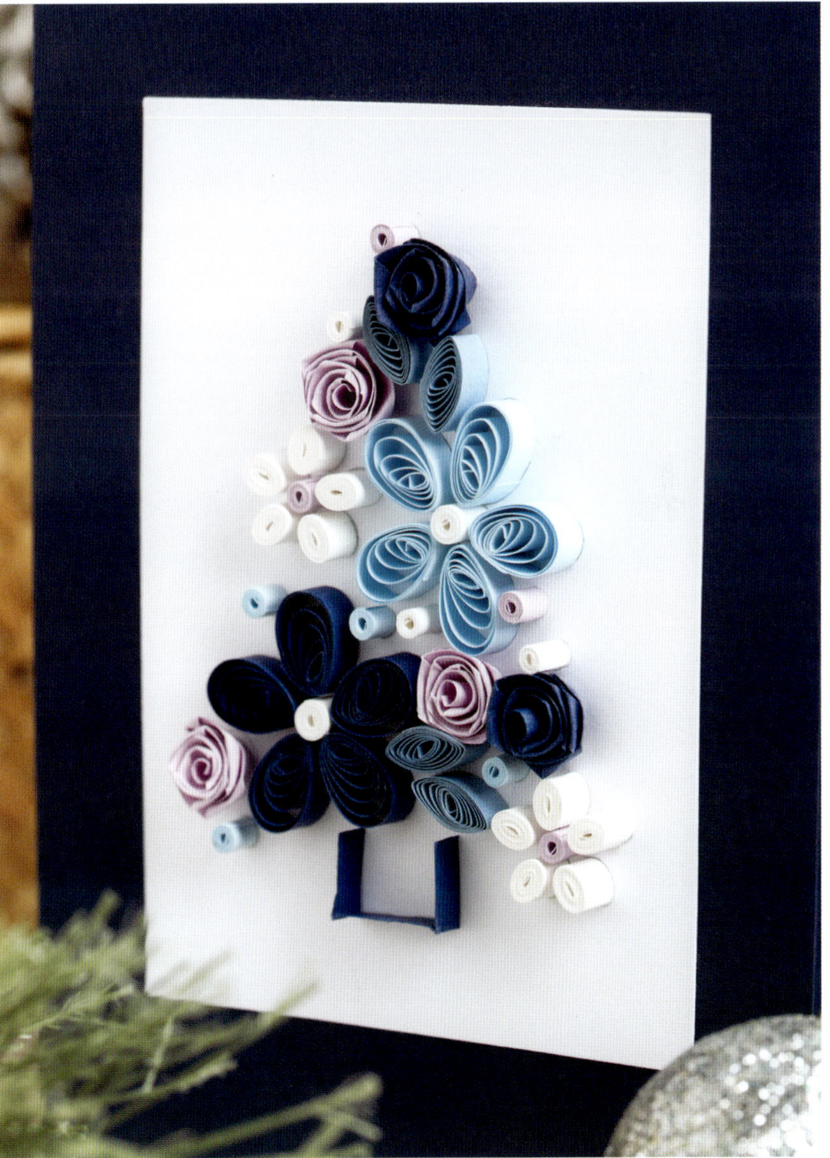

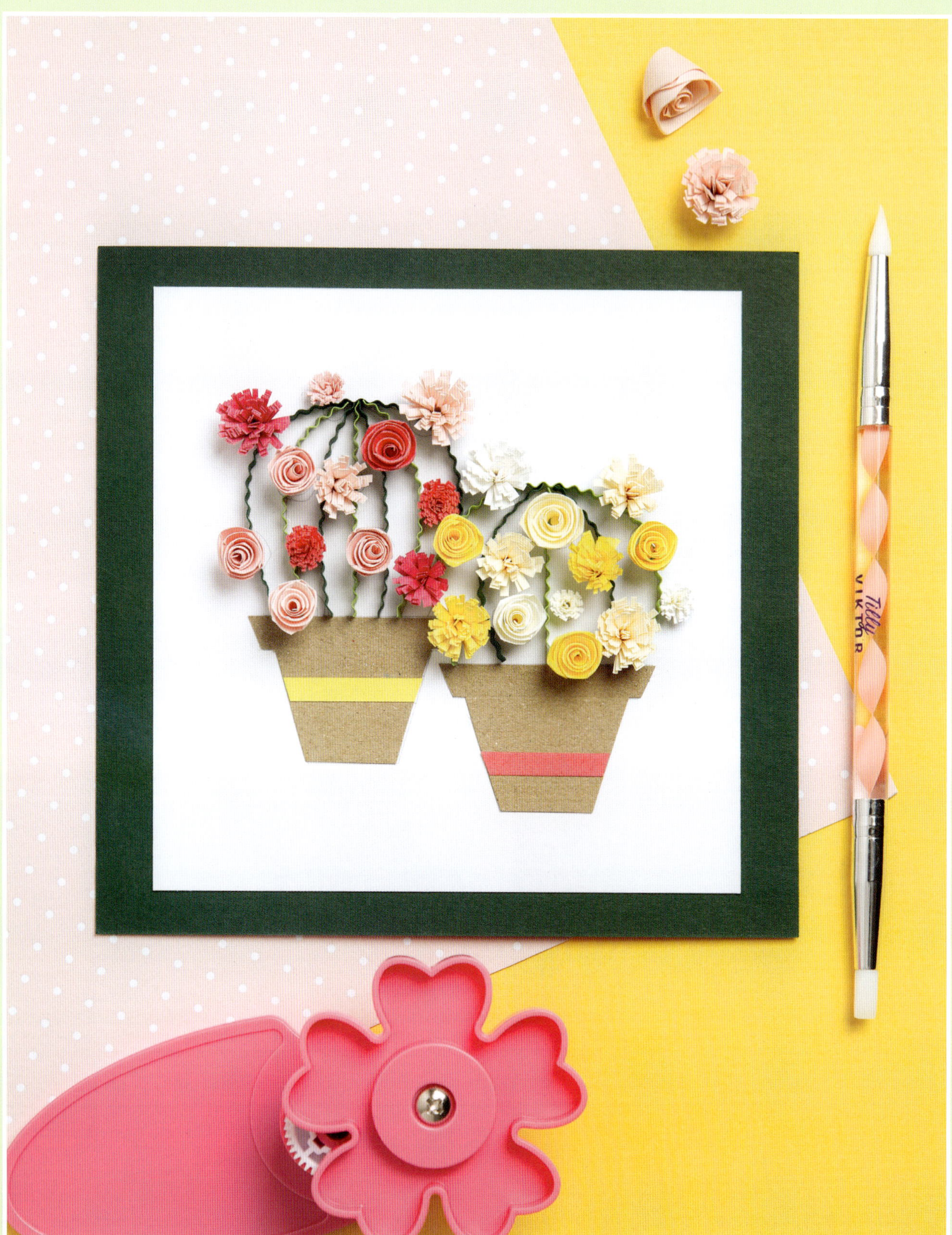
Tilly
VIKTOR

ROSE SHRUBS

This project focuses more on the art of edge quilling than specific quilled elements. This floral artwork is ideal for the green-fingered of you out there! Made in beautiful fresh summer colours, it would be perfect mounted on the front of a card or even framed as a standalone art piece.

TIPS

You can make this piece without the use of a paper crimper; the crimped paper simply adds a little interest to the finished piece.

Some of the shrub outlines cross through the rose and fringed coil template spaces. Don't worry too much about that, just fix them as closely as possible to the outlines.

Plant pots

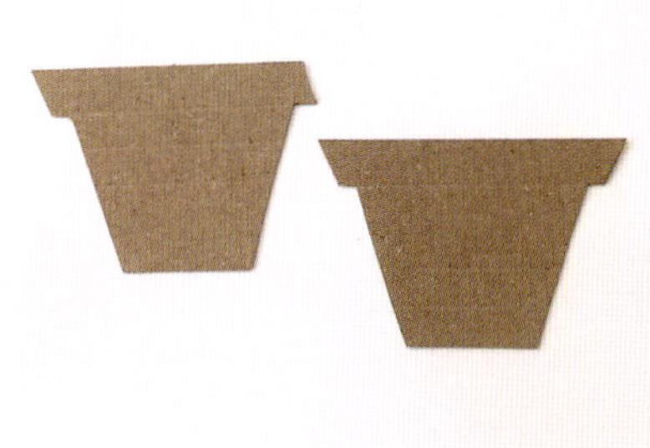

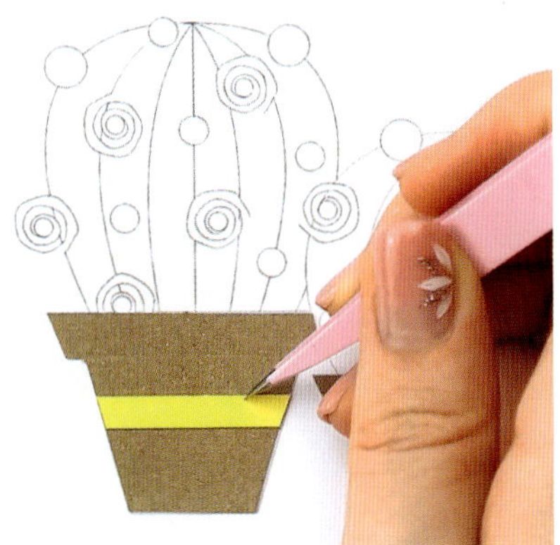

1 Start this project by tracing and cutting out the plant pots from a sheet of brown card.

2 Add a little glue to the base of each pot and fix them down to the template. Take a strip of quilling paper in both lemon and pink and trim down to sit on top of each pot, then glue them down.

Rose shrubs

3 Take a strip of forest green and viridity quilling papers and run them through a quilling crimper (this step is optional).

4 Take the crimped forest green strip, and starting with the taller of the two shrubs, stick down the outer edge first. Apply a little glue to the first couple of centimetres (an inch) of the strip edge using the tweezers to guide your strip in place. Hold in place with your tweezers for a moment to allow the glue to bond. Once the first section has stuck, apply a little glue to your glue brush and paint it directly onto the template as shown. Use tweezers to guide your strip into place, sticking down as you go. When you reach the end of the printed template use sharp scissors to trim the excess part of the strip.

5 Moving on to the next section, take a crimped strip in viridity and use the same technique as above to continue to build the shrub outline. Alternate the green shades with each new section.

6 Now move on to the smaller shrub. Follow the same method as above, but this time start the outline with a strip in viridity.

Roses

7 Each open rose has a tight coil base to prop it up. Cut 10 strips measuring 5cm (2in), five in baby pink and five in cream. Follow the instructions on page 100 to make the tight coils. Apply a little glue to the base of these and fix down to the template in the centre of the roses, as shown.

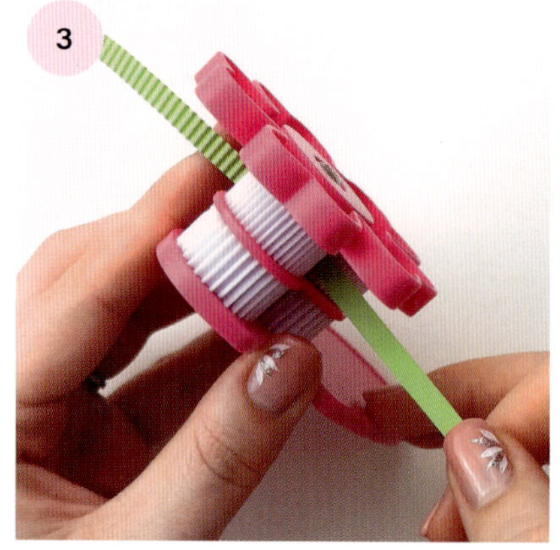

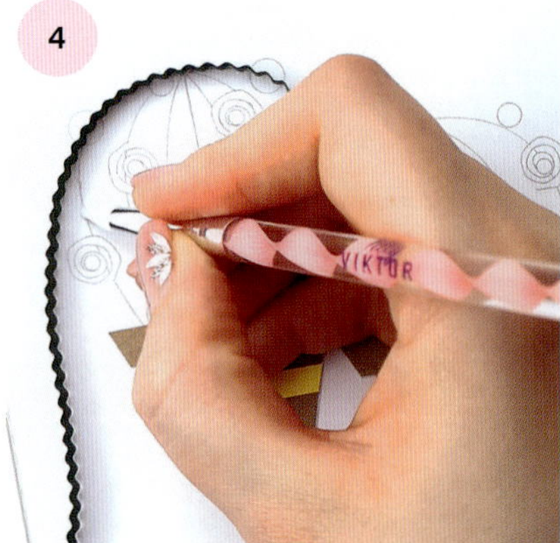

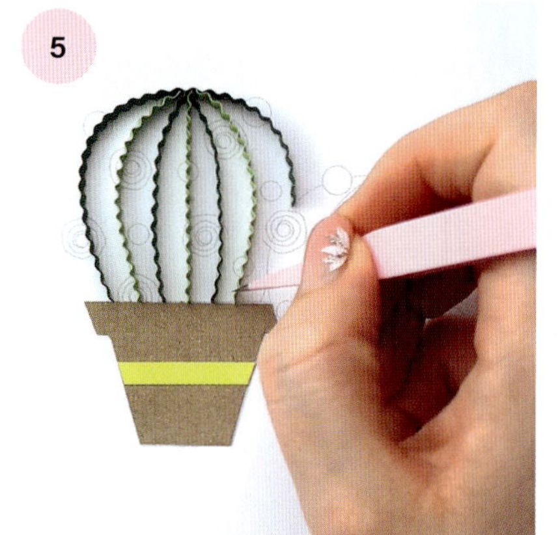

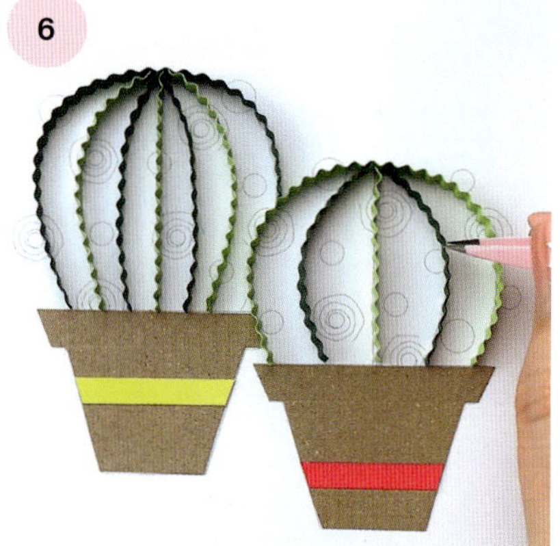

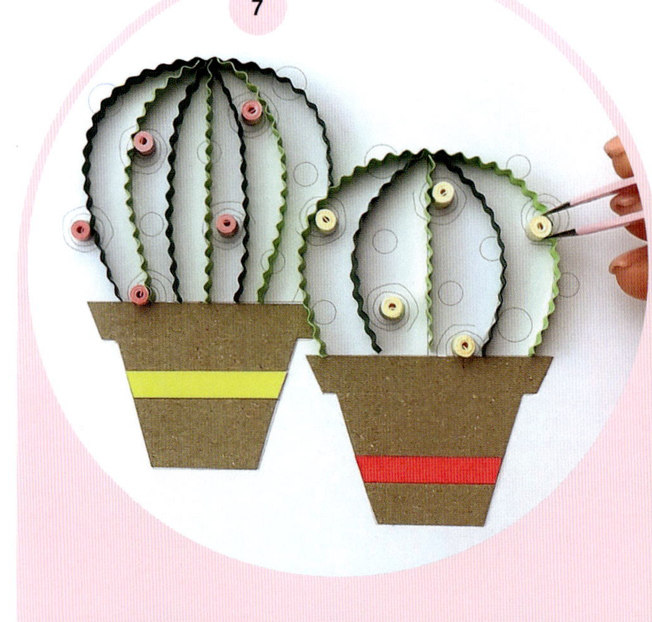

Rosebuds

8 There are 10 roses in total. Cut 11cm (4⁵⁄₁₆in) strips of the following colours: three in lemon, two in cream, one in magenta, three in pink and one in baby pink. Follow the instructions on page 115 to make the roses. Once all roses are made, apply a generous amount of glue to the tight coil bases, fixing the pink roses to the pink coils, and the yellow and cream roses to the cream coils.

9 The fringed tight coils give the perfect impression of a rose bud! There are 15 in total, four large and 11 small in a mix of cream, bleach, lemon, magenta and baby pink shades. Take a strip in each colour and fringe as shown (see page 105). For each large fringed tight coil, cut strips of 15cm (6in) and for each small fringed coil, cut strips of 10cm (4in).

10 Follow the instructions on page 105 for making fringed tight coils, once they are all made, apply a little glue to the base of each shape and fix down to your template. Once the glue has dried, fluff out your fringed elements by spreading the cut papers.

Mount and frame

11 To finish this piece trim around the template and use double-sided tape or glue to mount the artwork onto a base card of your choice and frame. I have chosen a deep green to give extra contrast to the piece – it really makes the bright flowers pop!

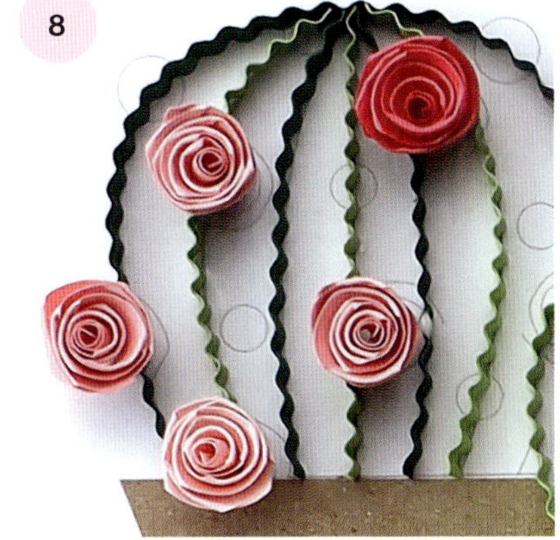

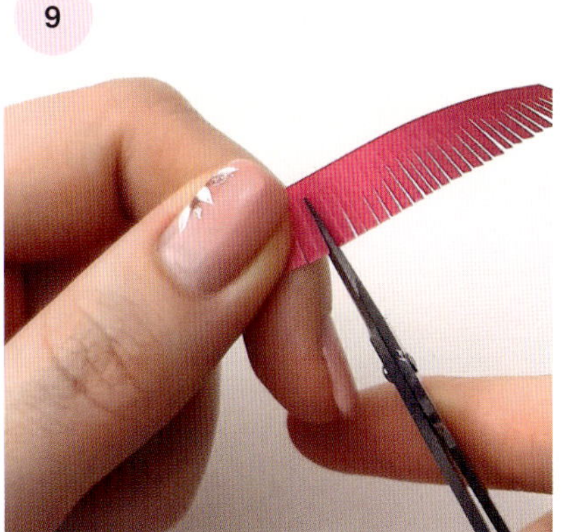

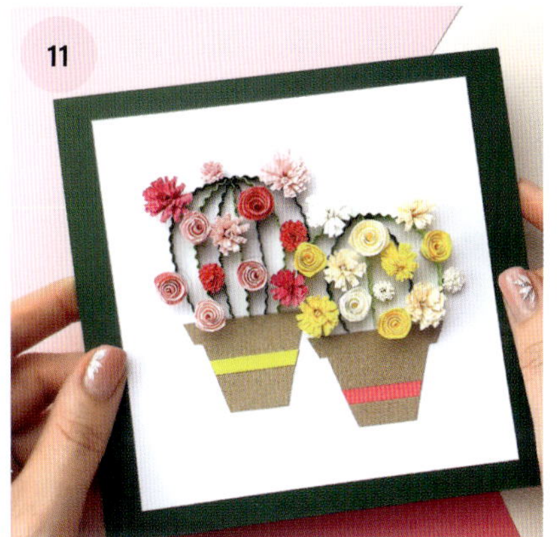

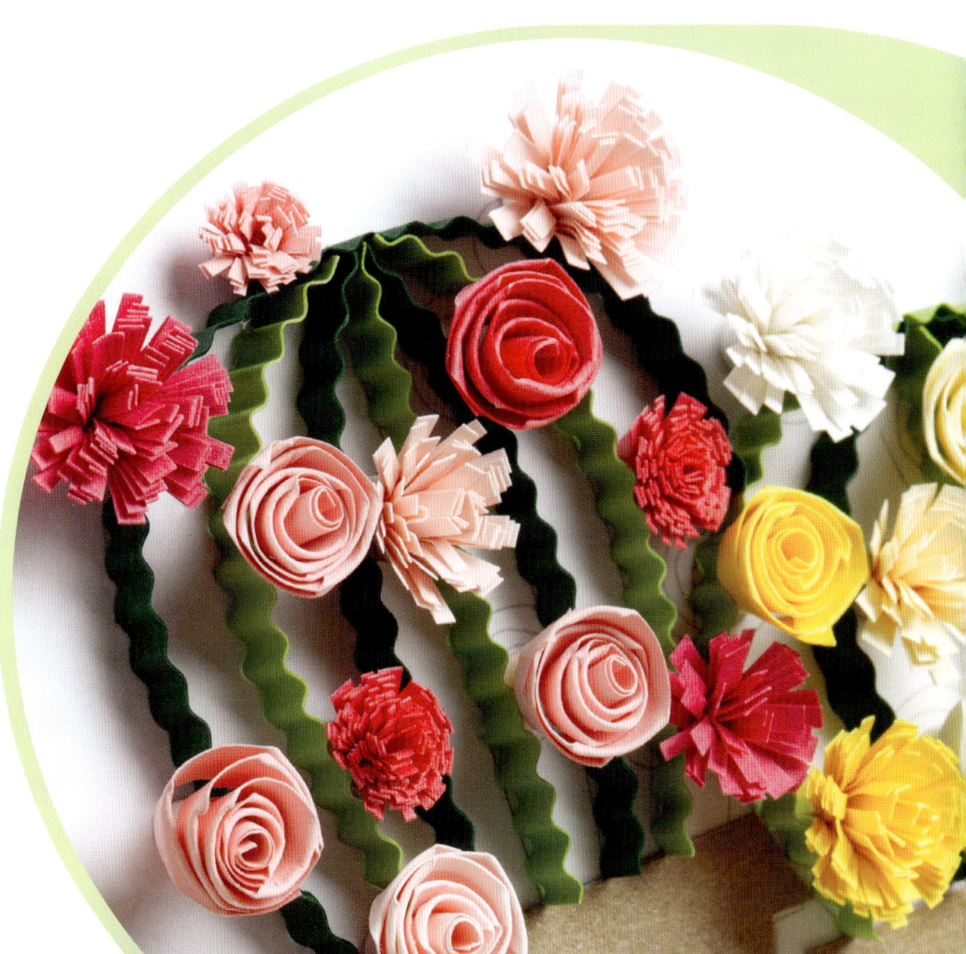

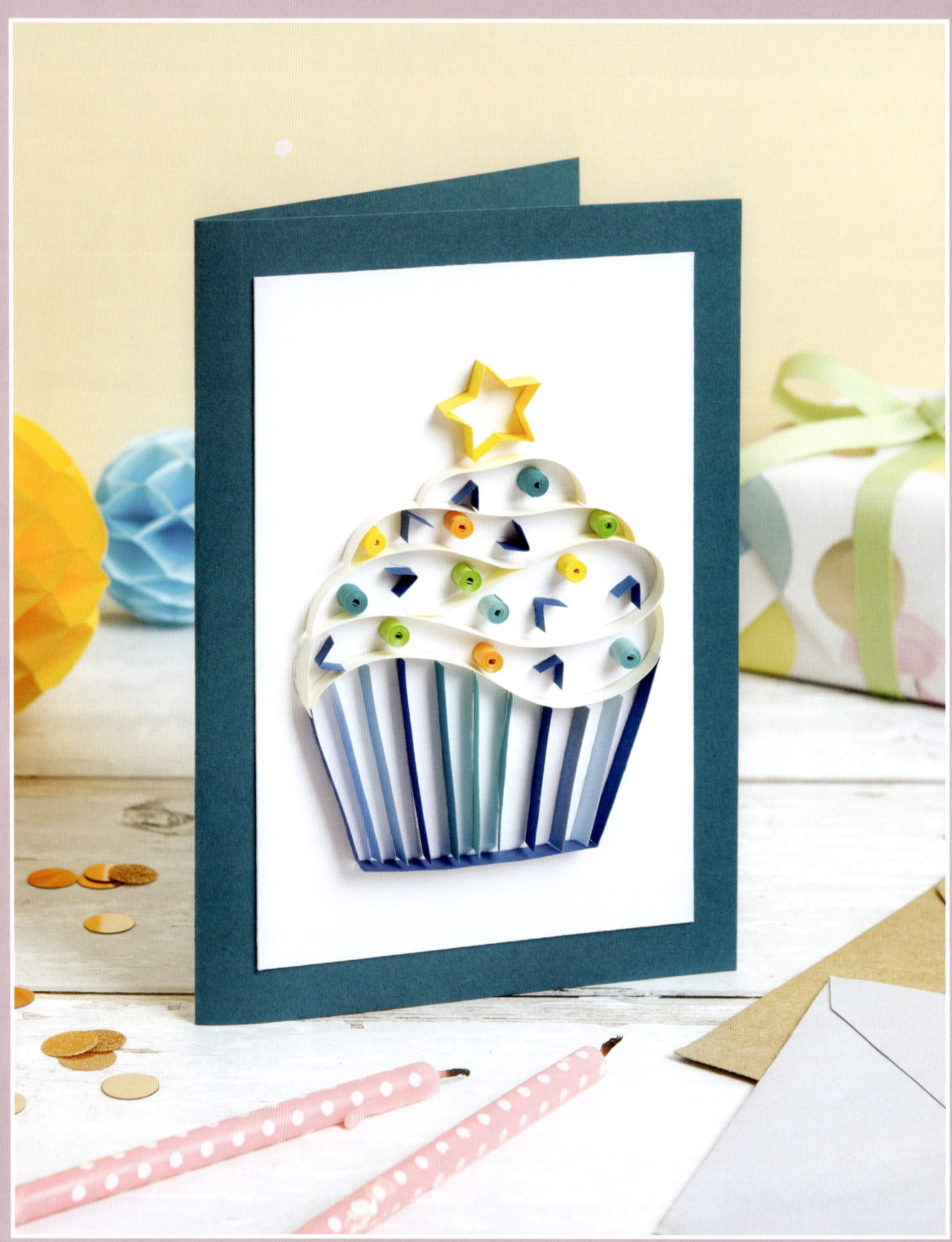

CUPCAKE

This project focuses more on the art of edge quilling than on specific quilled elements. This super cute cupcake with vanilla icing and lashings of rainbow sprinkles is the perfect way to celebrate any occasion!

Start this project by quilling the cupcake icing – take your time with this section, it can be fiddly, but it will be worth it for the end result! Work through the steps in order sticking the elements down as you go.

Icing

1 Take a full 54cm (21¼in) strip of cream quilling paper and apply glue to the first couple of centimetres (an inch), as shown.

2 Place the strip onto the template guiding it into place with your tweezers. Hold in place for a couple of moments to allow the glue to bond.

3 Using your glue brush paint a little glue directly onto the template line as shown then use your tweezers to guide more of the strip into place.

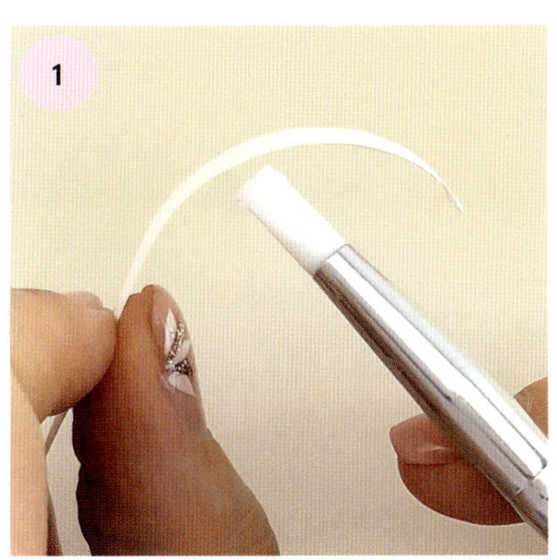

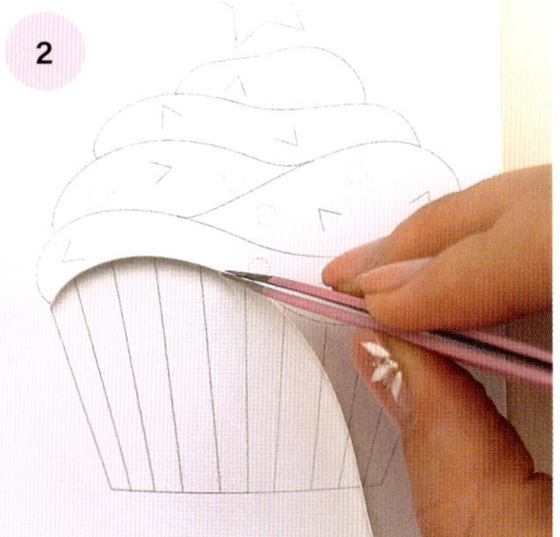

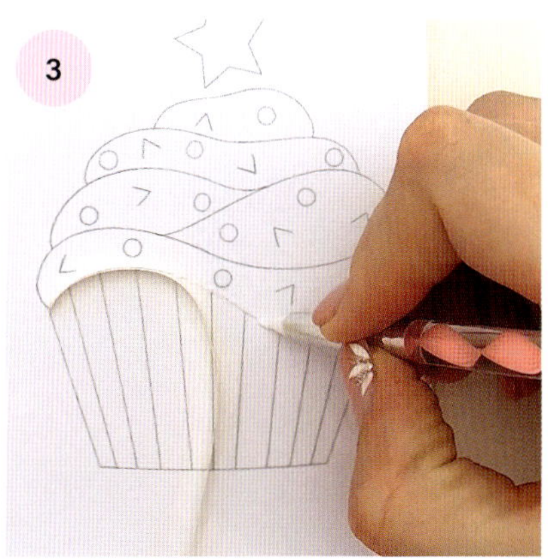

4 Once you reach the end of the printed line, trim the quilling strip with sharp scissors, as shown.

5 Continue this process with the rest of the printed lines until the icing section is complete.

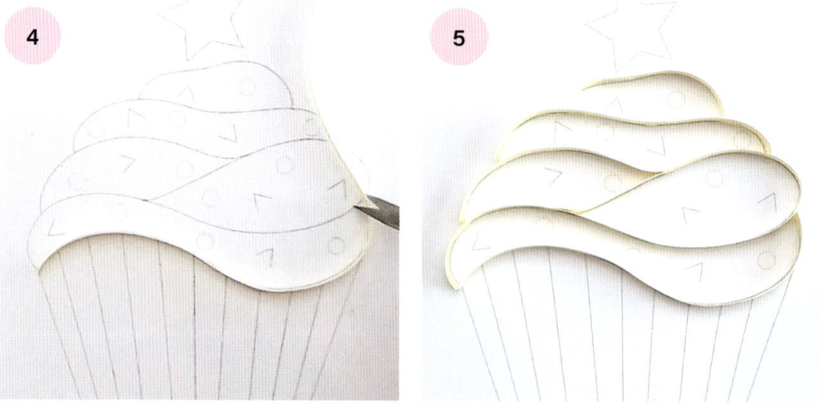

Case

6 Make the outline of the case by cutting three strips in deep blue: the left-hand side measures 3.2cm (1¼in), the bottom piece measures 4.3cm (1¹¹⁄₁₆in) and the right-hand side measures 3.5cm (1⅜in). Apply glue to the base of these strips and fix down to the template, as shown.

7 Take a selection of blue shades to complete the stripes on the cupcake case: I've used sky blue, royal blue and turquoise. You can alternate the colours in any way you like. To measure the interior sections, hold the strip up to the template as shown, using this as a rough guide, then cut the strip longer than needed. Hold the strip up to the template as shown, using this as a guide, then cut the strip to size.

8 Apply glue to the edge of the strips and fix them to the template.

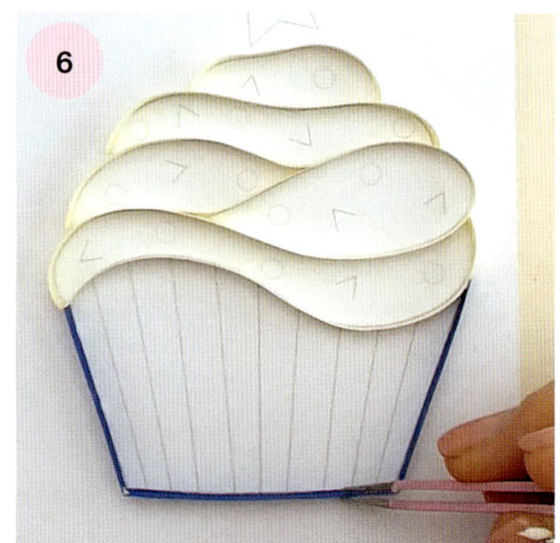
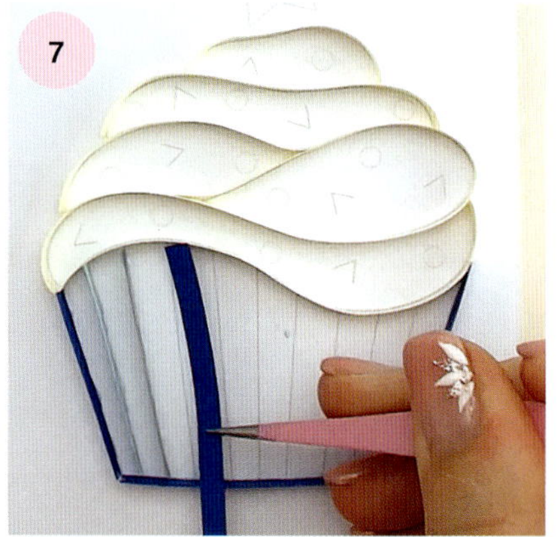
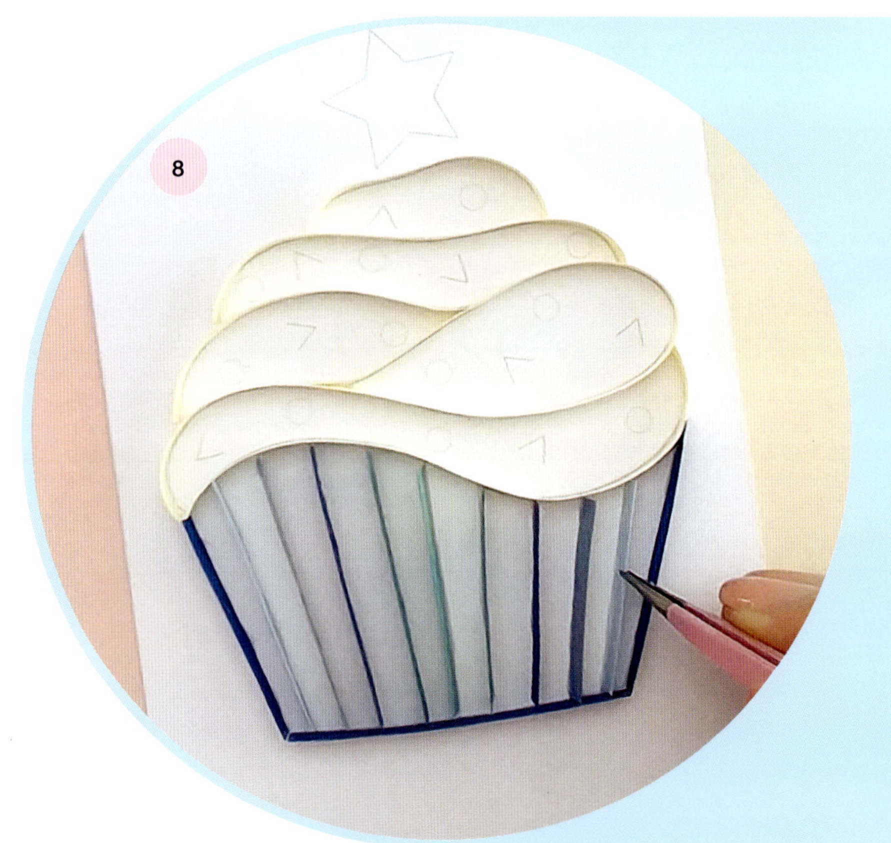

Sprinkles

9 The cupcake is decorated with rainbow sprinkles: 11 tight coils and eight triangles. For the tight coils, cut 8cm (3⅛in) strips: two of each in lemon, turquoise, emerald and orange, and three in viridity. For the triangle sprinkles, cut eight 1cm (⅜in) strips in royal blue, and fold in half to make the triangle shape. Apply glue to the base of each element and fix down to the template using tweezers.

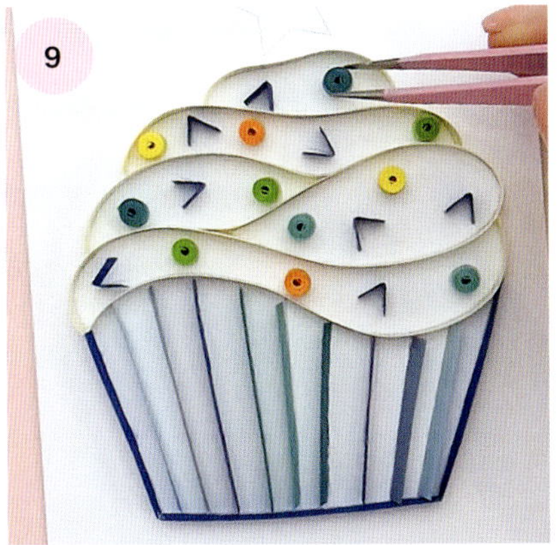

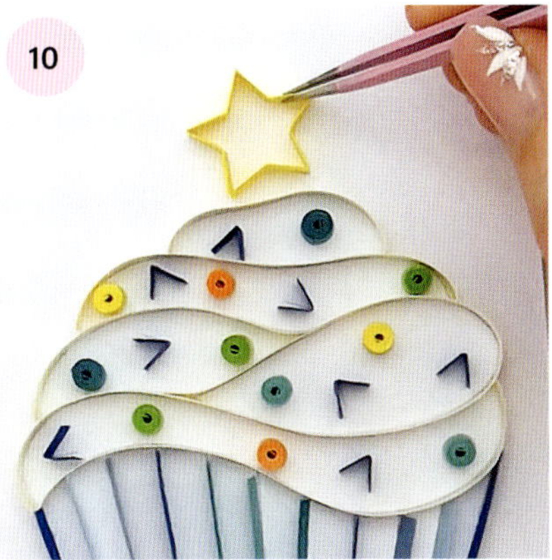

Finishing touches

10 No cupcake would be complete without the addition of a topper! Take a full strip in lemon and follow the instructions on page 111 to make a star. Once made, apply glue to the back of the star and fix to the template at the top of the icing.

11 To finish the cupcake, mount the artwork to a coloured base of your choice.

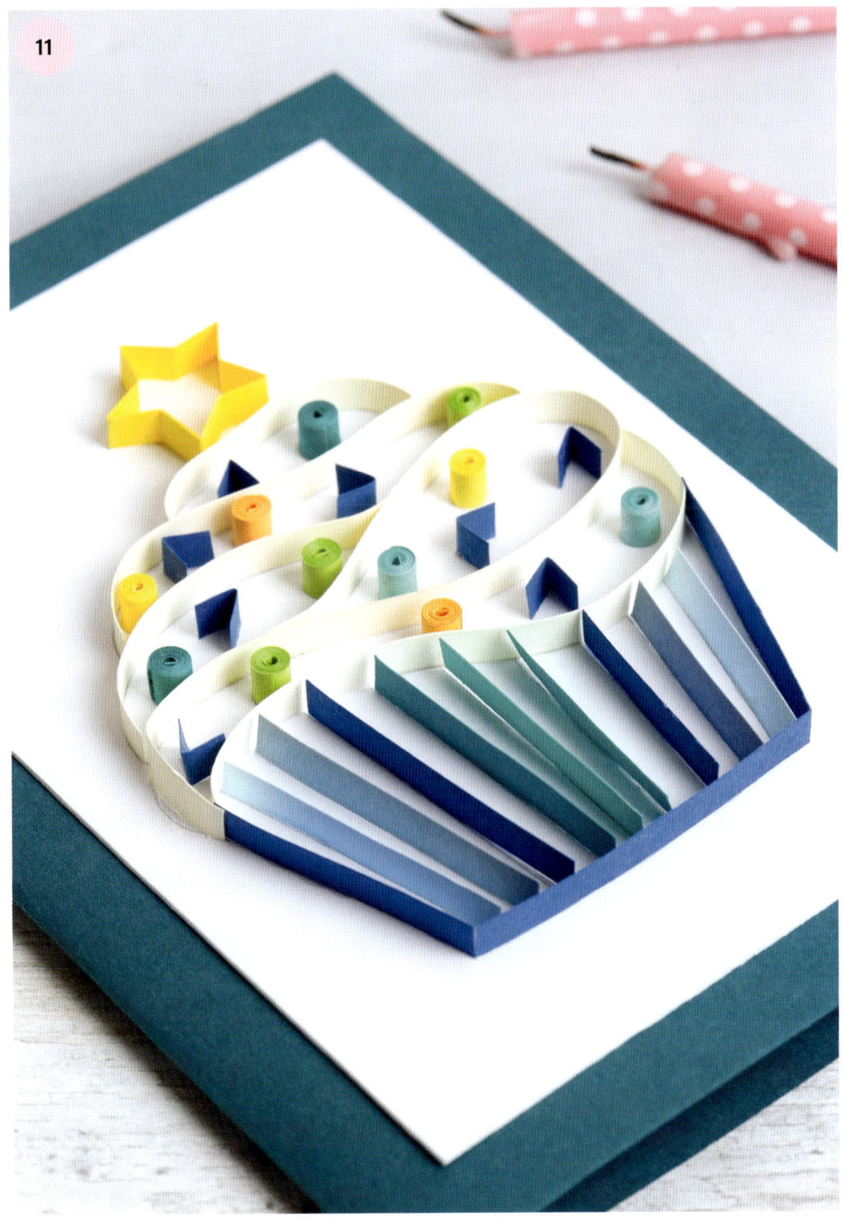

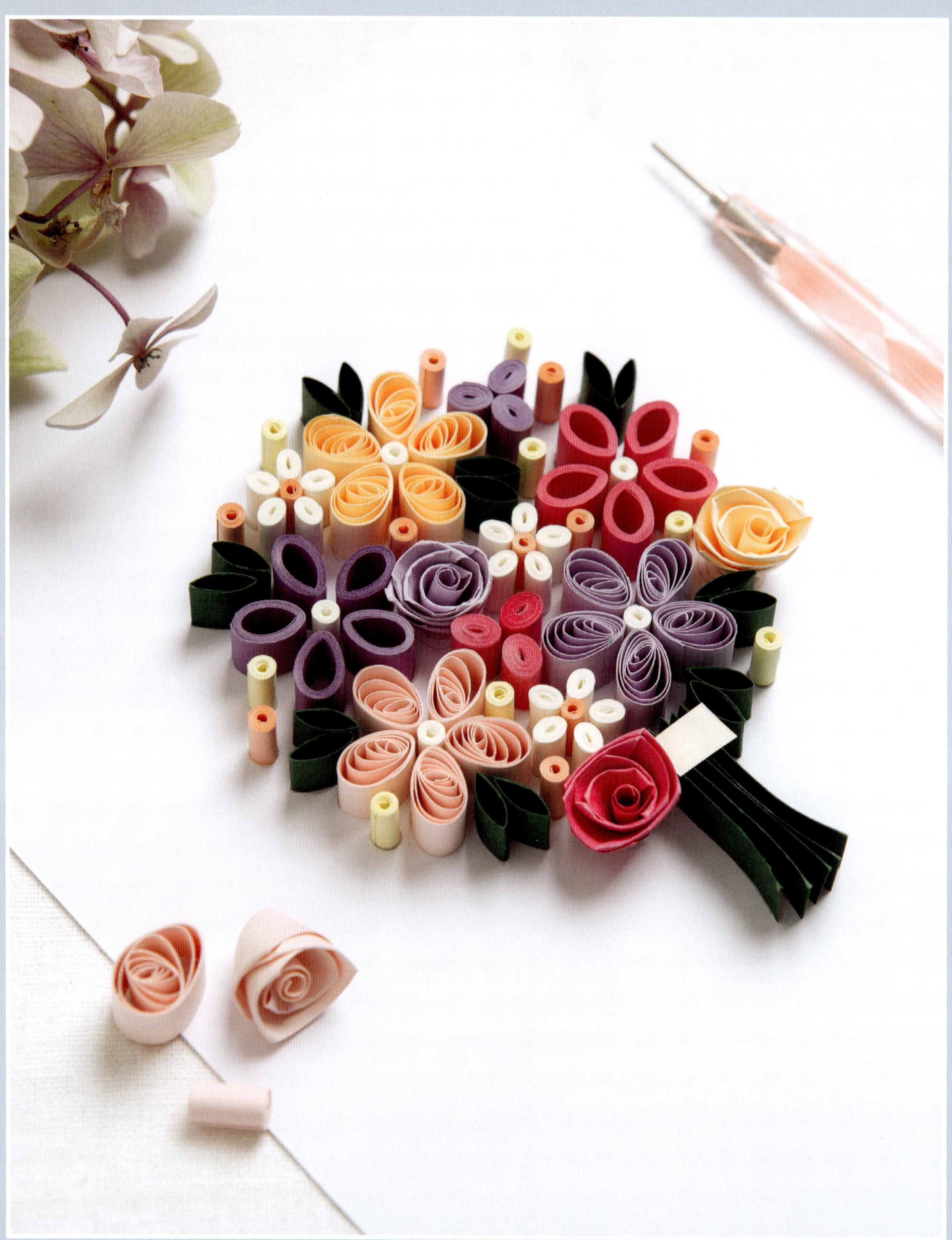

SUMMER BOUQUET

This stunning bouquet is made using six different quilled shapes in nine bright summery shades. Work through the elements one by one, sticking them down as you go. Attach the tight coils, roses and floral stems last so you can fit them around the other elements.

TIP

When making the flowers, always make and stick down the tight coil at the centre before adding any of the petals. This will ensure you don't run out of space for the central coil.

Flower design 1

1 There are three of this flower type, each in a different colour. They are made by assembling five rounded teardrop shapes around a tight coil. Cut five strips, each measuring 13cm (5⅛in), in apricot, baby pink and light purple for the petals, and cut three 7cm (2¾in) strips in cream for the tight coil flower centres.

2 To make the rounded teardrop shapes, follow the instructions on page 98 using the 10mm (⅜in) hole on the quilling board. Once all the elements are made, dab a little glue onto the template and fix down starting with the centre tight coils.

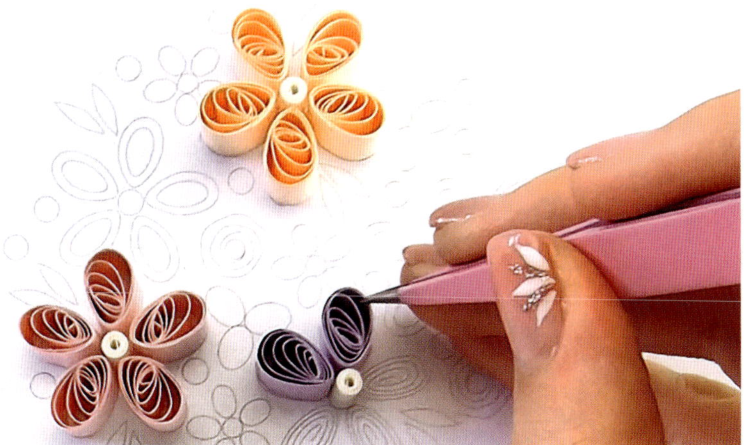

You will need

Summer Bouquet template, page 118
Quilling papers, I used 10mm (⅜in)
Quilling tool 10mm (⅜in)
Scissors
Tacky PVA glue
Glue brush
Quilling board
Tweezers

Quilling paper colours

Baby pink (2)
Purple (6)
Light purple (7)
Peach (15)
Cream (37)
Light yellow (38)
Magenta (51)
Apricot (52)
Forest green (54)

Quilled elements

Rounded teardrop
Tight coil
Ring teardrop
Ellipse coil
Hollow marquise
Rose
Arch

Flower design 2

3 There are two of these flowers in this bouquet, one in purple and one in magenta. These flowers are made by assembling five ring teardrop shapes around a tight coil. Cut five strips measuring 20cm (7⅞in) in each colour and cut three 7cm (2¾in) strips in cream and make the tight coil flower centres. Using a glue brush, dab a little glue on the base of each tigh coil and fix down to the template.

4 To make the ring teardrop shapes follow the instructions on page 113, using the 9mm (⅜in) hole on your quilling board. As these elements are hollow, it is best to be precise when adding glue. Using a glue brush, dab a little glue on the base of the ring teardrop and fix down to the template.

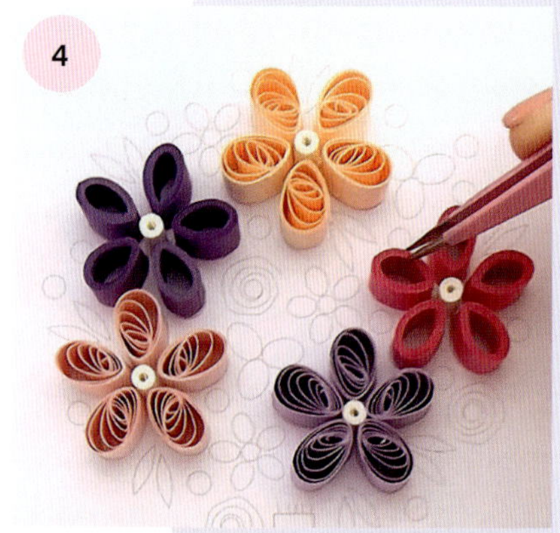

Flower design 3

5 There are three of this flower type in the bouquet, all in the same cream colour with an apricot centre. These flowers are made by assembling five ellipse coils around a tight coil shape. Cut 15 strips measuring 9cm (3⁹⁄₁₆in), five for each flower, and cut three 4cm (1⁹⁄₁₆in) strips in peach for the tight coil flower centres. To make the ellipse coils, follow the instructions on page 103. Once all the elements are made dab a little glue onto the template and fix down, starting with the centre tight coils.

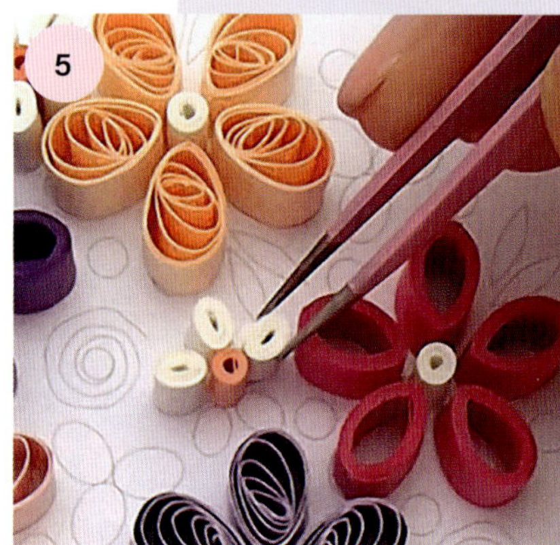

Flower design 4

6 There are two of these flowers in this bouquet, one in purple and one in magenta. They are made by gluing three ellipse coils together. Cut six strips measuring 19cm (7½in), three in each colour and follow the instructions on page 103. Once all the elements are made dab a little glue onto the template and fix down.

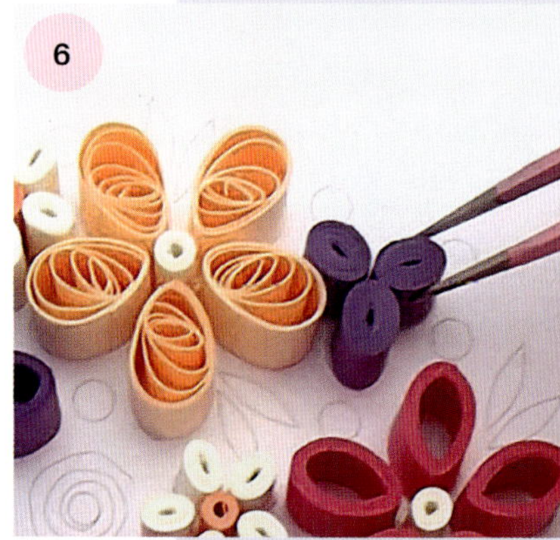

Leaves

7 To make these hollow marquise shapes cut 16 strips of 2.5cm (1in) in green and follow the instructions on page 106. As these elements are hollow it is best to be as precise as you can with the glue. Using a glue brush, dab a little glue on the base of the hollow marquise and fix down to the template.

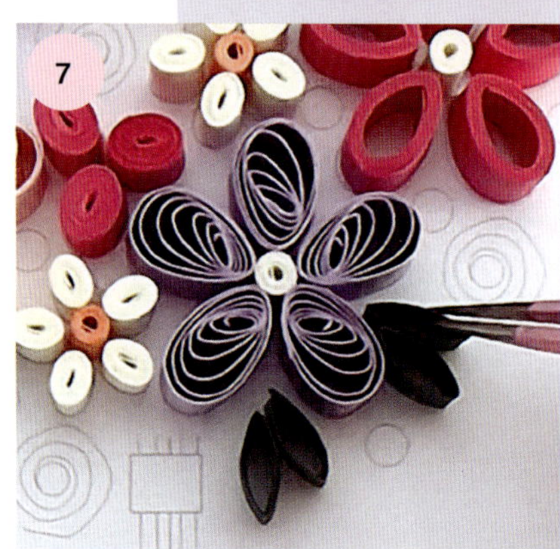

Tight coils

8 There are 16 tight coils in this bouquet, half in light yellow and half in peach. Cut eight strips in each colour all measuring 7cm (2¾in) and follow the instructions on page 100 to make the tight coils. Using a glue brush, dab a little glue on the base of each coil and fix down to the template.

Roses

9 There are three roses in this bouquet, one in magenta, one in light purple and one in apricot. They are made by winding and folding a single strip around a quilling tool. Cut one 13cm (5⅛in) strip in each shade and follow the instructions on page 115 to make. Add a generous amount of glue to the base of the roses and hold them in place on the template until they stick securely.

Flower stems

10 Cut one 3.2cm (1¼in) strip in forest green for the centre stem, two 3.1cm (1¼in) strips for the inside stems and two 3cm (1³⁄₁₆in) strips for the outside stems. Apply a little glue to each strip edge and stick them one at a time to the template. Hold in place to allow the glue to bond.

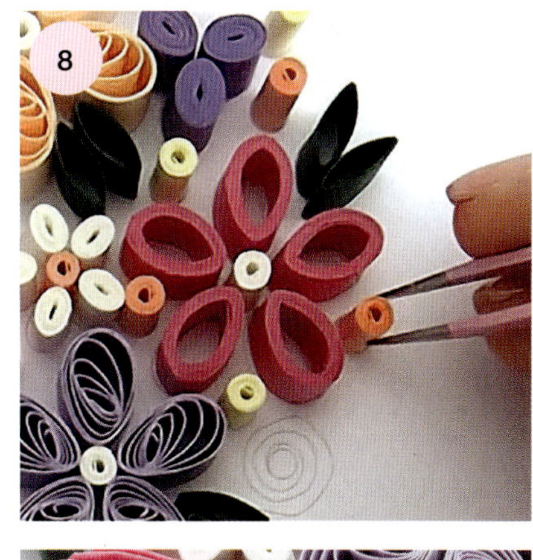

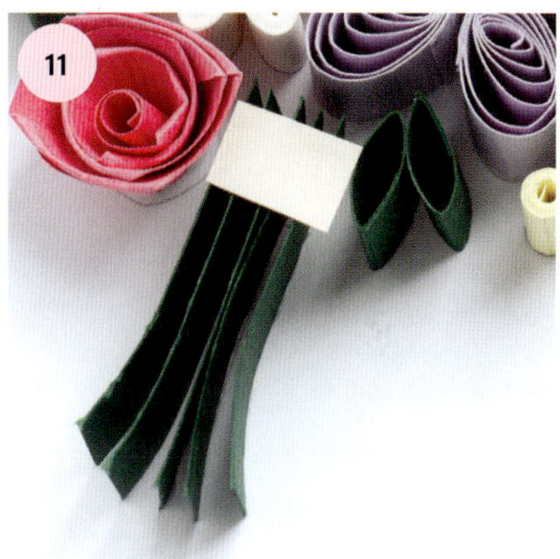

11 To finish the stems, cut and glue a 5mm (³⁄₁₆in) peach strip on top, as shown.

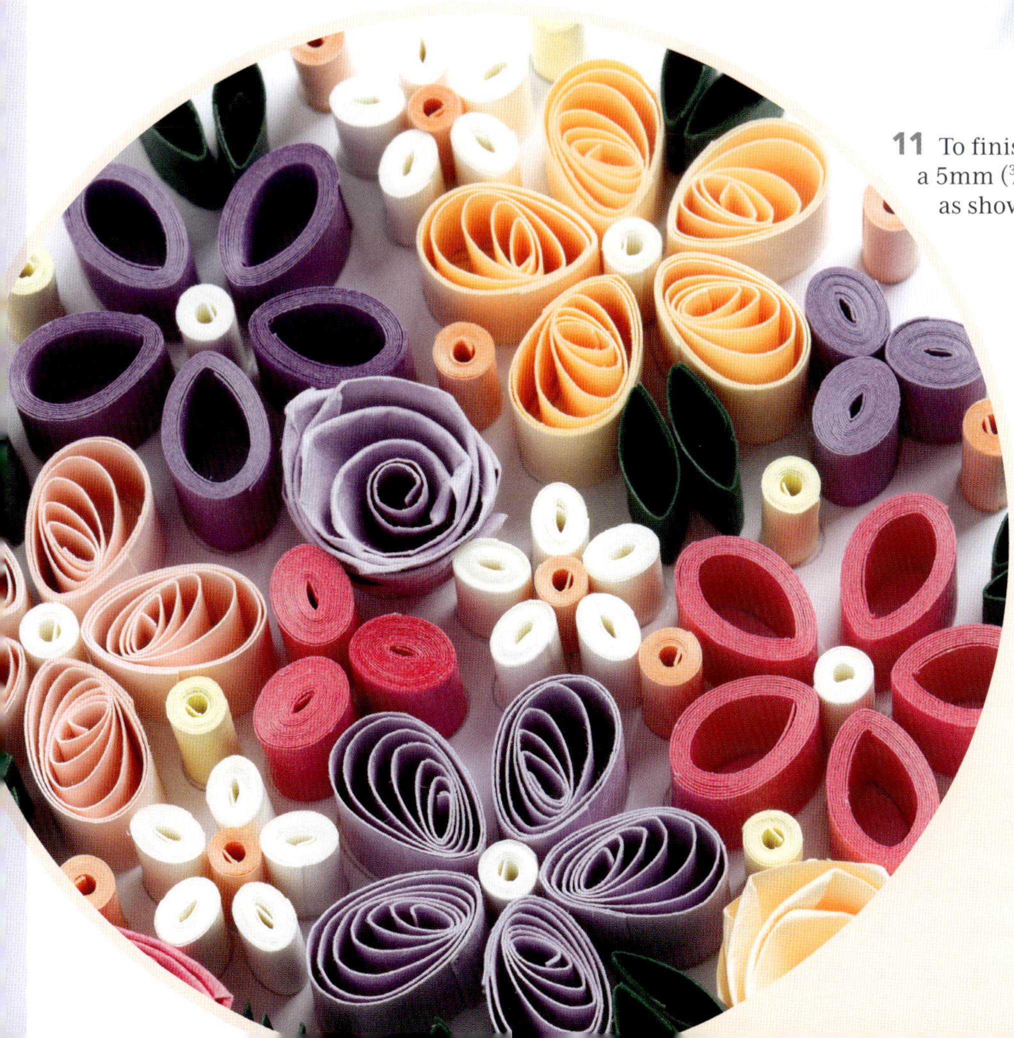

Quilling know-how: making the shapes

Use the instructions on the following pages to make the quilled elements required for each project.

Rounded teardrop

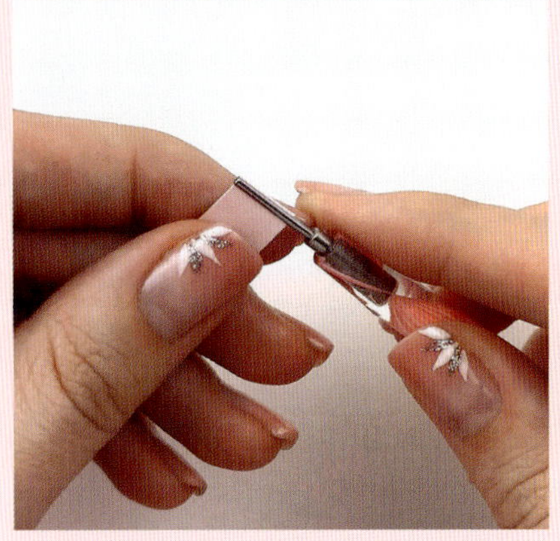 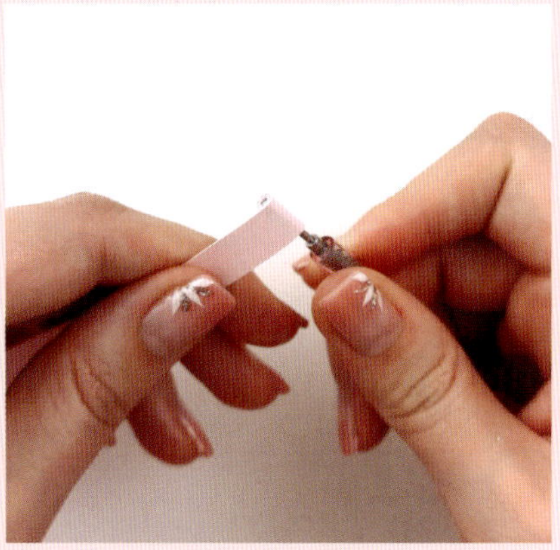 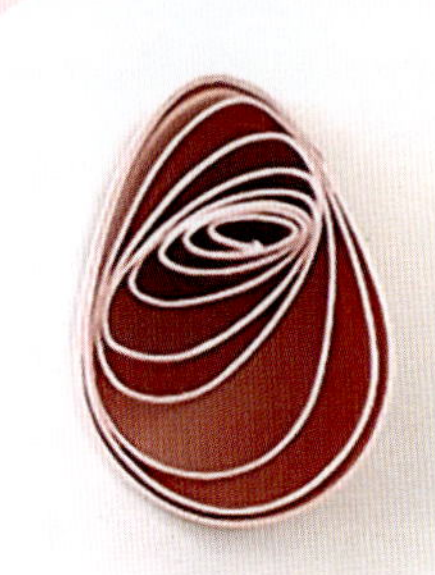

1 Hold the quilling tool in your dominant hand, the paper in the other hand and insert the tip of the paper strip into the tool.

2 Turn the tool to roll the paper keeping the paper taut as you roll.

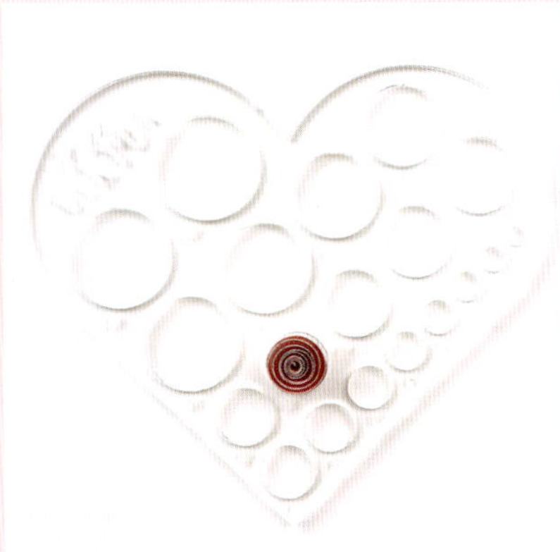 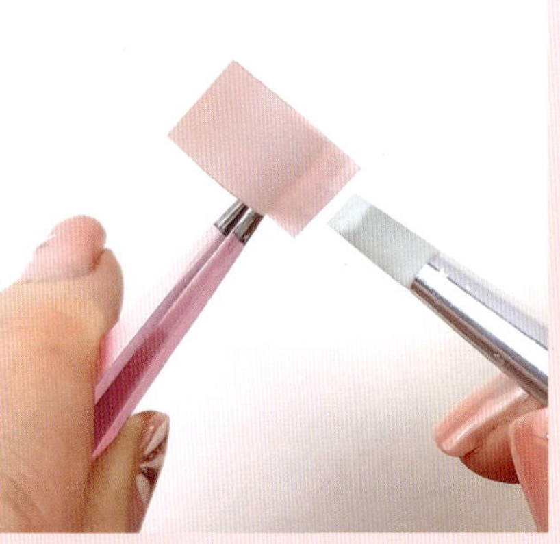 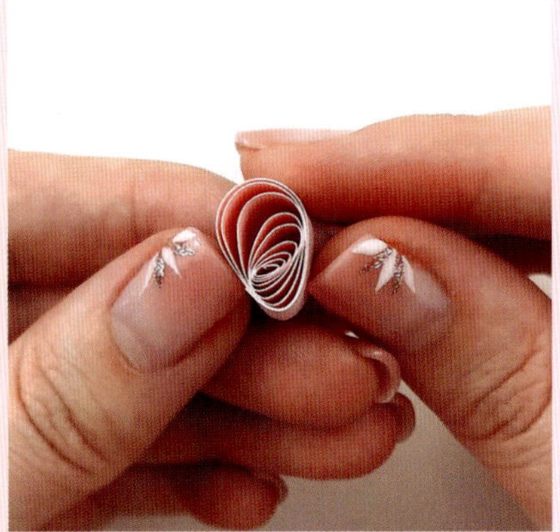

3 Remove the shape from your quilling tool and place into the required size hole on the quilling board. Allow the shape to unravel to fill the hole.

4 Insert one tip of the tweezers in the centre of the shape and the other tip on the outside, pinch both tips together to pick up the shape. Apply a little glue to the tail end and close the shape.

5 Pinch into a point with your index finger and thumb to make a rounded teardrop.

Pointed teardrop

Follow steps 1–4 for the rounded teardrop before continuing with steps 5 and 6 below.

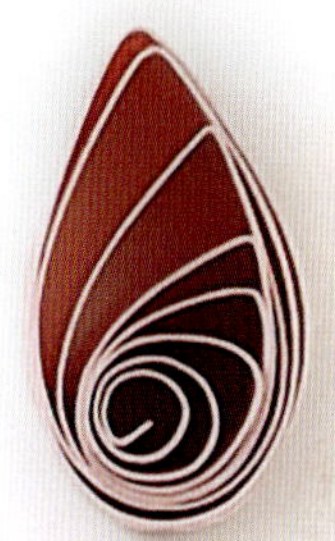

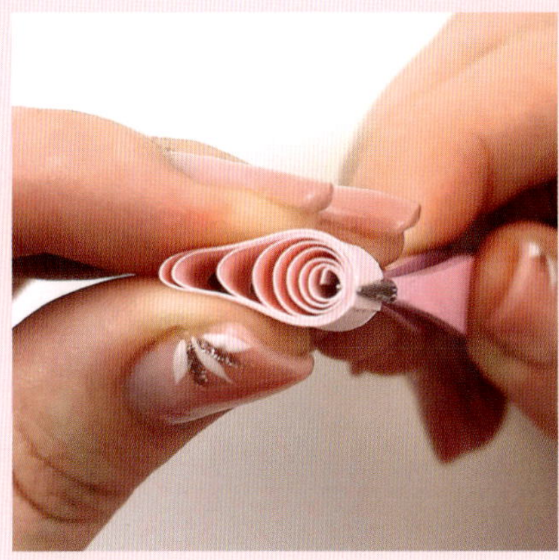

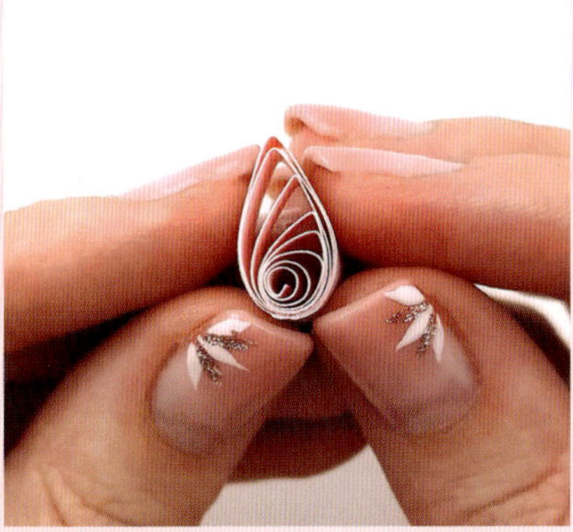

5 Pinch the end opposite to the one held by the tweezers to make a point.

6 Take the shape off the tweezers and let it relax in your fingers, making sure the point stays crisp.

Tight coil

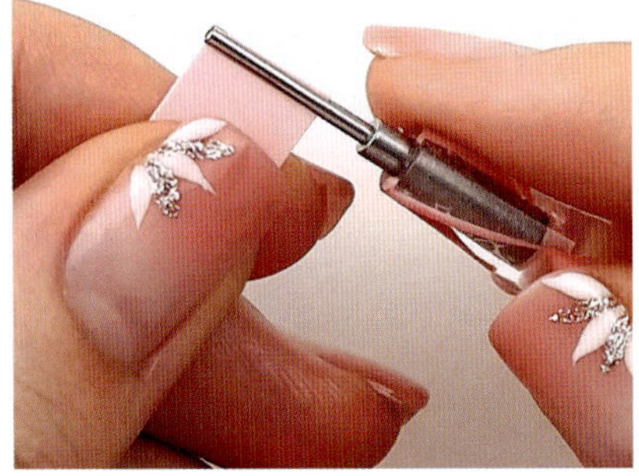

1 Hold the tool in your dominant hand, the paper in the other hand, and insert the tip of the strip into the quilling tool.

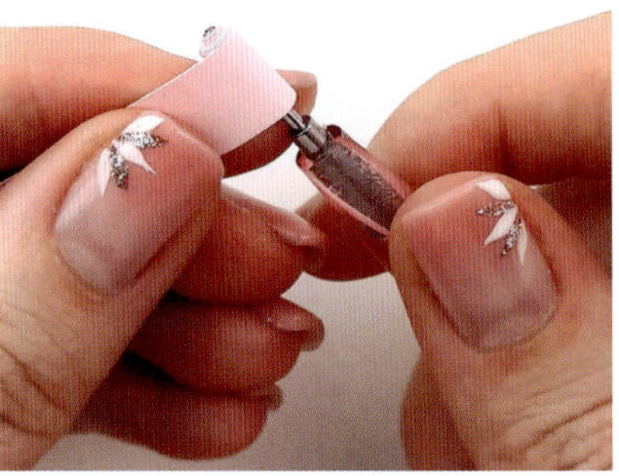

2 Turn the tool to roll the paper, keeping the paper taut as you roll.

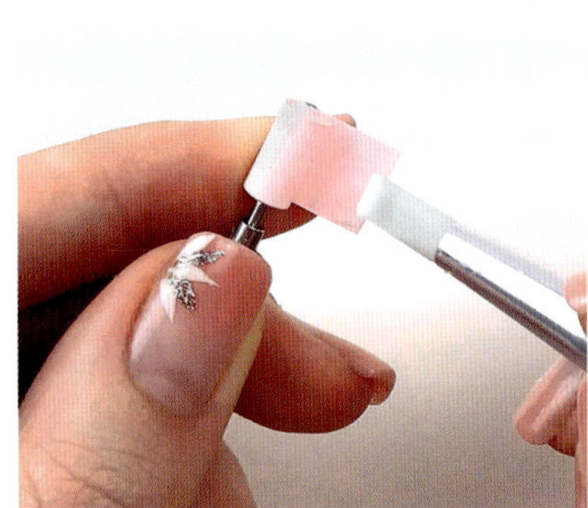

3 Apply a little glue to the tail end and roll to complete.

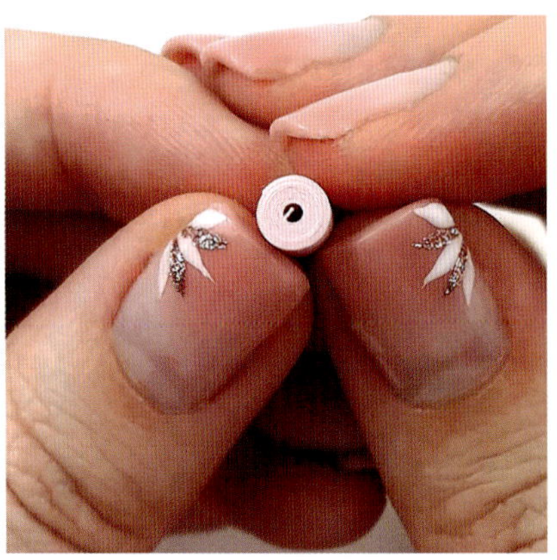

4 Hold to allow the glue to bond then remove from the tool.

Multi-coloured tight coil

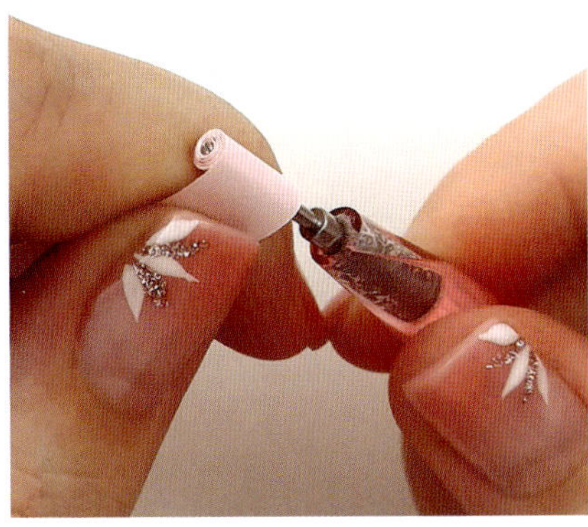

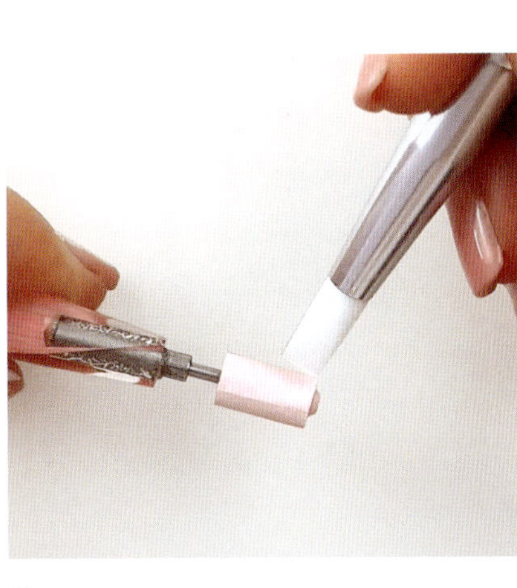

1 Hold the tool in your dominant hand, the paper in the other hand and insert the tip of the strip into the quilling tool. Turn the tool to roll the paper, keeping the paper taut as you roll.

2 Apply a little glue to the tail end and roll to complete. Add a little glue to the tip of the next coloured strip, hold to the coil for a few moments to allow the glue to bond.

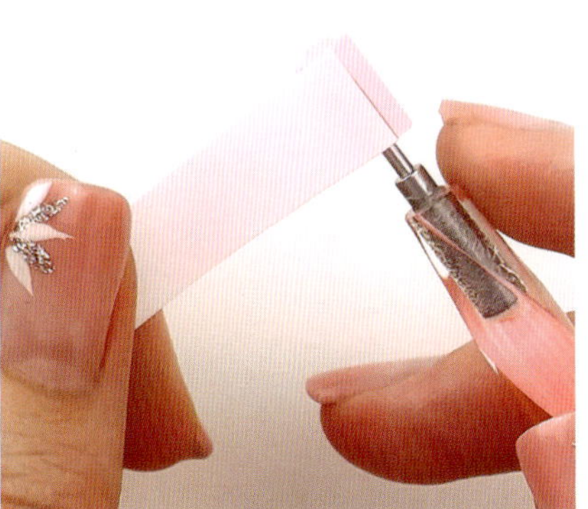

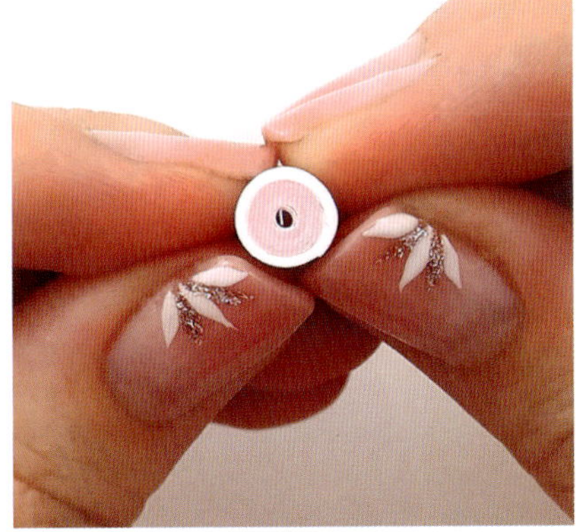

3 Roll the new coloured strip tightly around your base colour.

4 Add a little glue to the tail end and roll to complete. Repeat this process for each new colour you want to add.

Ring coil

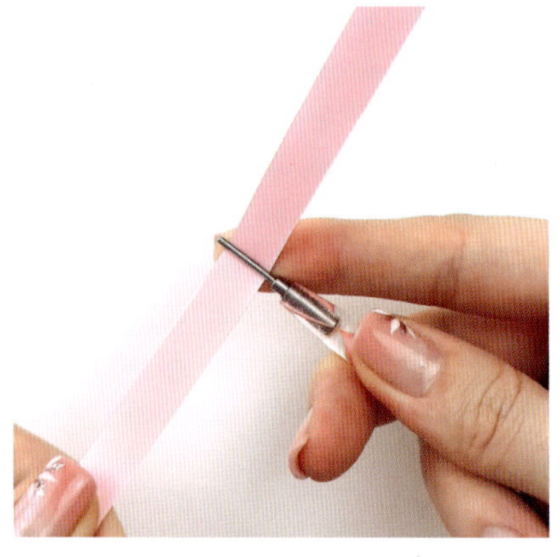 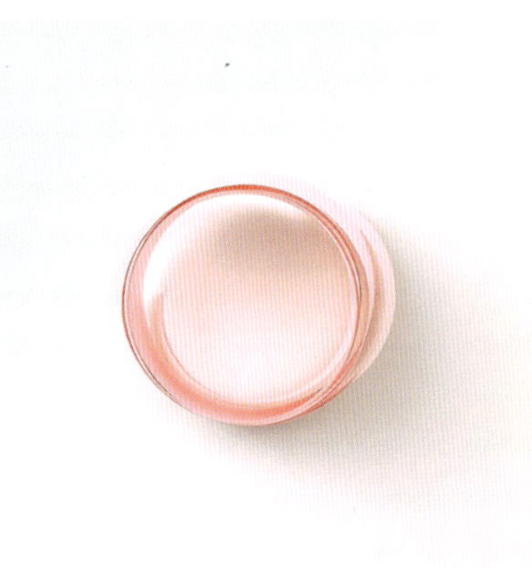 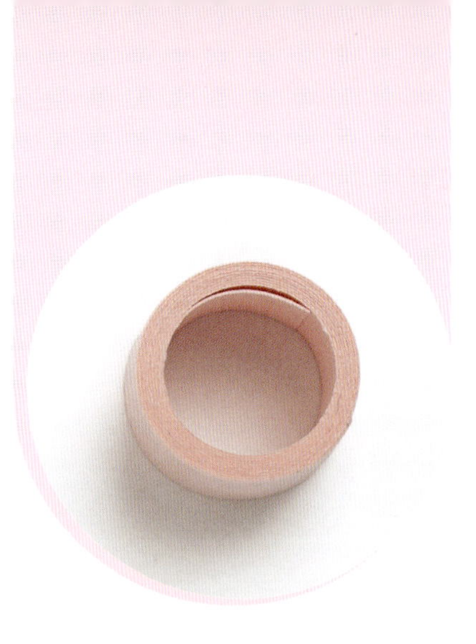

1 Hold the tool in your dominant hand, the paper in the other hand and drag the metal tip across the paper length to curl the paper. Set the tool aside.

2 The paper will now be curled into a circle shape.

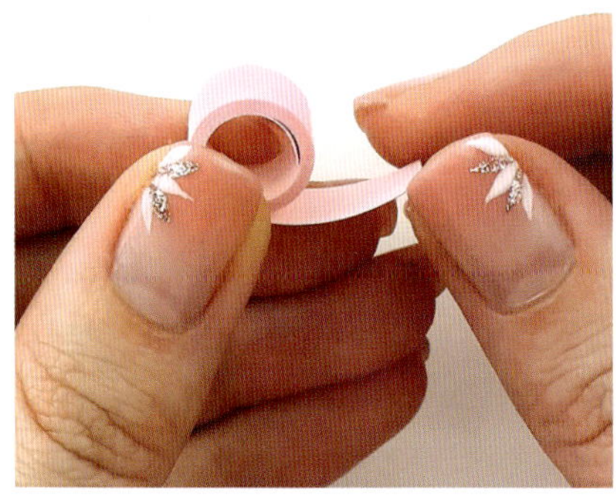 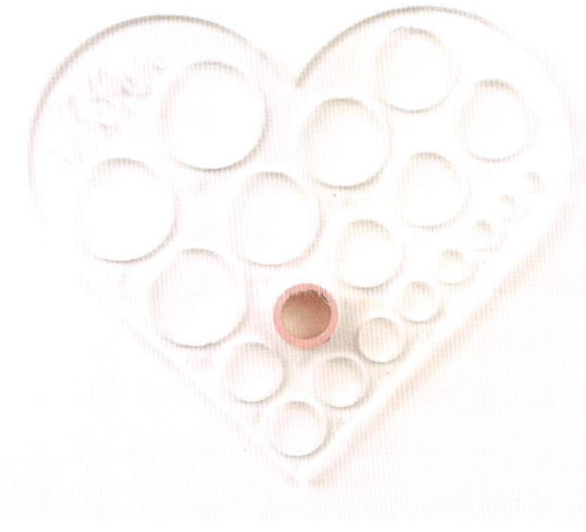 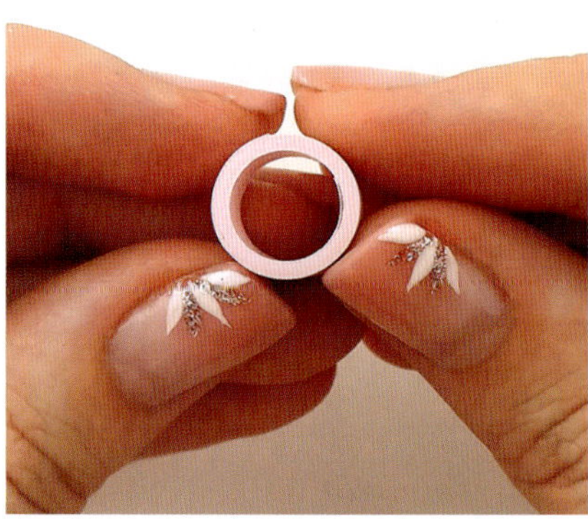

3 Using your hands, wind the strip into a smaller, more compact circle shape.

4 Pop into the quilling board in the size hole indicated on the project instruction page. Allow the shape to expand to fill the hole.

5 Apply a little glue to the tail end and stick down to close the shape.

Ellipse coil

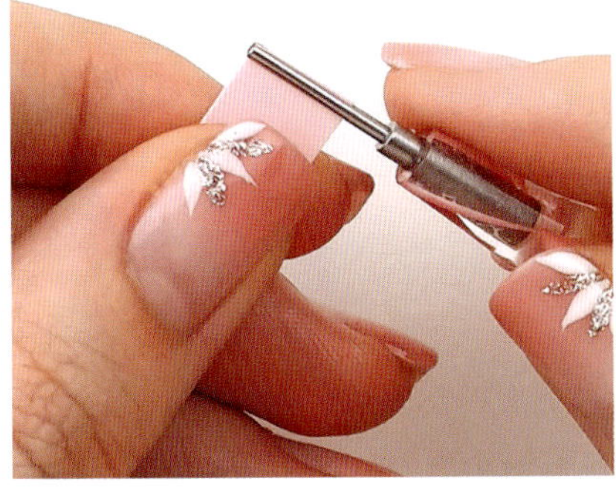

1 Hold the tool in your dominant hand, the paper in the other hand and insert the tip of the strip into the quilling tool.

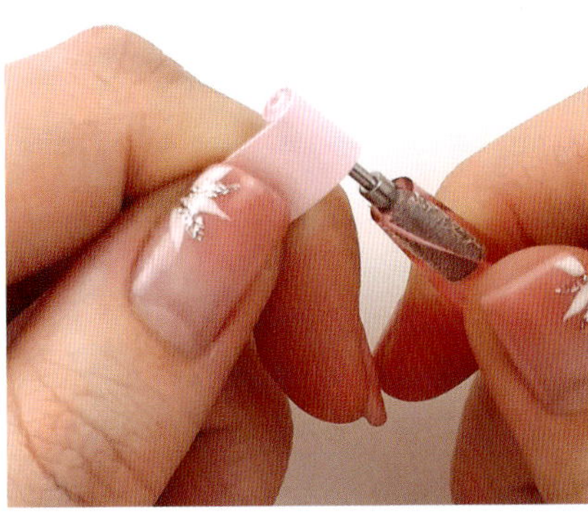

2 Turn the tool to roll the paper, keeping the paper taut as you roll.

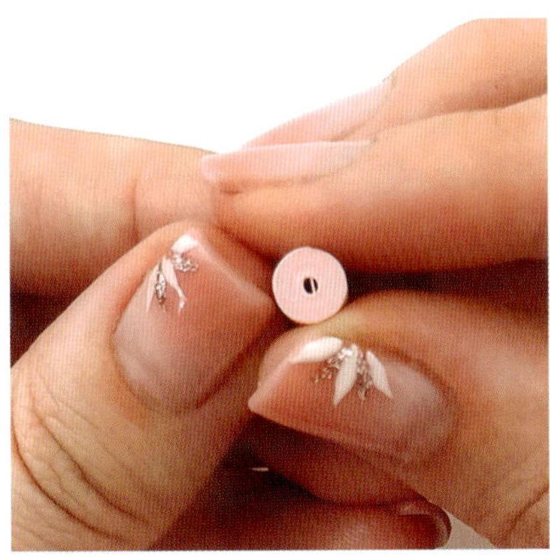

3 Apply a little glue to the tail end and roll to complete. Hold to allow the glue to bond then remove from the tool.

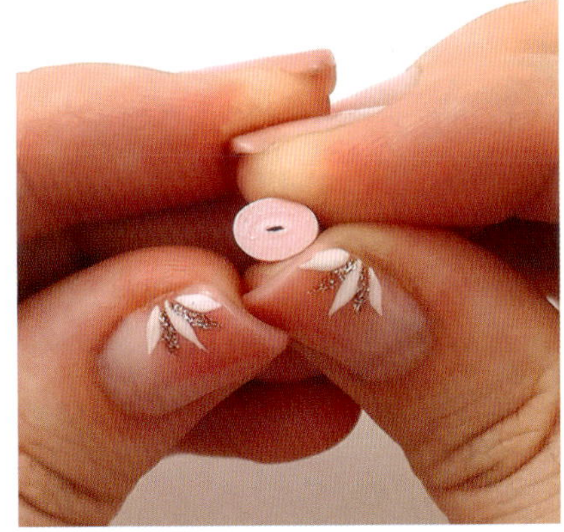

4 Apply pressure to the top and the bottom of the tight coil to make an ellipse coil.

Loose coil

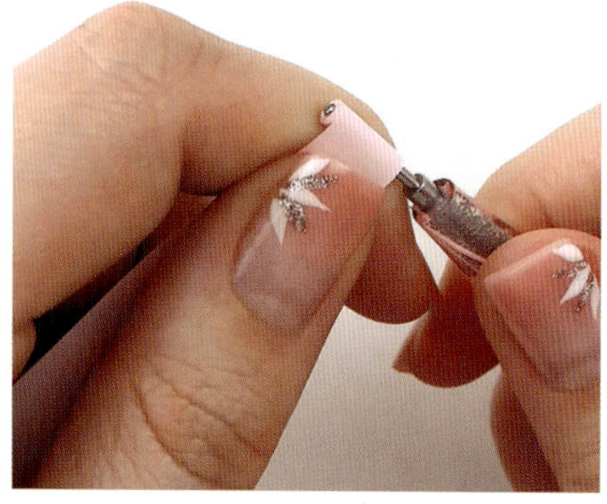

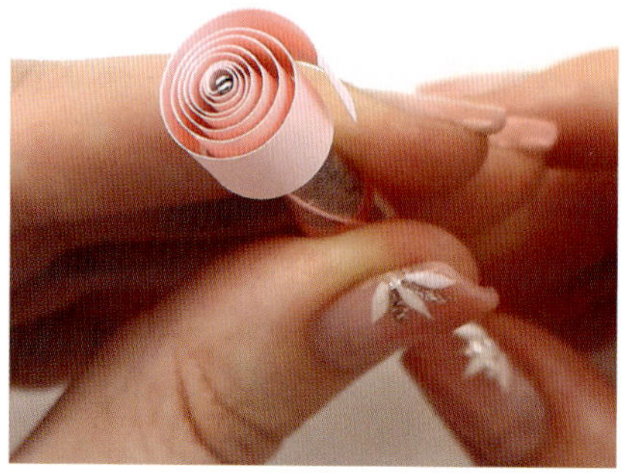

1 Hold the tool in your dominant hand, the paper in the other hand and insert the tip of the strip into the quilling tool. Turn the tool to roll the paper, keeping the paper taut as you roll.

2 When you reach the end of the strip, allow the coil to unwind while still on the tool.

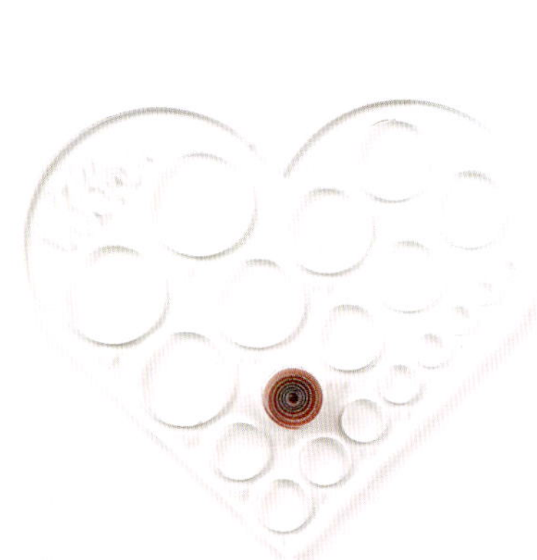

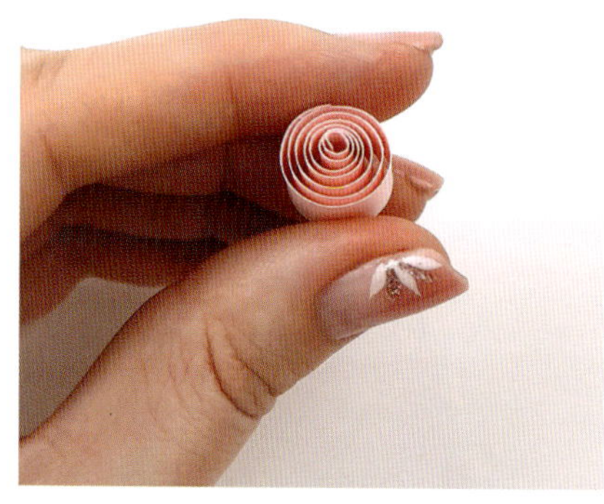

3 Remove the shape from your quilling tool and place into the quilling board in the size hole indicated on the project instruction page. Allow the shape to unwind to fill the hole.

4 Insert one tip of the tweezers in the centre of the shape and the other tip on the outside, pinch both tips together to pick up the shape. Apply a little glue to the tail end and fix closed.

Fringed tight coil

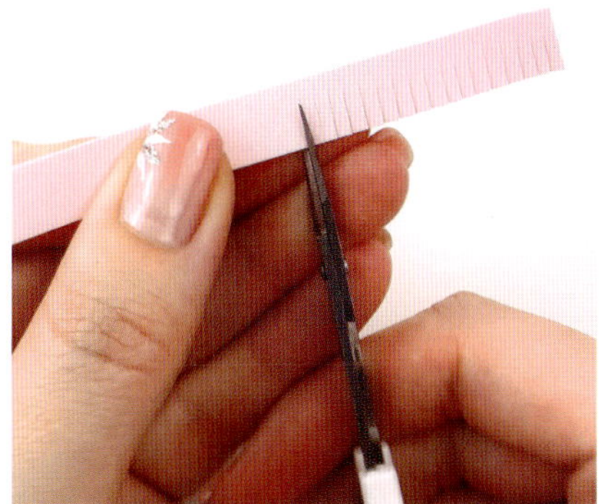 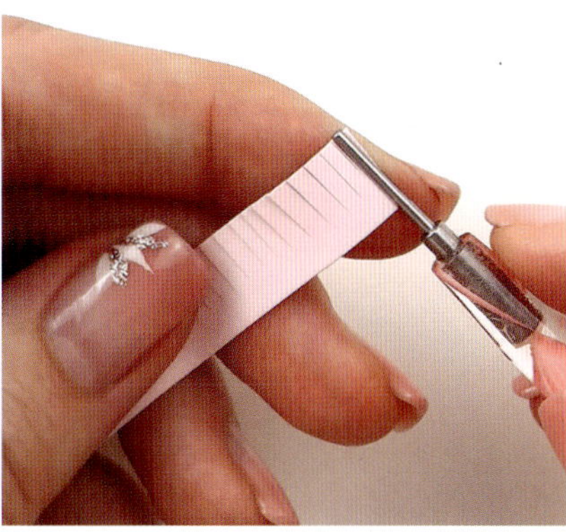 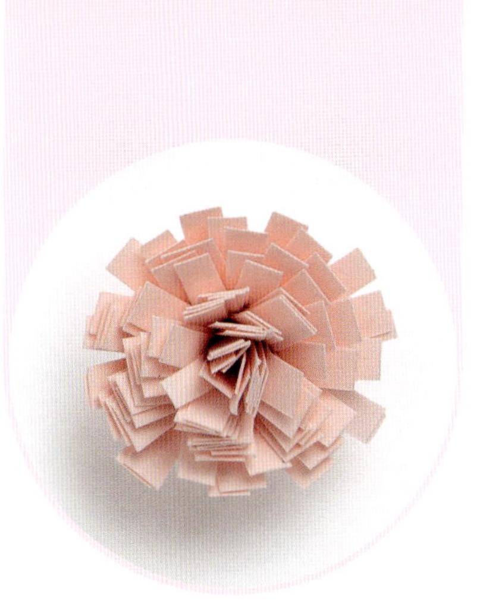

1 To fringe a strip, you need scissors that are sharp to the tip – quilling scissors are best to use. Take a strip and cut at regular intervals. Be careful not to cut through the whole strip, cutting to around two thirds of the width. Go slow and take your time.

2 Hold the tool in your dominant hand, the paper in the other hand and insert the tip of the strip into the quilling tool with the fringing at the top as shown.

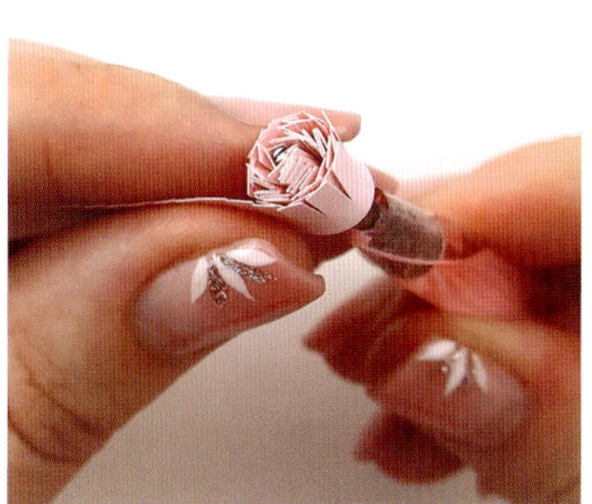 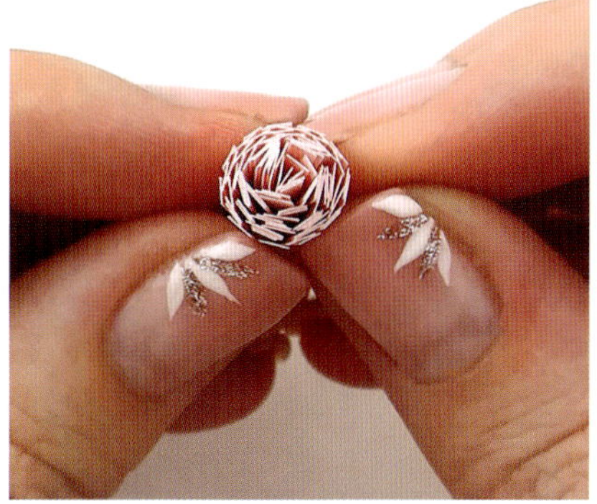 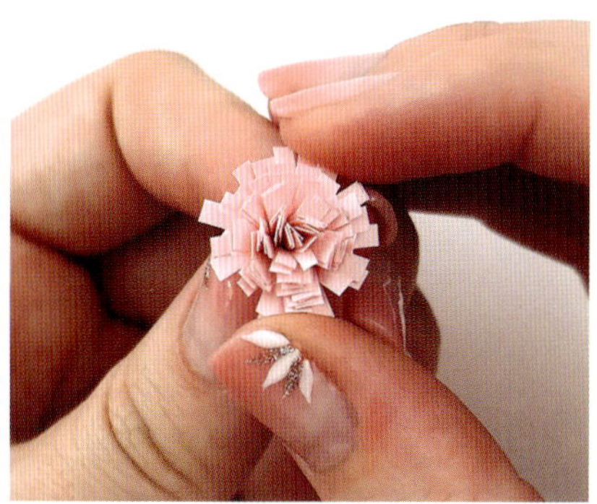

3 Turn the tool to roll the paper, keeping the paper taut as you roll.

4 Apply a little glue to the tail end and roll to complete. Hold to allow the glue to bond then remove from the tool.

5 Once quilled, spread out the edges with your fingers and thumb to give a fuller appearance.

Hollow marquise

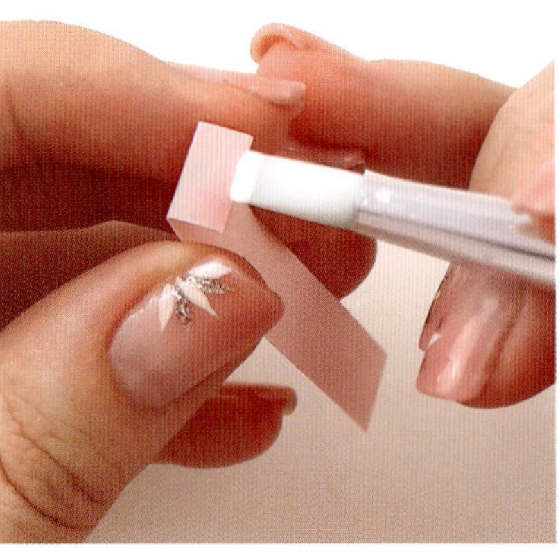

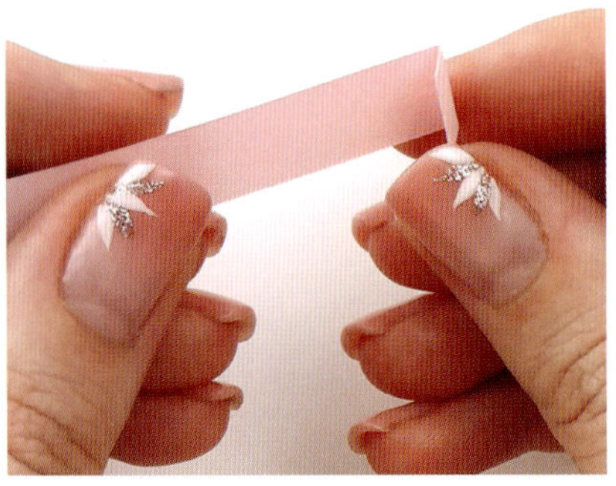

1 Cut a strip to the desired length. Fold a 5mm (³⁄₁₆in) tab at one end.

2 Apply a little glue to the tab and fold the strip in half.

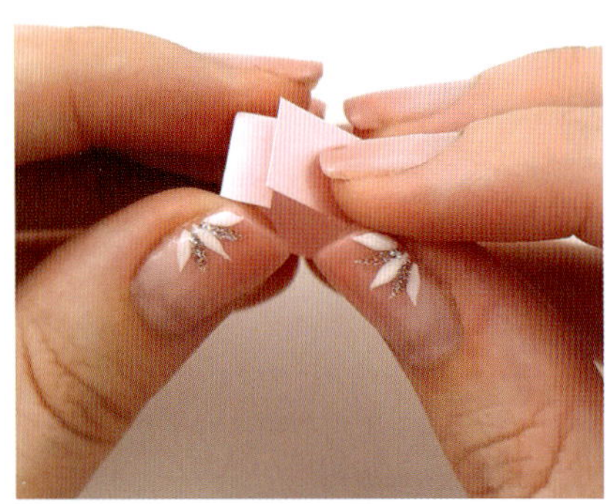

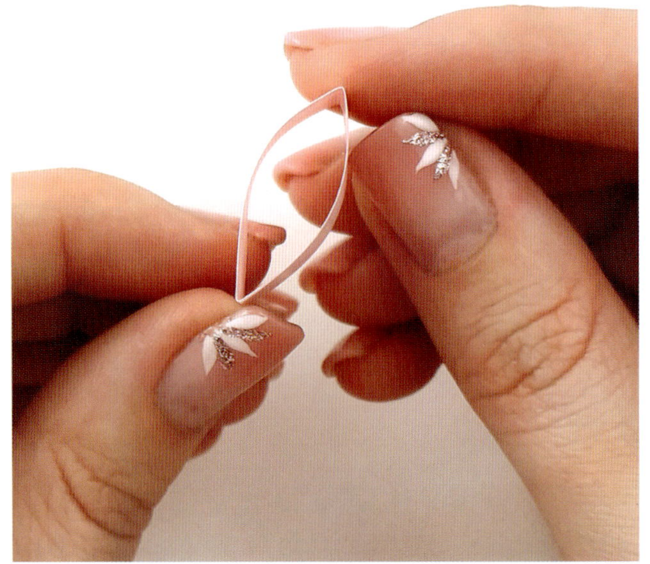

3 Stick the end of the strip to the tab to form a marquise shape.

Marquise

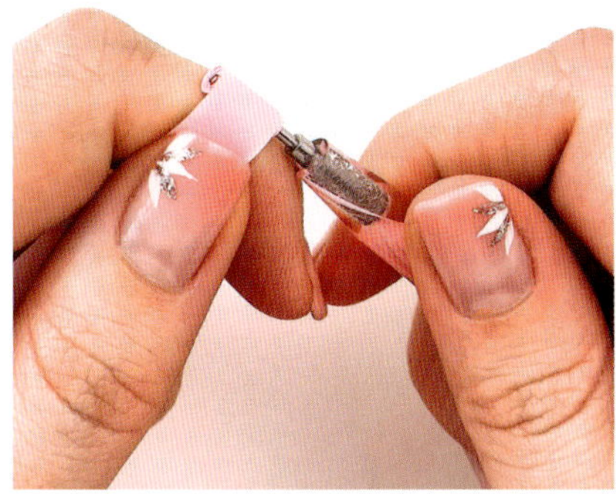 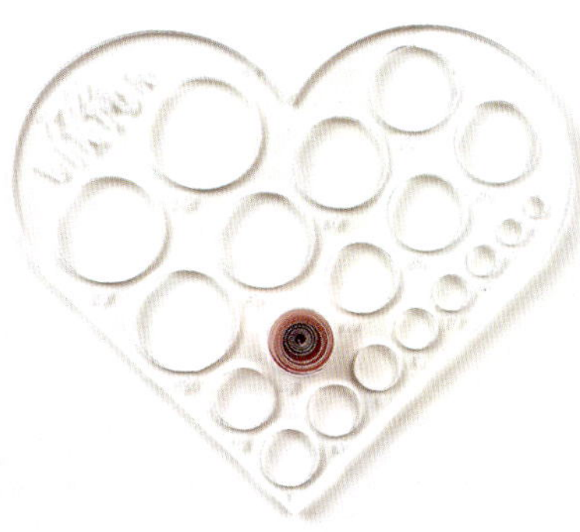 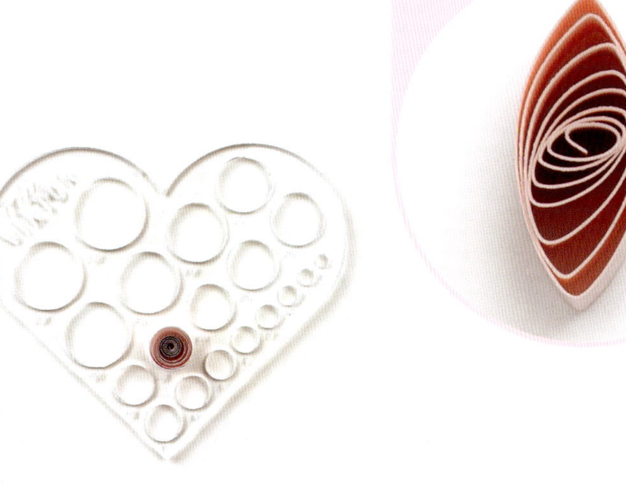

1 Hold the tool in your dominant hand, the paper in the other hand and insert the tip of the strip into the quilling tool. Turn the tool to roll the paper, keeping the paper taut as you roll.

2 Remove the shape from your quilling tool and place into the quilling board in the size hole indicated on the project instruction page. Allow the shape to unwind to fill the hole.

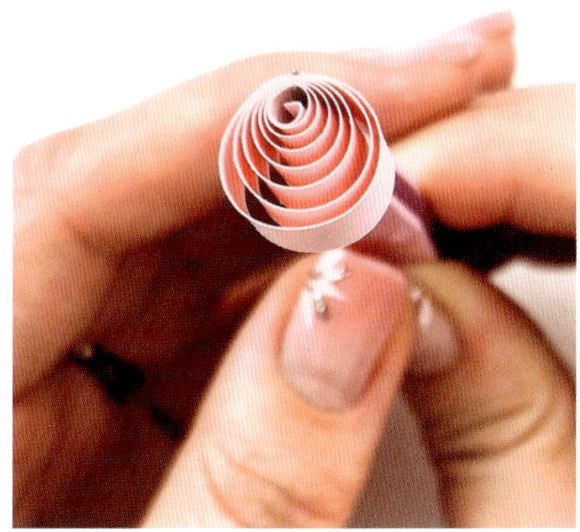 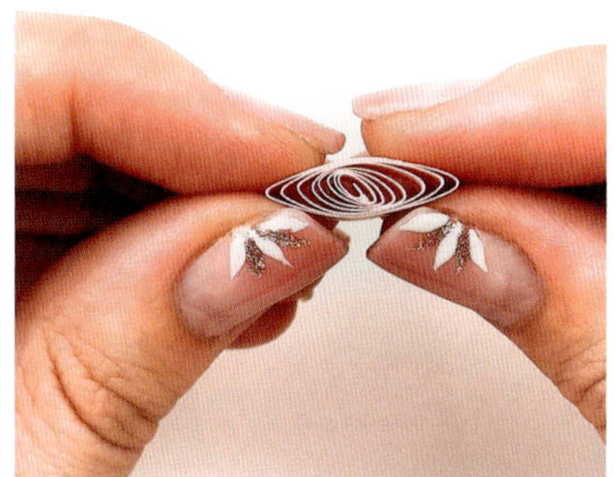

3 Insert one tip of the tweezers in the centre of the shape and the other tip on the outside, pinch both tips together to pick up the shape.

4 Apply a little glue to the tail end to close the shape, and pinch either side into a point to make a marquise shape.

Loose swirl/Open scroll

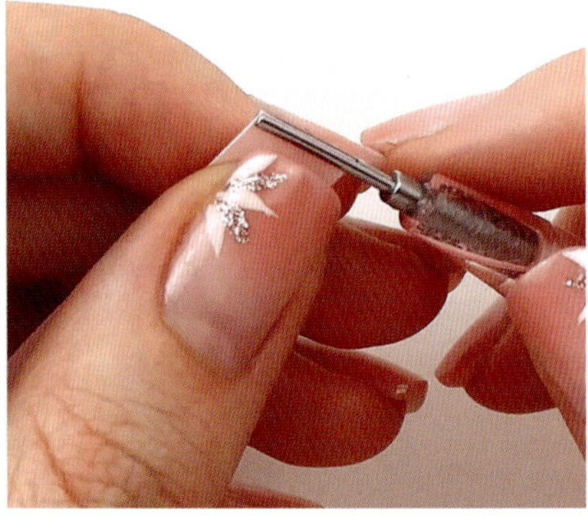

1 Hold the tool in your dominant hand, the paper in the other hand and insert the tip of the strip into the quilling tool.

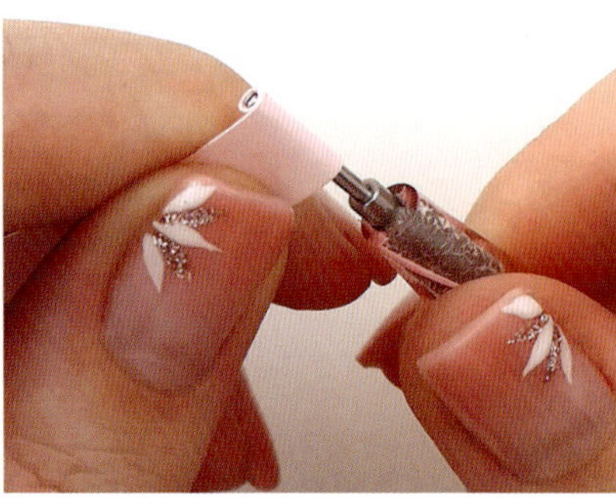

2 Turn the tool to roll the paper, keeping the paper taut as you roll.

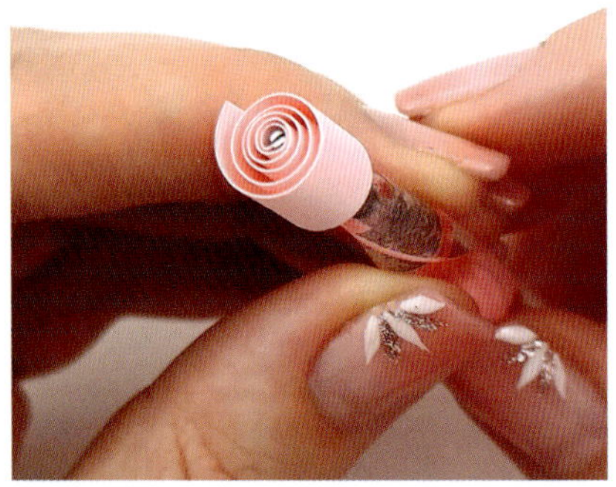

3 When you reach the end of the strip allow the scroll to unwind while still on the tool.

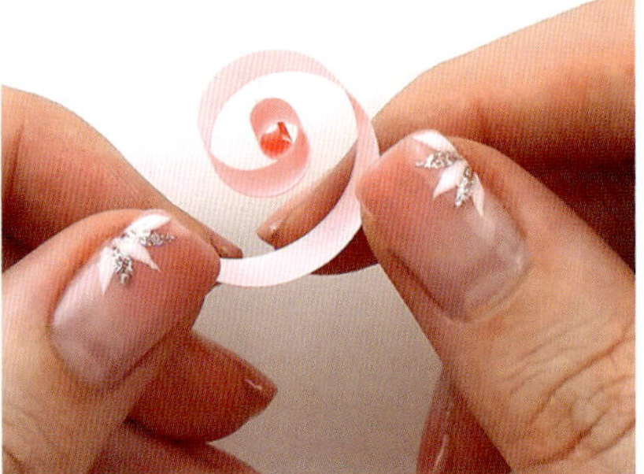

4 Remove the shape from your quilling tool and using your fingers unwind slightly to form an open scroll shape.

Arch

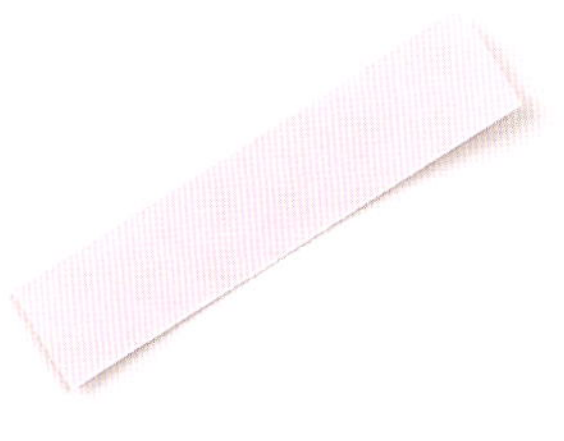

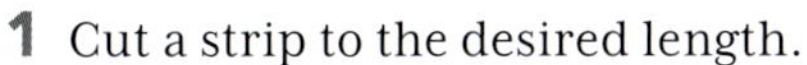

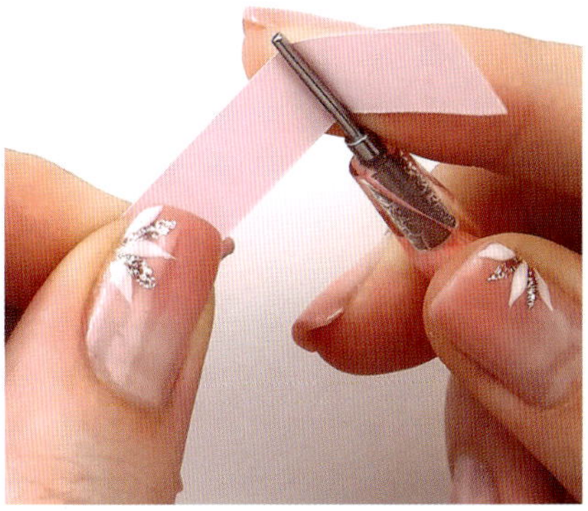

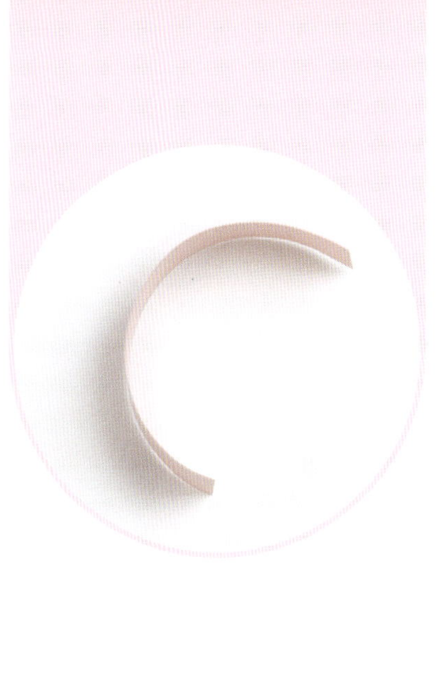

1 Cut a strip to the desired length.

2 Hold the tool in your dominant hand, the paper in the other hand and drag the metal tip across the paper length to curl the paper.

Triangle

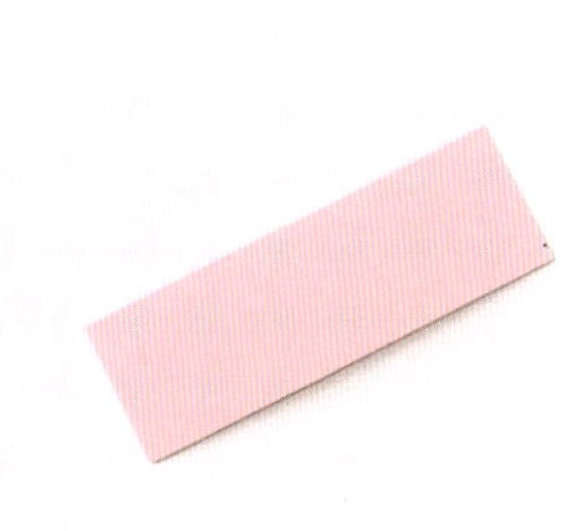

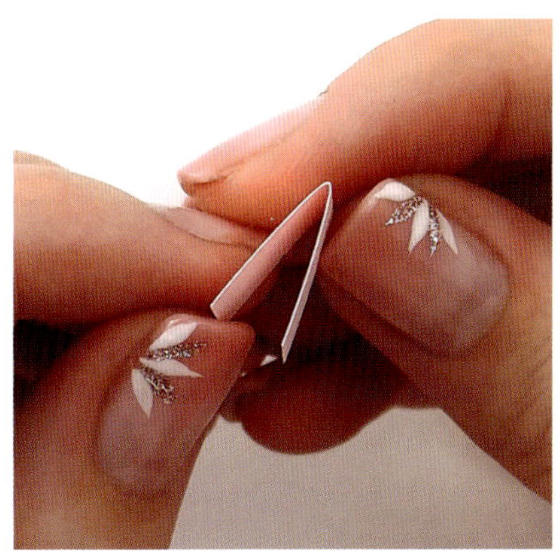

1 Cut a strip to the desired length. **2** Fold in half.

Pointed heart

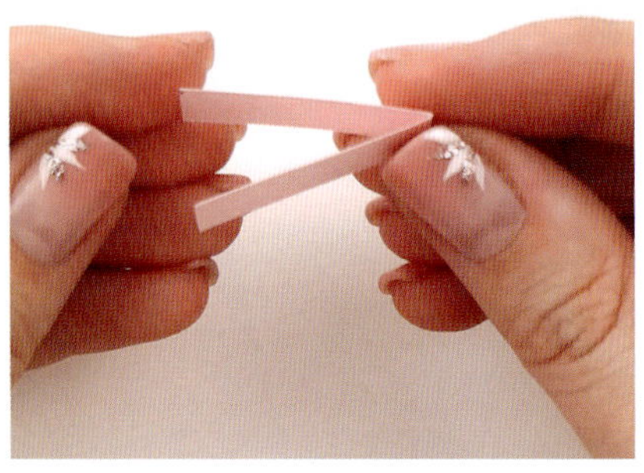

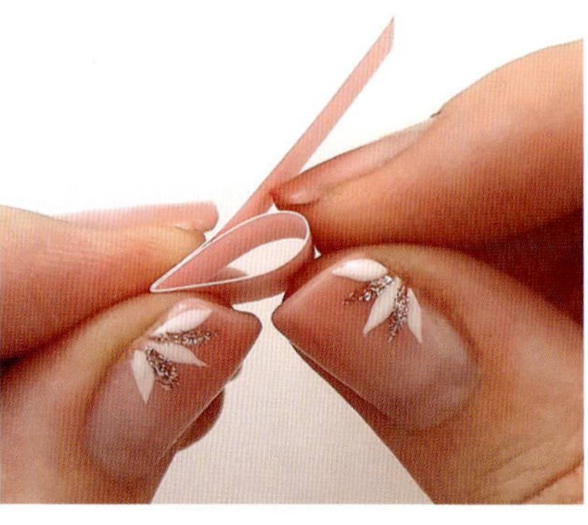

1 Cut a strip to the desired length and fold in half to form a V shape.

2 Make another fold in each side, folding in towards the centre.

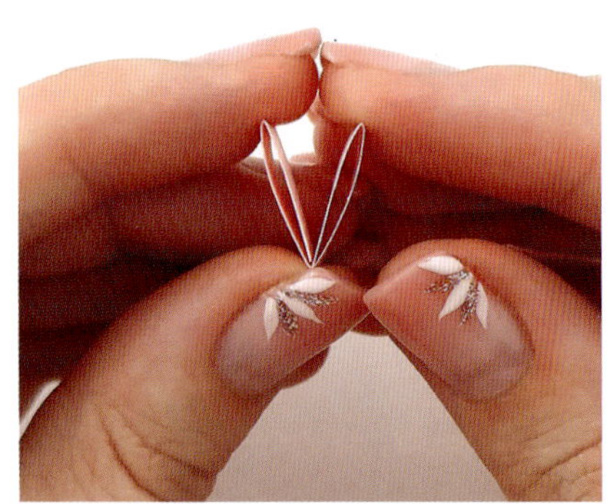

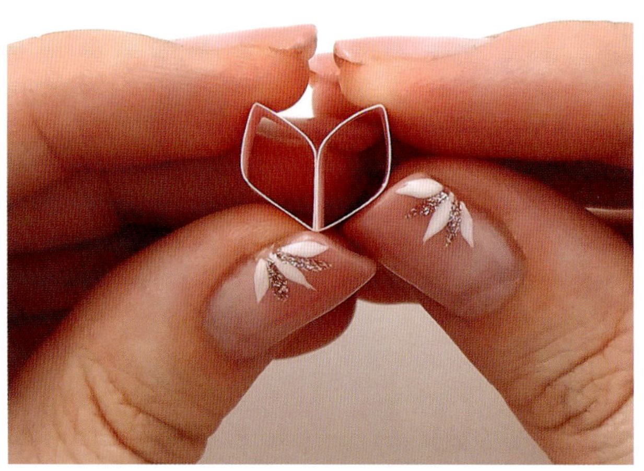

3 Take each half of the shape between your index finger and thumb and apply a little pressure so that each side forms its own kite shape.

Star

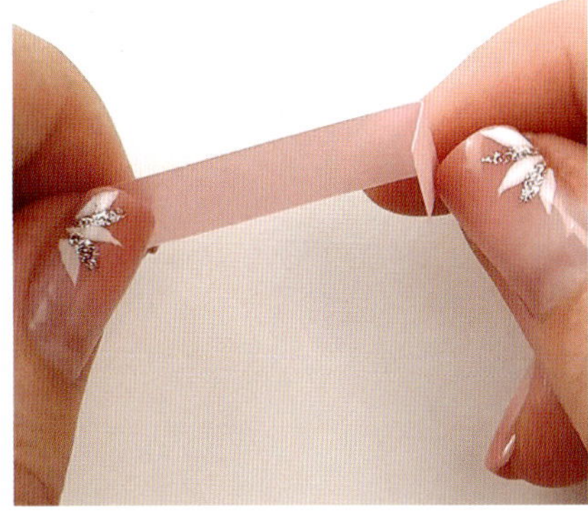

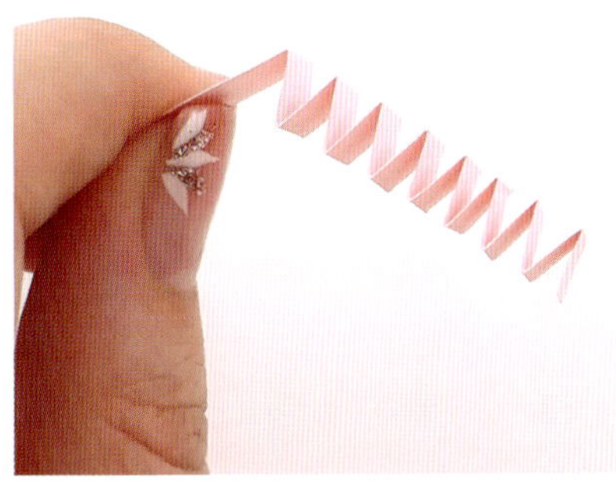

1 Take a full-length strip and make an initial 5mm ($\frac{3}{16}$in) fold at one end, this will be your 5mm ($\frac{3}{16}$in) tab to measure the rest of the folds.

2 Turn the tab back on itself, line the length up to the edge and make another fold. In a concertina style continue to fold the strip every 5mm ($\frac{3}{16}$in) until the whole strip is folded. Take time and make sure the folds are straight, pinching them tight as you go.

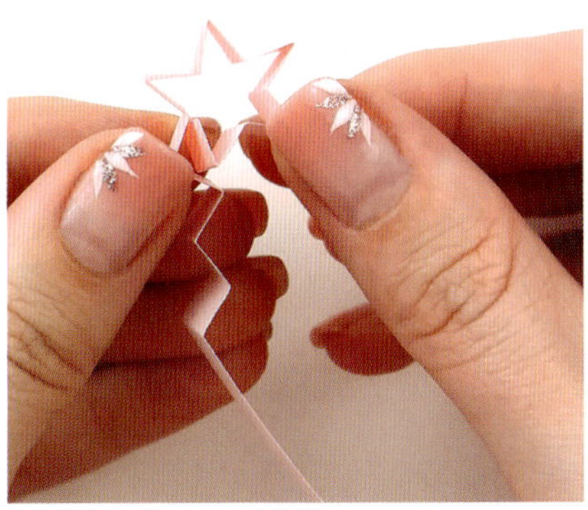

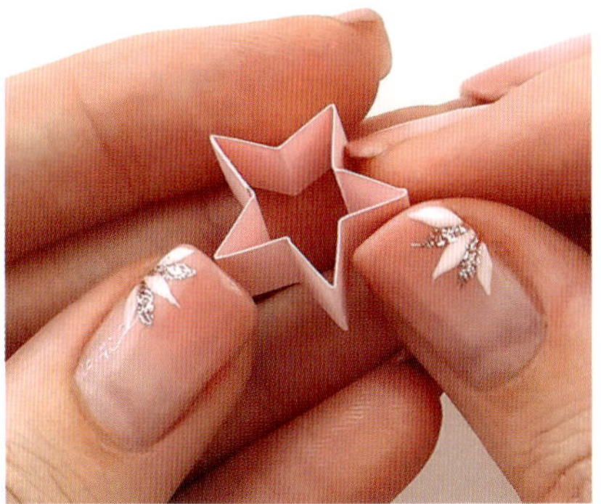

3 Stretch out the strip, count 11 tabs and cut off the excess. Take the eleventh tab and bend it round to meet the starting tab of your star.

4 Fix the end two tabs together to make a star shape.

Hollow teardrop

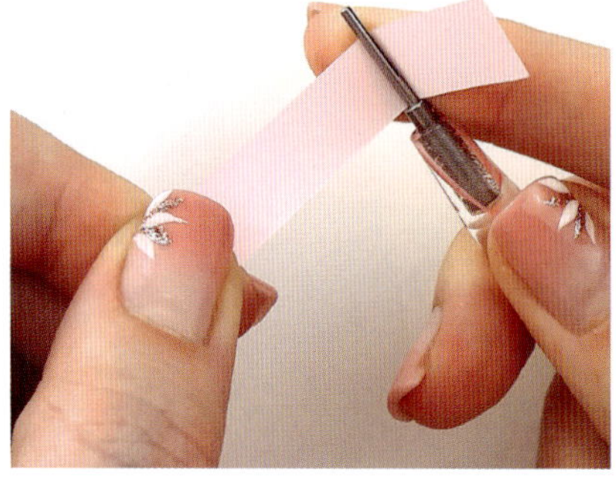

1 Hold the tool in your dominant hand, the paper in the other hand and drag the metal tip across the paper length to curl the paper. Set the tool aside.

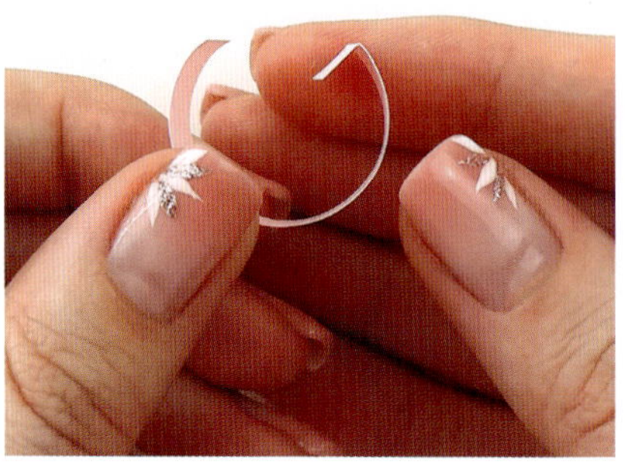

2 Fold a 5mm (³⁄₁₆in) tab at one end.

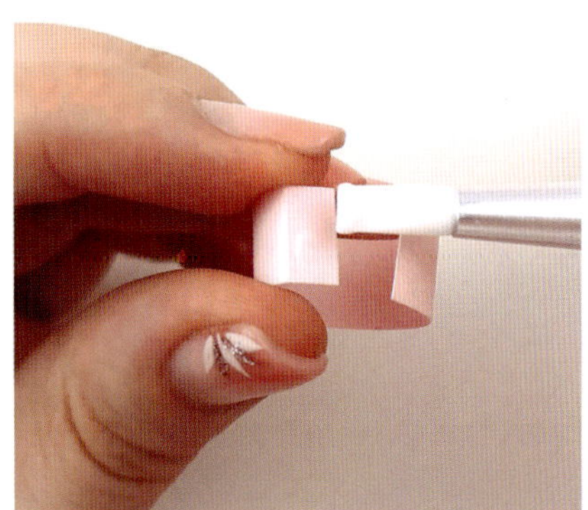

3 Apply a little glue to the tab.

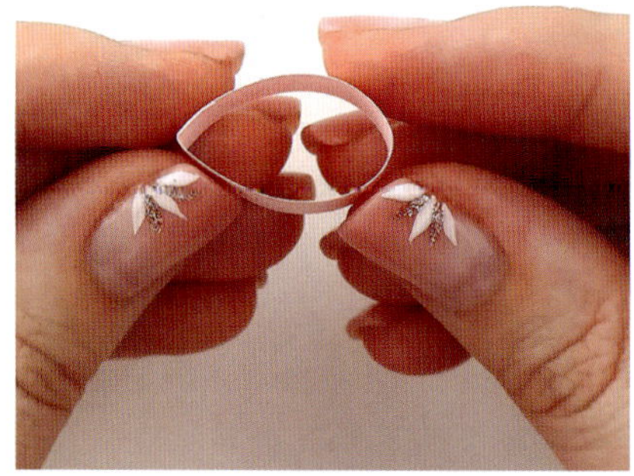

4 Bend the paper round and stick the tab to the other side to form a teardrop shape.

Ring teardrop

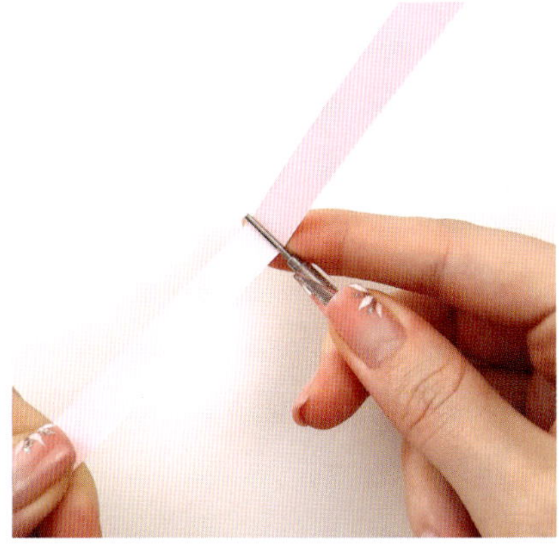 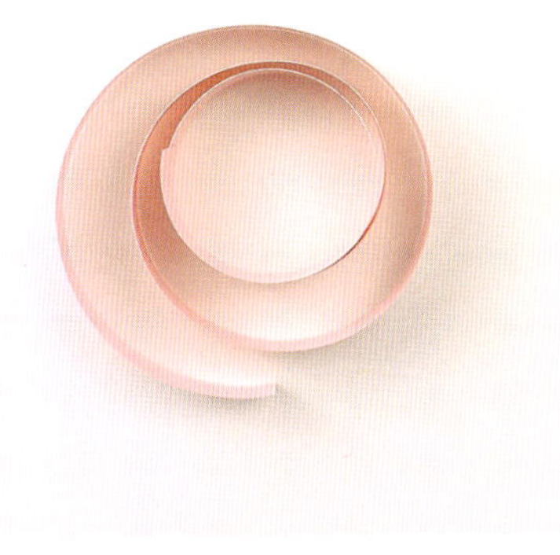 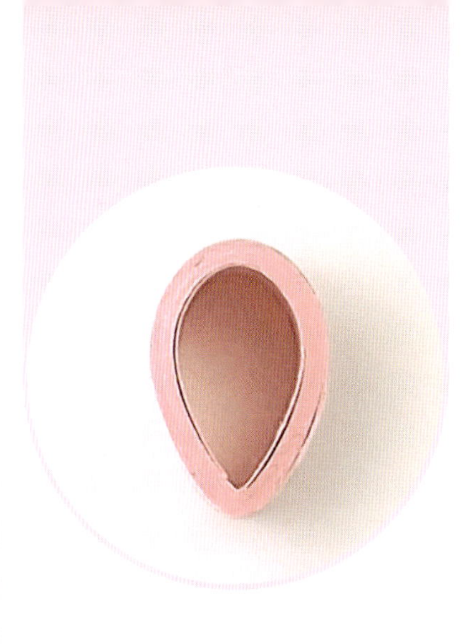

1 Hold the tool in your dominant hand, the paper in the other hand and drag the metal tip across the paper length to curl the paper. Set the tool aside.

2 The paper will now be curled into a circular shape.

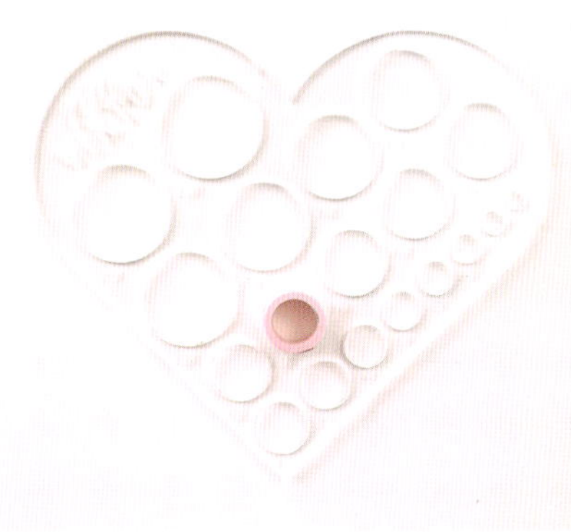 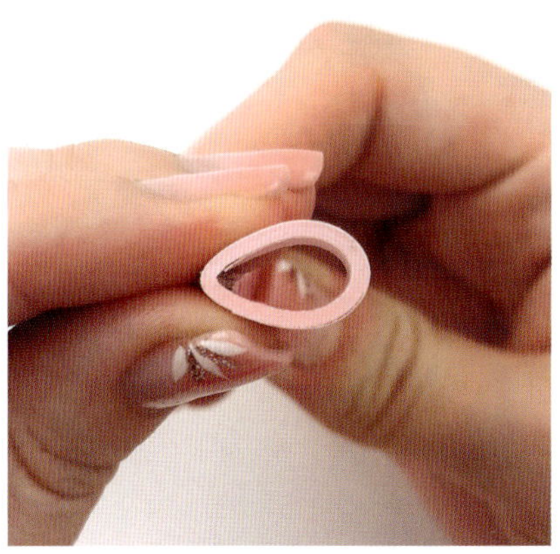

3 Using your hands, wind the strip into a smaller, more compact circle shape.

4 Pop into the quilling board in the size hole indicated on the instruction page. Allow the shape to expand to fill the hole. Using your tweezers, remove the shape from the quilling board and apply a little glue to close the shape.

5 Pinch into a point with your index finger and thumb to make a rounded ring teardrop.

Hollow ellipse

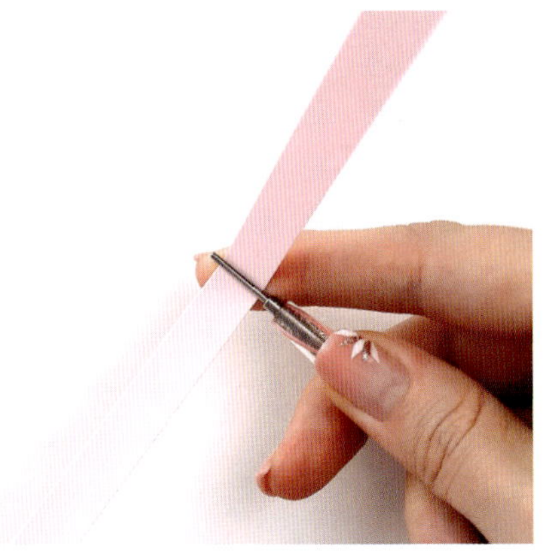

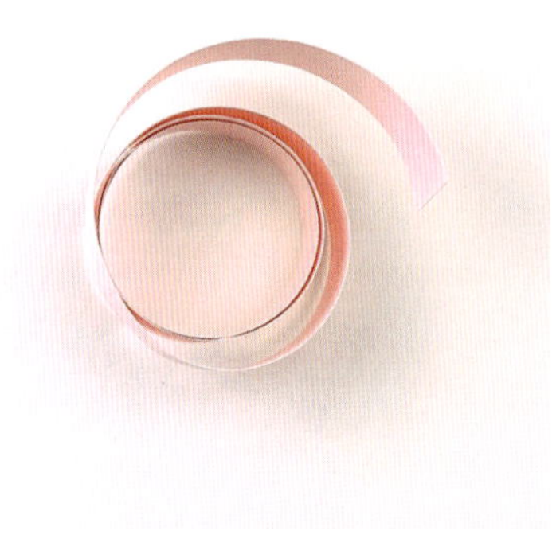

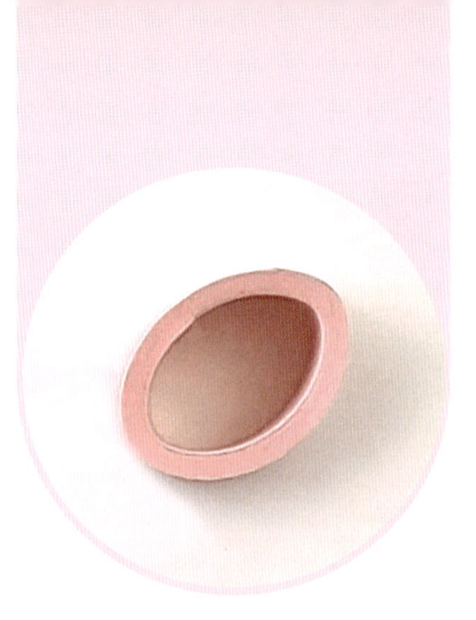

1 Hold the tool in your dominant hand, the paper in the other hand and drag the metal tip across the paper length to curl the paper. Set the tool aside.

2 The paper will now be curled into a circular shape.

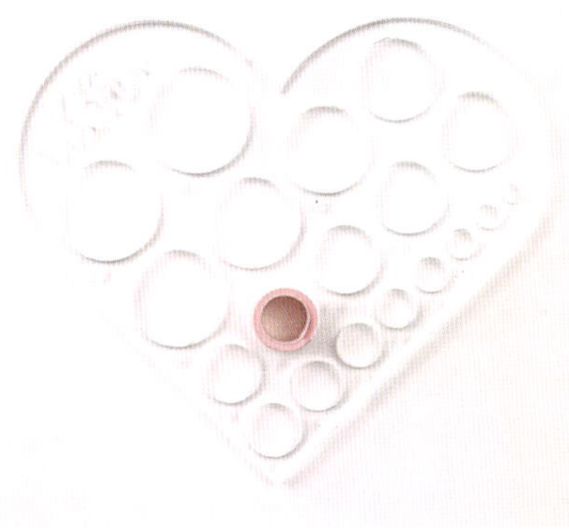

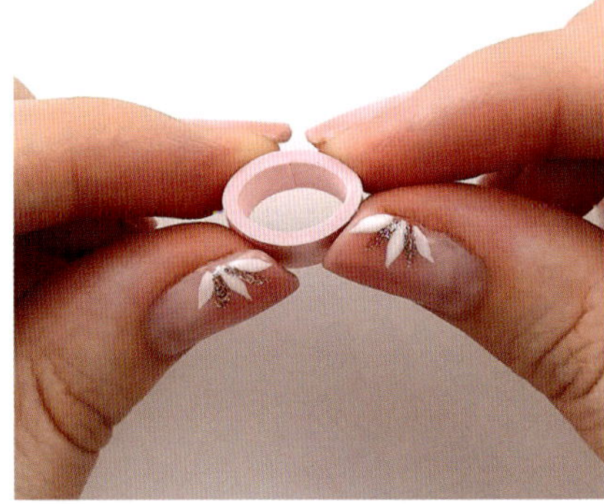

3 Using your hands, wind the strip into a smaller, more compact circle shape.

4 Pop into the quilling board in the size hole indicated on the instruction page. Allow the shape to expand to fill the hole. Using your tweezers, remove the shape from the quilling board.

5 Add a little glue to the tail end to close the shape. Apply a little pressure on each side to squash slightly into an ellipse shape.

Rose

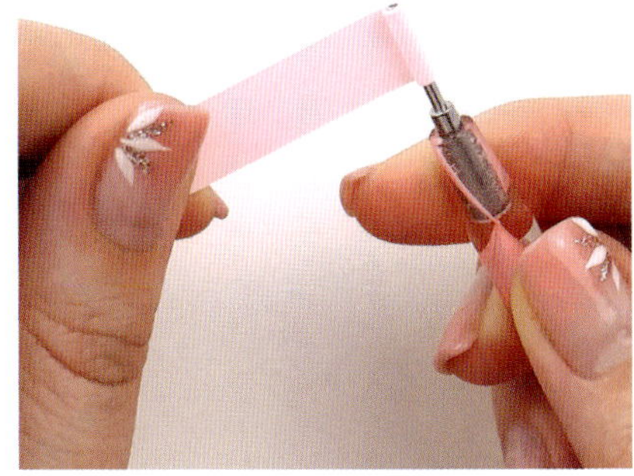

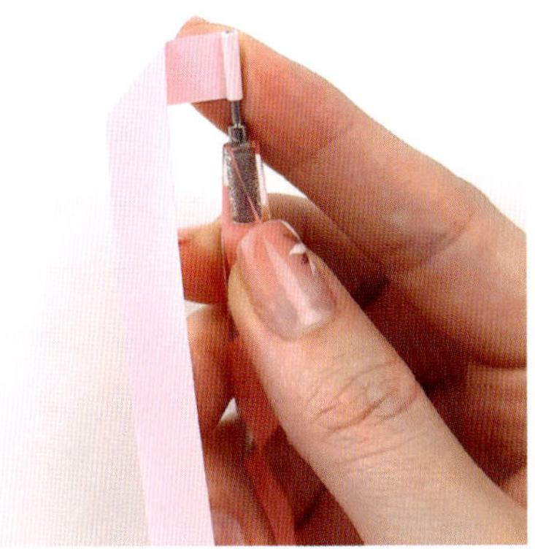

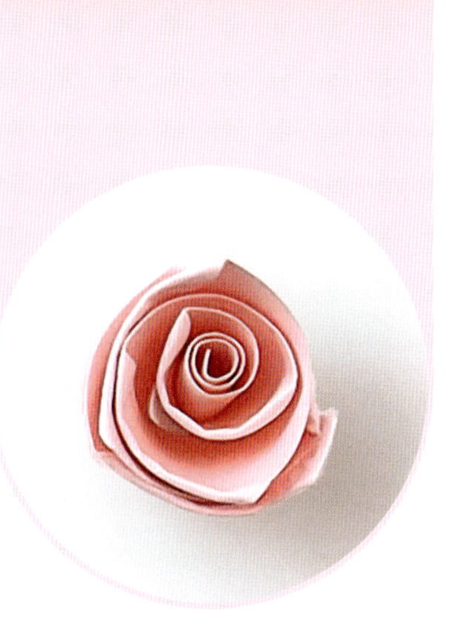

1 The rose seems quite complicated at first but stick with it and trust the process. Hold the tool in your dominant hand, the paper in your other hand and insert the tip of the strip into the quilling tool. Make two or three revolutions towards you to secure the strip and make the rose centre.

2 Using your other hand, make a 90-degree fold so that the tail end now points down, parallel to the tool.

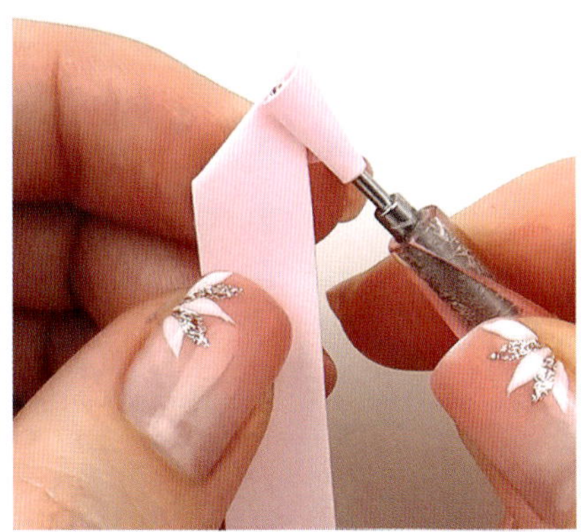

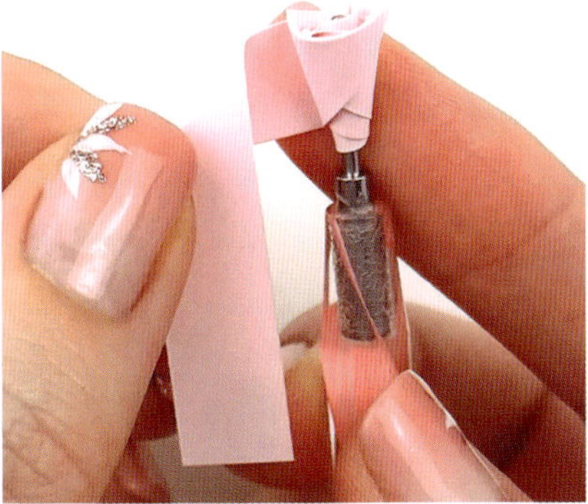

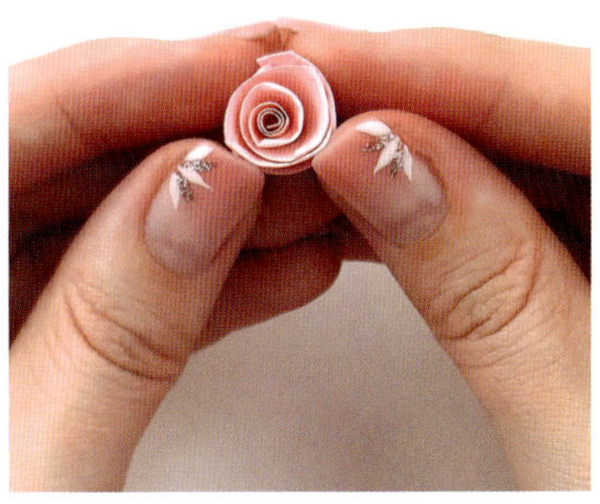

3 Make another two or three revolutions, rolling over the fold. Notice that that strip will now lie perpendicular to the tool.

4 Continue to fold and roll until the full strip is rolled.

5 Remove from the tool and allow the rose to expand slightly. Apply a little glue to the tail end to complete.

Templates

These templates are also available to download free from the Bookmarked Hub: www.bookmarkedhub.com. Search for this book by title or ISBN: the files can be found under 'Book Extras.' Membership of the Bookmarked online community is free.

Templates are printed at actual size. Photocopy the template you wish to use, or print it out from the Bookmarked Hub onto the card you'd like to use as the background to your quilled design (see page 15 for more on choosing card for your base). When printing, ensure you print at 100% scale, otherwise the paper lengths on the project instructions will be invalid. Remember to leave enough blank space around the edges of your template if you would like to frame your finished quilled piece.

Rose shrubs, page 86

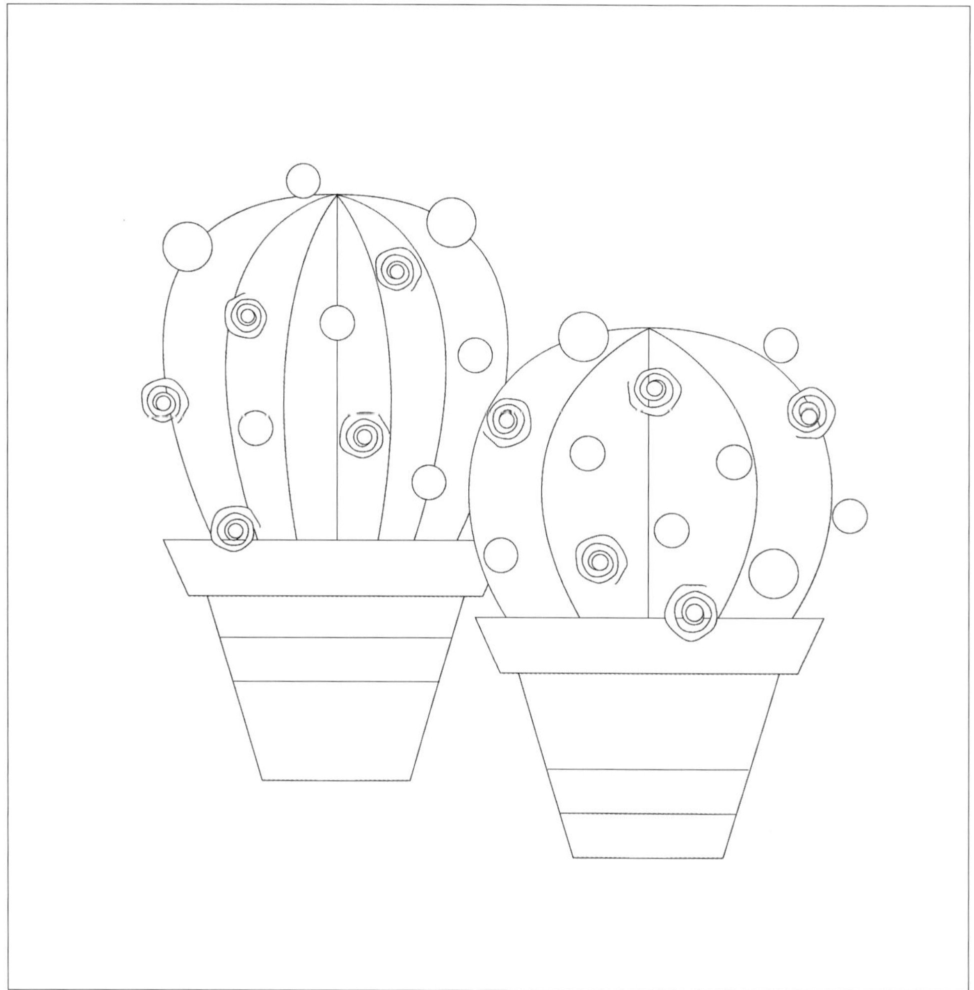

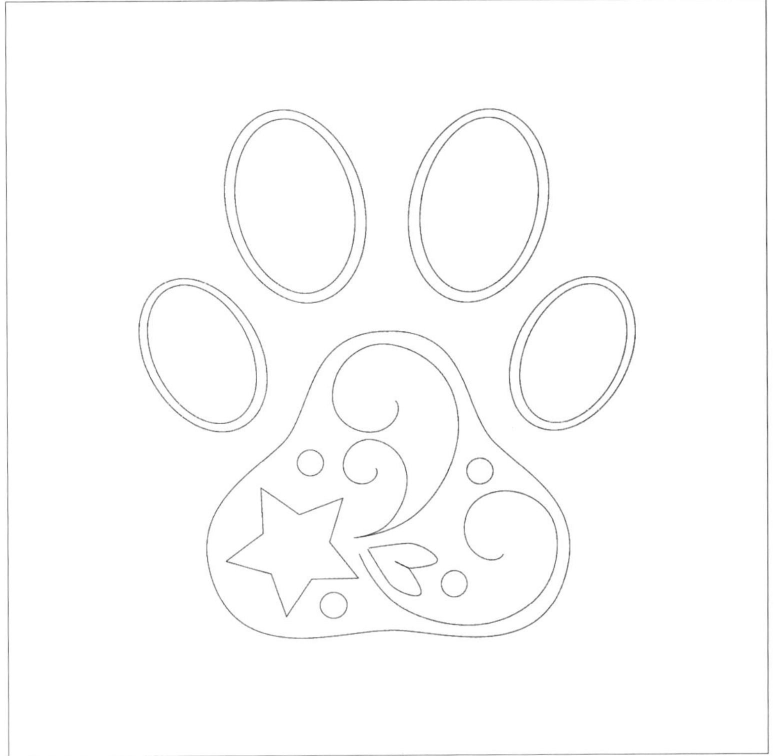

Paw print, page 70

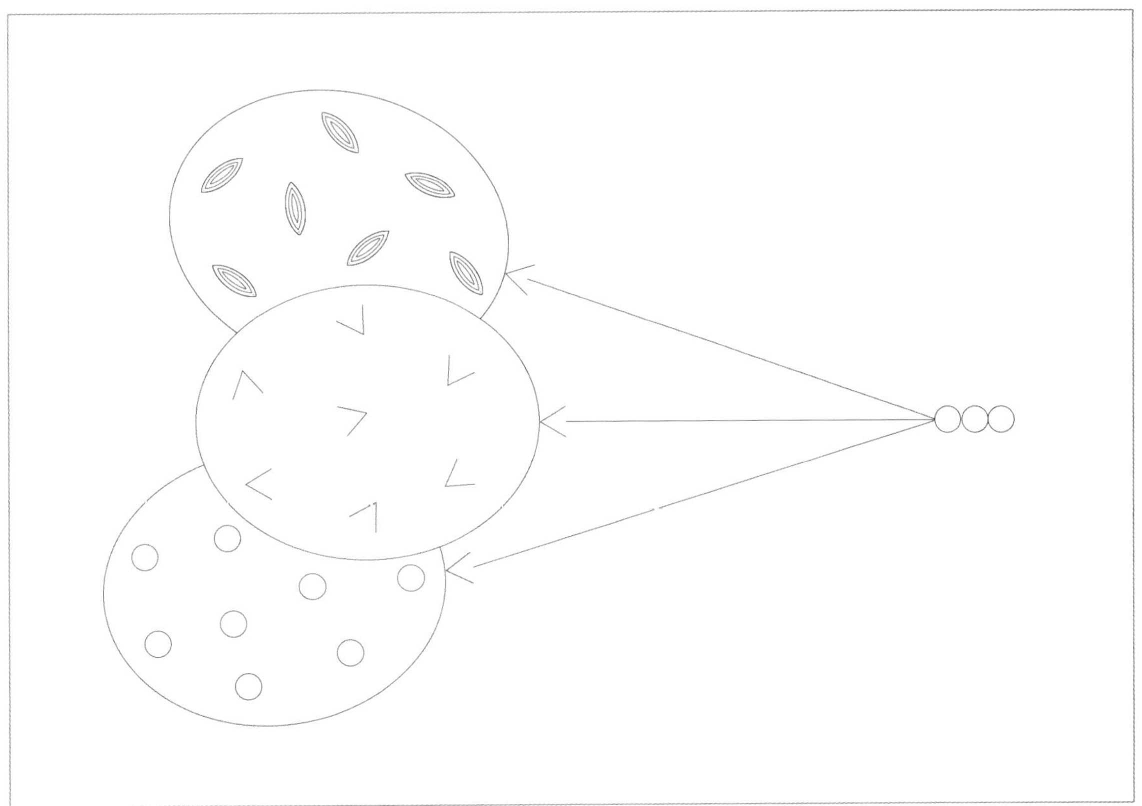

Balloons, page 50

Summer bouquet, page 94

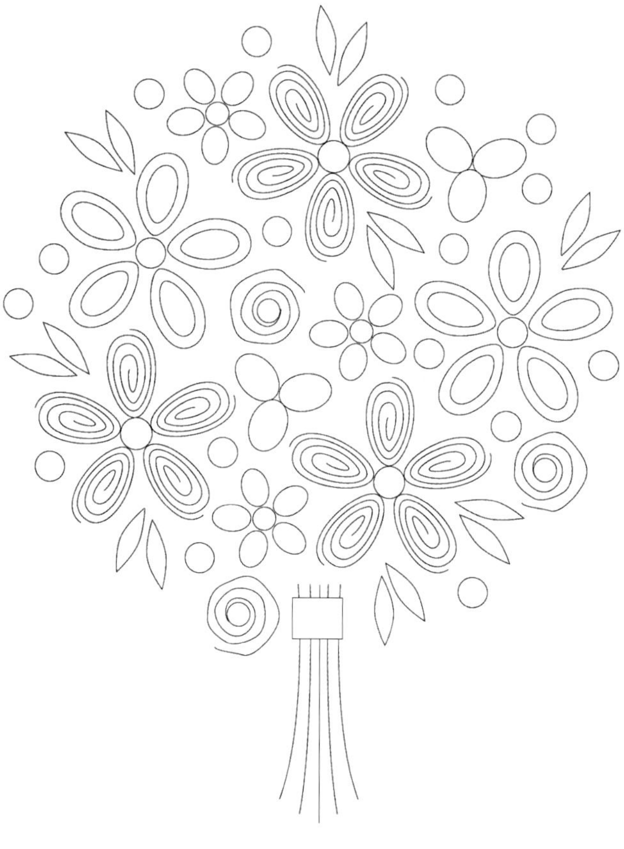

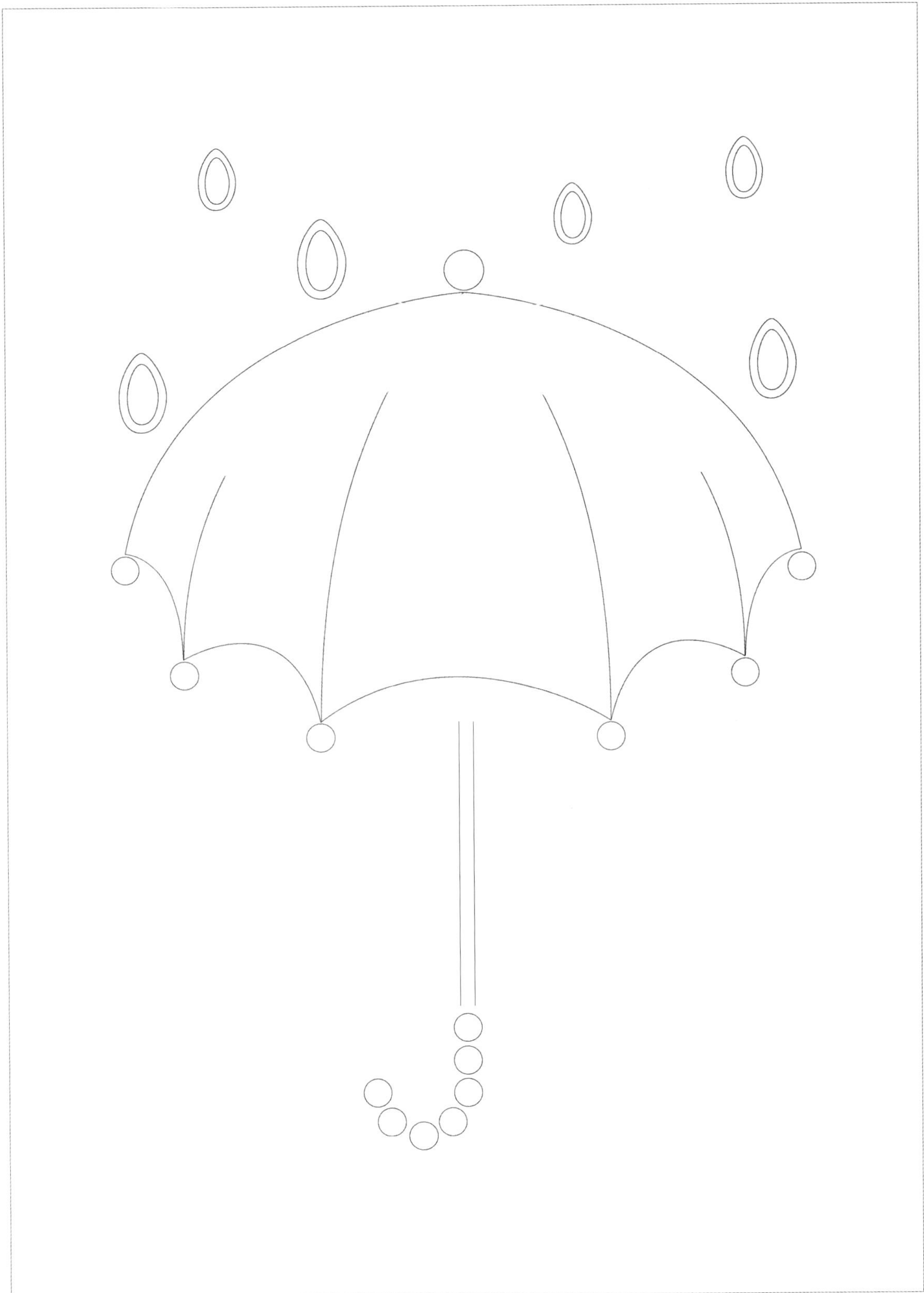

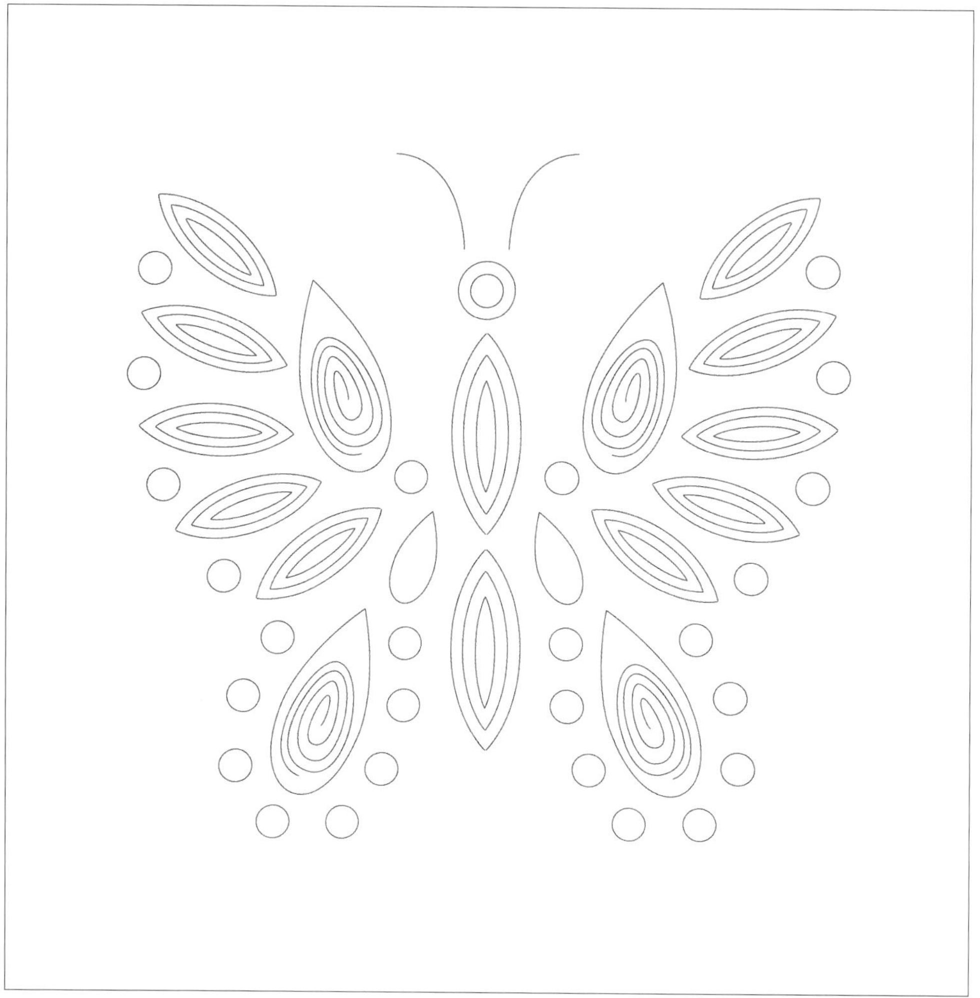

Candles, page 18

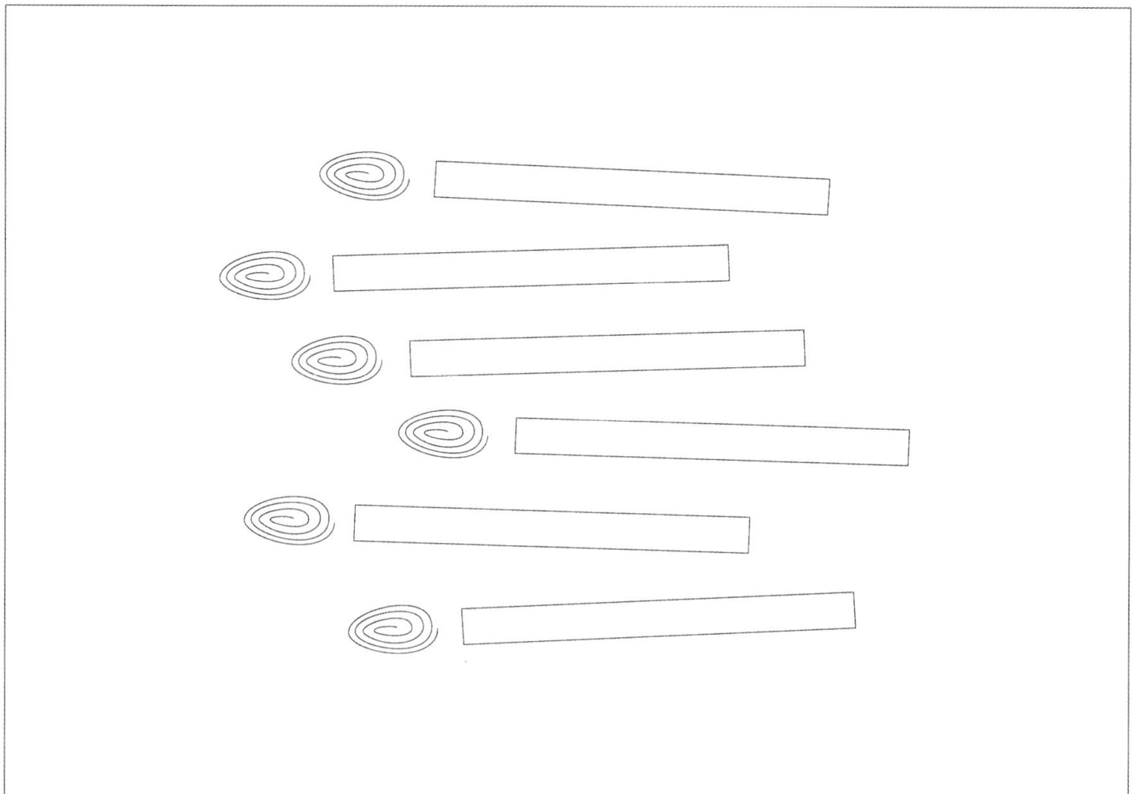

Cupcake, page 90

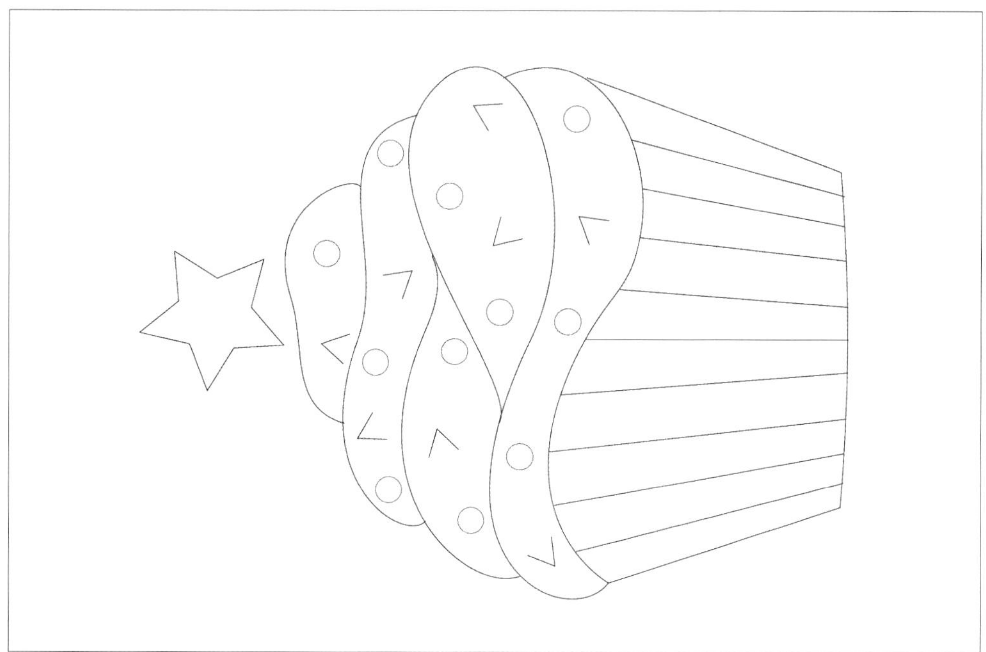

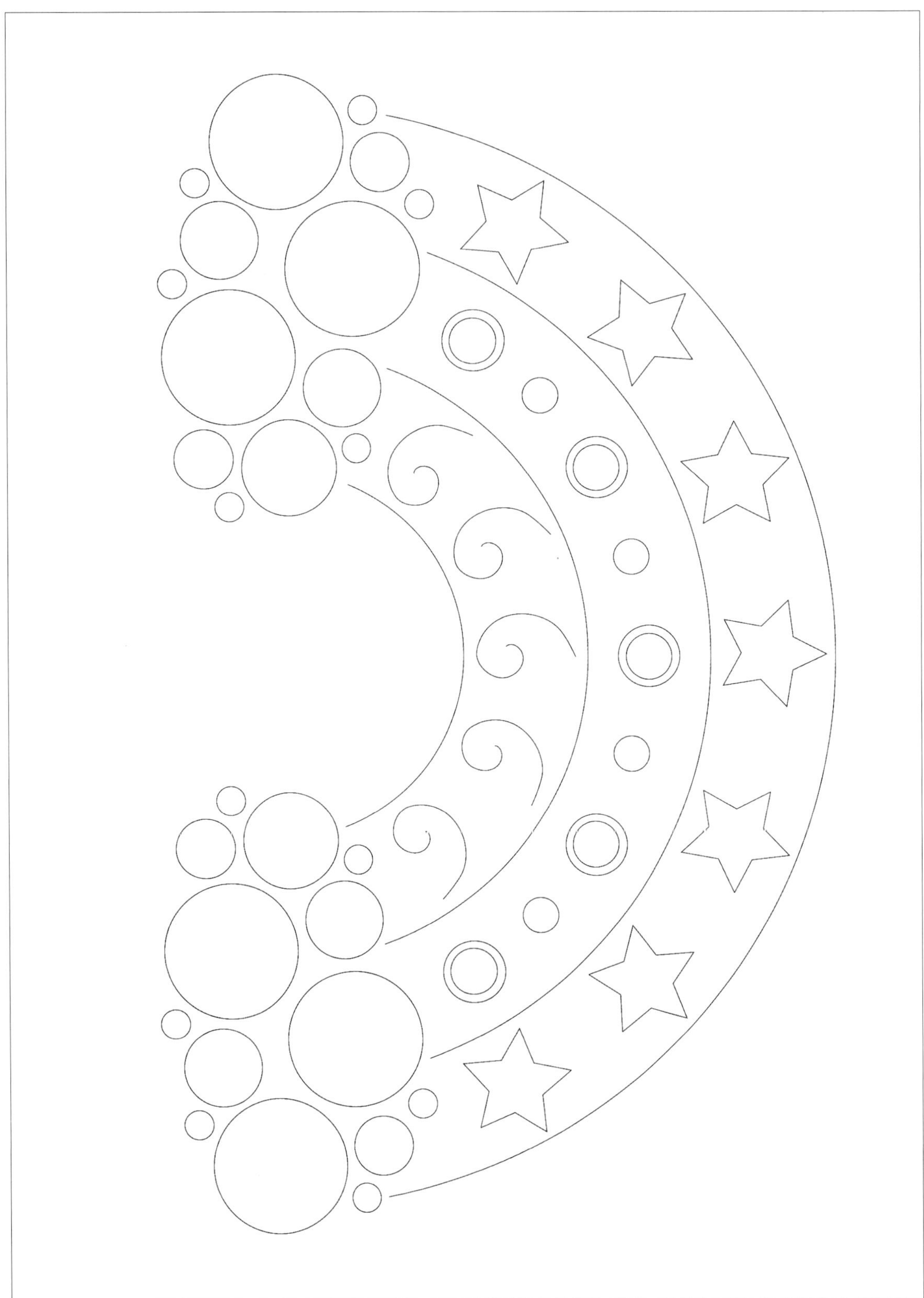

Daisy, page 26

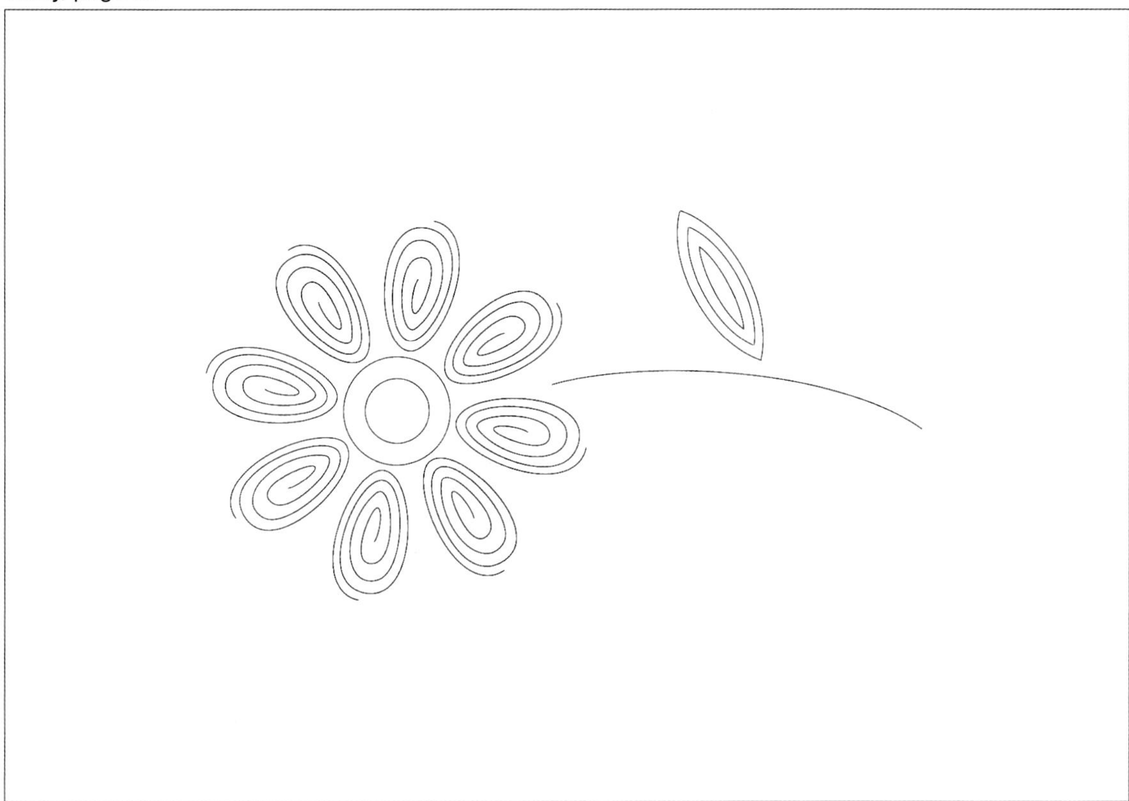

Gifts, page 30

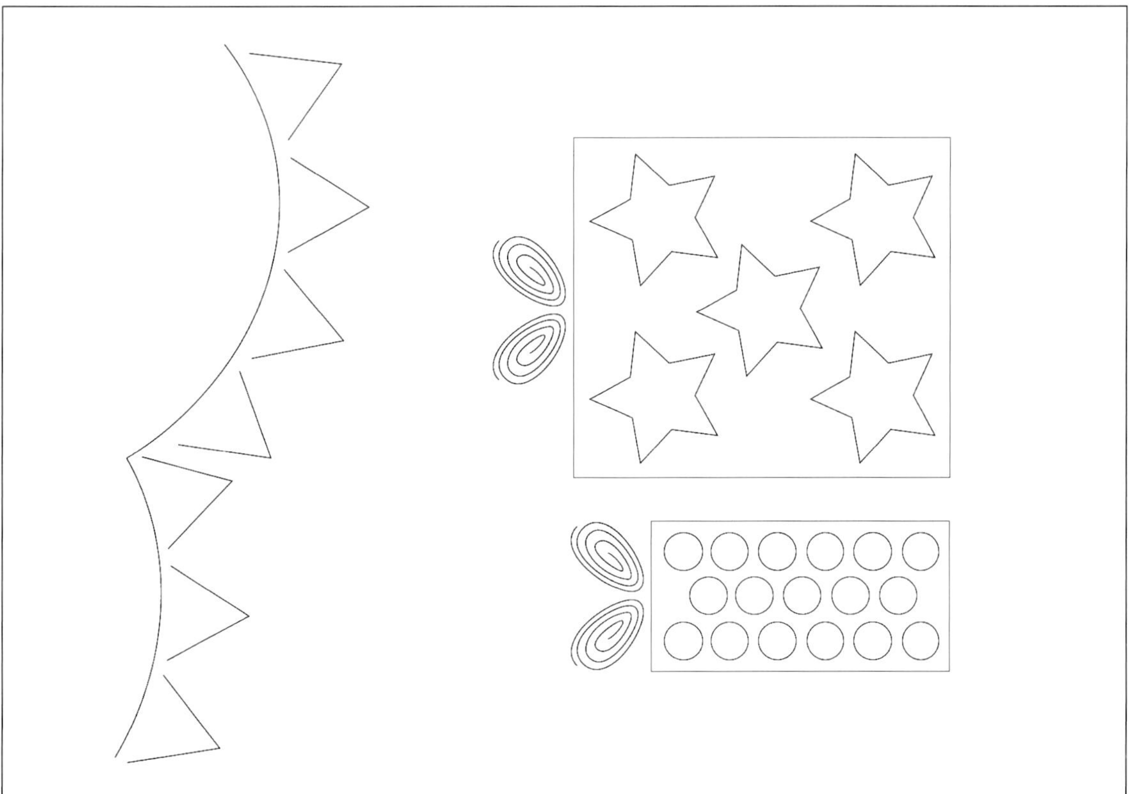

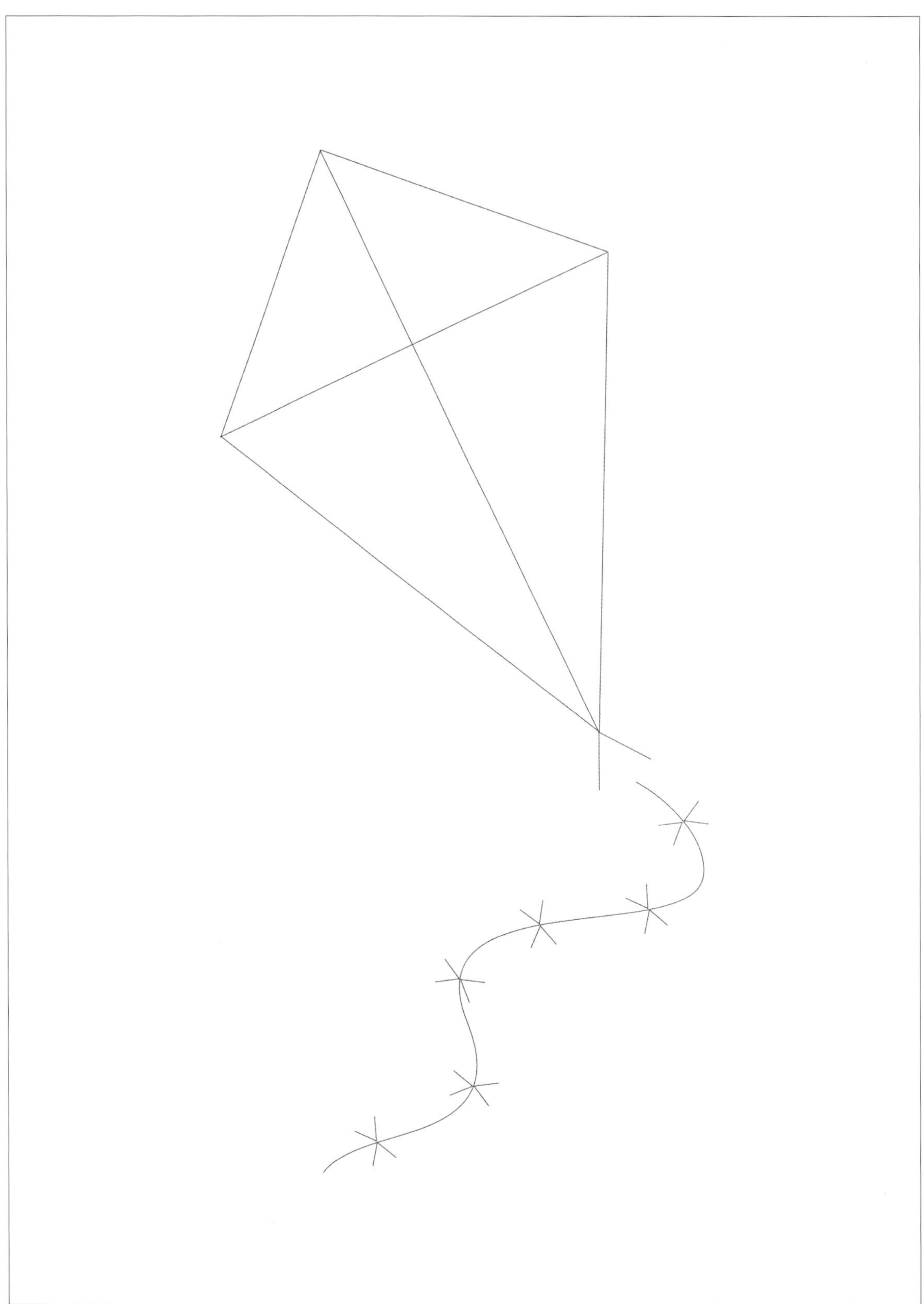

Heart duo, page 62

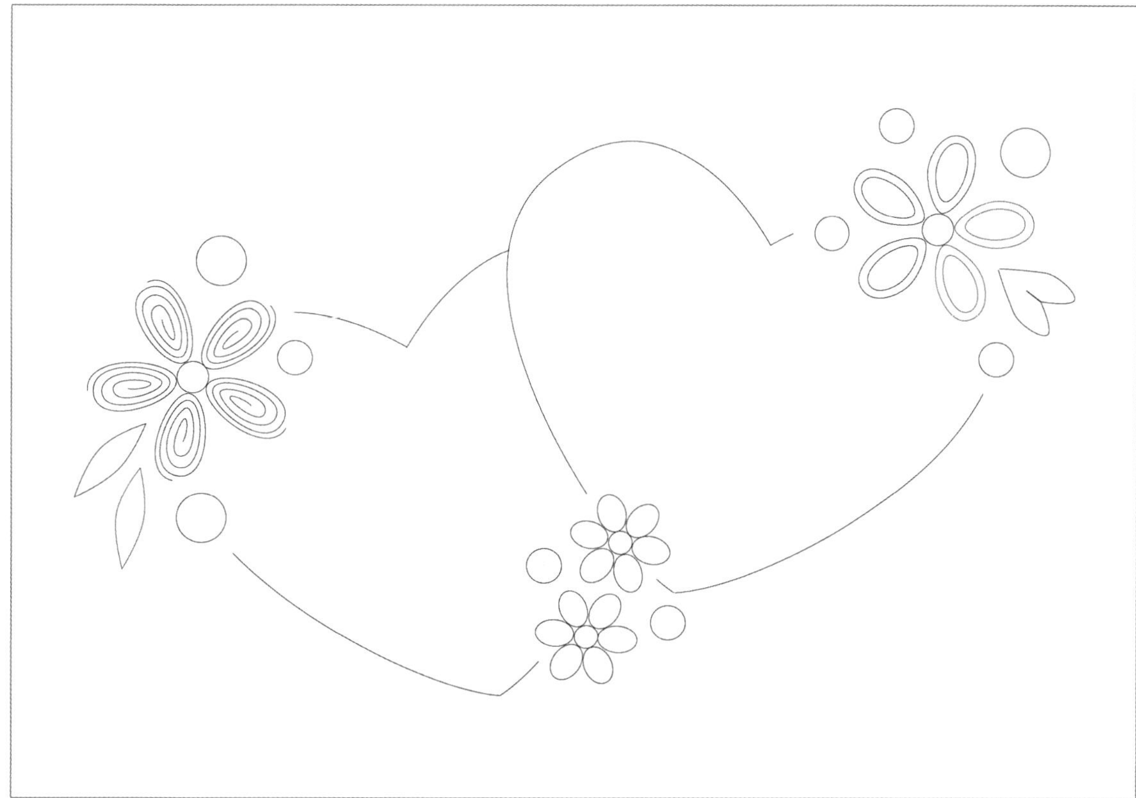

Hummingbird, page 58

Winter wonderland tree, page 82

Leaves,
page 34

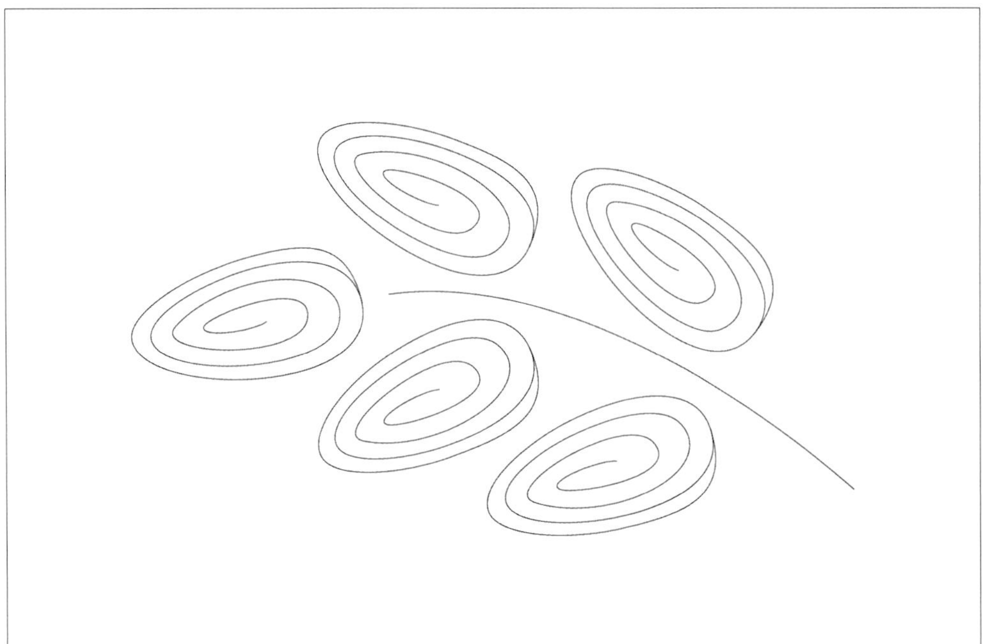

Dreamy
cloud,
page 66

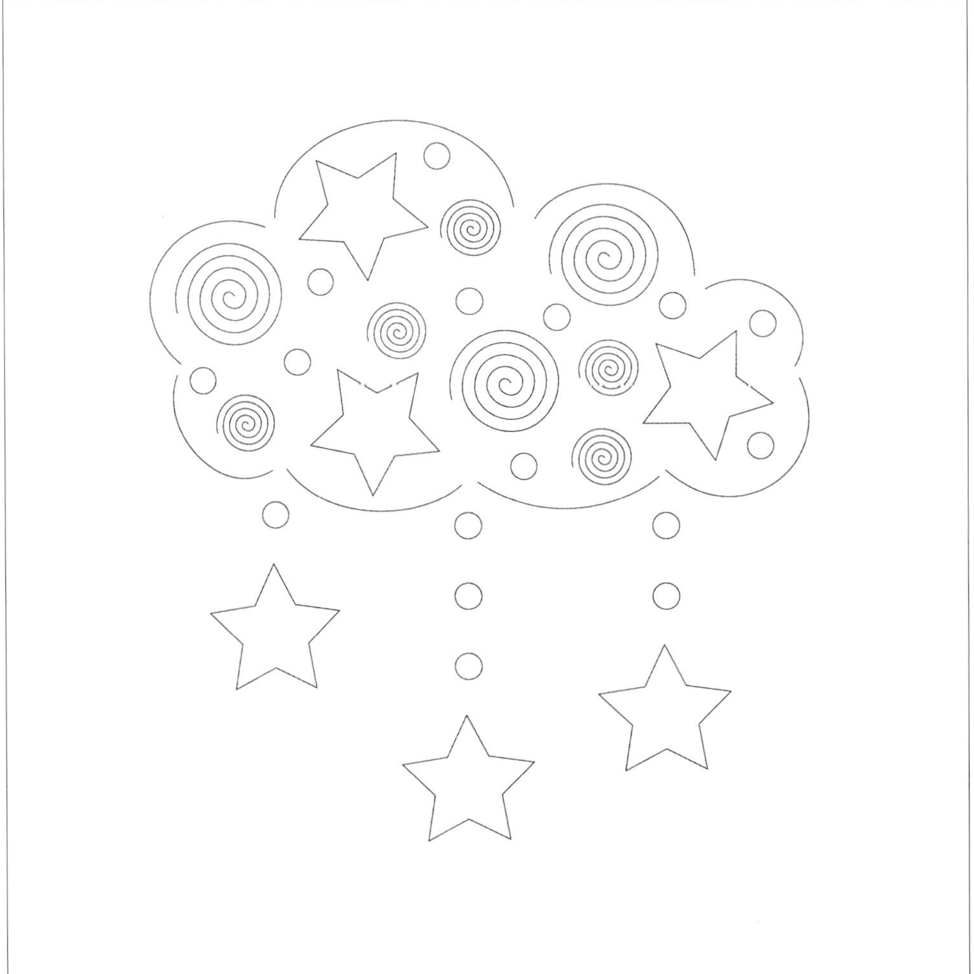

Tulips, page 78

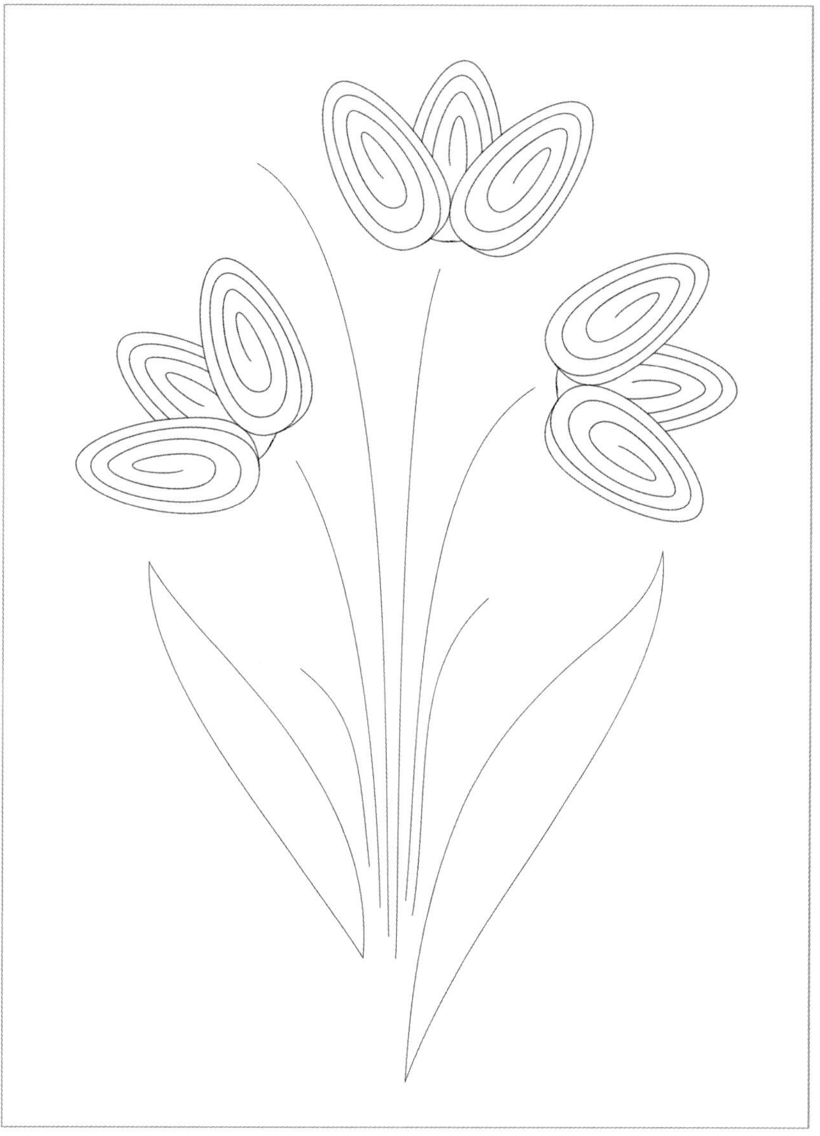

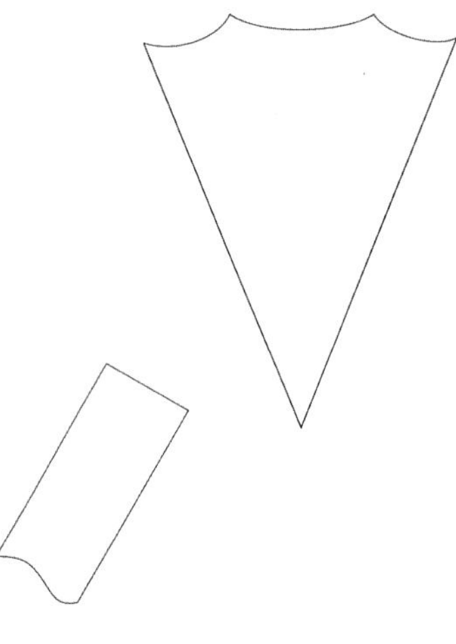

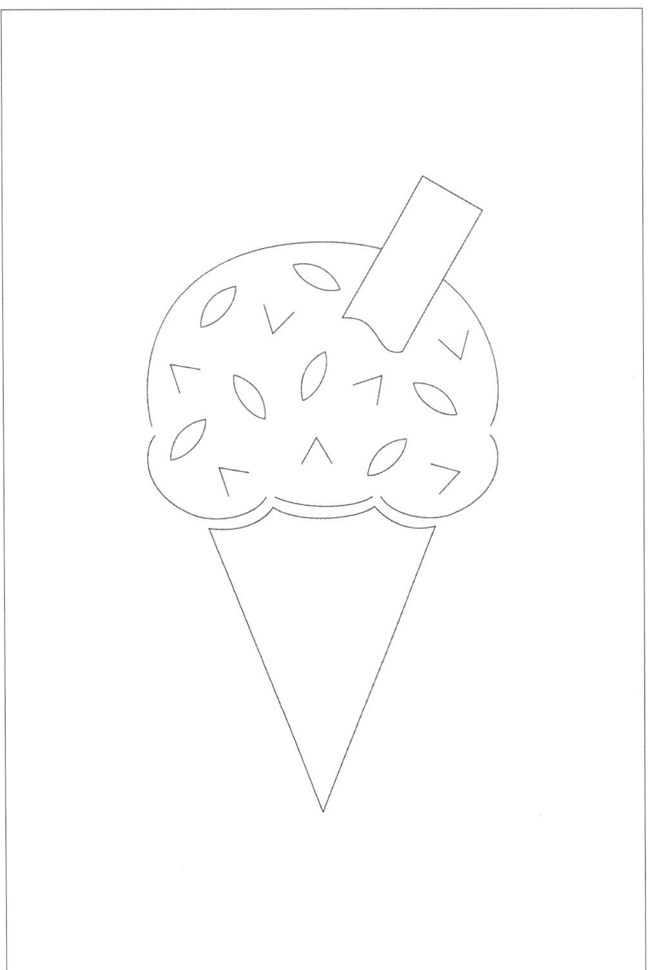

Snowflake,
page 54